HOW THE
Aid Industry
WORKS

SECOND EDITION

HOW THE
Aid Industry
WORKS

The Politics and Practice
of International Development

Arjan de Haan

 Kumarian Press

A Division of Lynne Rienner Publishers, Inc. • Boulder & London

Published in the United States of America in 2023 by
Kumarian Press
A division of Lynne Rienner Publishers, Inc.
1800 30th Street, Boulder, Colorado 80301
www.rienner.com

and in the United Kingdom by
Kumarian Press
A division of Lynne Rienner Publishers, Inc.
Gray's Inn House, 127 Clerkenwell Road, London EC1 5DB
www.eurospanbookstore.com/rienner

Library of Congress Cataloging-in-Publication Data
Names: de Haan, Arjan, author.
Title: How the aid industry works : the politics and practice of
    international development / Arjan de Haan.
Description: 2nd edition. | Boulder, Colorado : Kumarian Press, 2023. |
    Includes bibliographical references and index. | Summary: "A concise
    introduction to the business of development"— Provided by publisher.
Identifiers: LCCN 2022038912 (print) | LCCN 2022038913 (ebook) | ISBN
    9781955055895 (pbk. ; alk. paper) | ISBN 9781955055987 (ebook) | ISBN
    9781685852801 (ebook other)
Subjects: LCSH: International economic relations. | Economic
    assistance—Developing countries. | Economic assistance—International
    cooperation. | Development economics. | Developing countries—Foreign
    economic relations.
Classification: LCC HF1411 .H217 2023 (print) | LCC HF1411 (ebook) | DDC
    338.9109172/4—dc22/eng/20220817
LC record available at https://lccn.loc.gov/2022038912
LC ebook record available at https://lccn.loc.gov/2022038913

British Cataloguing in Publication Data
A Cataloguing in Publication record for this book
is available from the British Library.

Printed and bound in the United States of America

∞   The paper used in this publication meets the requirements
       of the American National Standard for Permanence of
       Paper for Printed Library Materials Z39.48-1992.

       5 4 3 2 1

Contents

Tables and Figures

Tables

Figures

Preface

INTERNATIONAL DEVELOPMENT, OR AID, IS BIG BUSINESS, ANNUALLY spending some $250 billion in lower-income economies. The Sustainable Development Goals, or SDGs, adopted by the United Nations in 2015, provide a unifying framework for aid and have been taken on by many private companies as well as by official aid agencies. However, the SDGs unify development agencies only at the normative level; the framework does not include agreements on how aid is to be provided and how the impact of aid is to be measured, nor does it suggest mechanisms of accountability.

In 2007, the Development Assistance Committee of the Organisation for Economic Co-operation and Development noted that the number of aid organizations was "baffling," and that number has continued to increase. China has emerged as a global player in the aid industry, many smaller countries have started aid programs, and private donors have come to play an increasingly important role. Much has been written about how different these newer aid programs are from the older ones. However, those "old" donors have also operated in significantly varied ways, based on their own political and institutional circumstances.

A World Bank study in 1998 concluded that "foreign aid in different times and different places has . . . been highly effective, totally ineffective, and everything in between" (World Bank 1998). Twenty-five years later, that conclusion still holds, and scholars and journalists continue to variously praise the successes of aid, such as in combating diseases, and condemn its failure, such as in Afghanistan or in Africa, where the Zambian-born economist Dambisa Moyo concluded that aid is dead.

Against this ever-growing complexity and differences in how the results of aid are assessed, this book provides an overview of the practices of the "industry" of international development. It has been written as the Covid-19 pandemic is still very much present, and the climate crisis is growing, both requiring increased global action and solidarity. The ongoing momentous changes in the global political and economic order are creating opposing pressures on the aid industry with its postwar origins. Emerging economies are claiming their place at global forums, while populism in old-donor countries and debates on decolonization are impacting international development debates. September 11, 2001, and the invasion of Ukraine represent moments of heightened global tensions with major impacts on the aid industry.

The book is intended to fill a gap in the literature on international development, focusing on a description of aid practices around the world: what they are, how they evolved, and debates around them. Descriptions of practices and debates are illustrated with examples of projects and programs in specific contexts. Many of the examples are based on my personal experience in India and China, though these of course are by no means representative of all developing countries.

The experience of teaching a course on the practices of international development to undergraduate students at the University of Guelph in Ontario provided me the motivation and concept for this book. Students, generally aware of the critique of international development, are usually committed to the cause of international development but lack sufficient basis to assess the critique. They often express a desire to learn more about the practices and to get insight into the many different approaches to international aid. In 2005, I experienced a dearth of basic texts that could introduce students to the practices of international development; in 2022, with the aid industry even more complex, and with the growing roles of emerging economies and of private-sector actors, this is still the case. But much has changed, as well, motivating me to write this new edition. My hope is that it will be useful to students of international development, as well as to development practitioners, administrators, and managers seeking differing perspectives on the complex aid industry and its place in international relations and politics.

The text is as "neutral" as possible, in the sense that it provides the arguments of proponents and opponents, but also analytical, helping the reader to understand the practices from different perspectives. The book is neither a defense nor a critique of development aid; it is neither optimistic nor pessimistic. Given the diversity of development practices and ways of measuring results, it may be impossible to assess whether "aid works." I have much sympathy for many of the critiques of international development, but I also believe more systematic and well-informed commentary can make aid more accountable.

The people in the aid industry I know are extremely committed and have provided important contributions, recognized by partners in poor parts of the world. International organizations have contributed—though perhaps not enough or not quickly enough—to tackling the HIV/AIDS crisis, and they have often been faced with resistance from the North but also by governments in the South. Although the World Bank has provided misguided advice at times, and there is little doubt that it needs reform, I believe in senior fellow at the Council on Foreign Relations Sebastian Mallaby's observation that "most Bank staffers had joined the institution because they wanted to fight poverty" (Mallaby 2005, 47). I do not think that nongovernmental organizations are generally better, or worse, in providing aid. In this book, I try not to take sides, but to help readers form their own opinions.

Finally, a few words about the title of the book, particularly the reference to the "aid industry." The world of development or international aid, in my experience, is indeed—and should be—an industry, a branch of economic activity. Although it uses public (tax payers') and voluntarily donated money, professional administrators, many of whom have long-running careers in international development, disburse funds in a professional way, with generally strict procedures and reporting. Silke Roth's (2015) book is an excellent account of what drives these people. Though many of these officials are well paid, and indeed often fly business class instead of coach, most of the people in the aid industry are committed and "industrious."

I use the word *aid* rather than *development*. The desired outcome of the industry is development, leaving no one behind, as stated in the SDGs framework, but the focus of this book is how the aid industry contributes to this goal, and this is mostly through providing financial assistance. Many argue that the word *aid* suggests an imbalance in power relations. I agree, and I believe that relationships need to become much more equal; I recognize that the terms that we use—including in this book—can reinforce power relations (Khan et al. 2022). But the way the industry works is still primarily by disbursing aid, and many of its advocates continue to express paternalistic attitudes. There is still some way to go for the industry to become one of *development*. Merely changing the language will not change the practices.

*   *   *

Students of the international development program at the University of Guelph, Ontario, gave me the motivation for writing this book. During my short period there, I was amazed by their interest in and commitment to international development issues. Kendra Warner provided excellent help in preparing a bibliography for the book. I presented part of the text at the Institute of Social Studies in The Hague and learned much about the importance of acknowledging the position from which one writes. I have since had the opportunity to discuss aid practices with students at Carleton, Ottawa, and McGill universities, and with my colleagues at the International Development Research Centre. My time in Ottawa, on unceded Algonquin Anishinabe territory, also has made me understand better the deep roots of colonial practices in which we operate.

Working for the UK Department for International Development in China, I witnessed the emergence of a new world of international aid, with a South–South emphasis, and a historically unique transition from being an "aid recipient" to a "donor." Much inspiration came from colleagues and friends such as Qiao Jianrong, Sun Xuebing, Sarah Cook, James Keeley, Li Xiaoyun, Huang Chengwei, Adrian Davis, John Warburton, and Ellen Wratten. I presented the work at the International Poverty Reduction Center in China and benefited from the many questions and comments there.

I have also benefited from the comments, suggestions, and discussion of Shahin Yaqub, Rosalind Eyben, Paul Shaffer (particularly on the chapter on monitoring and on methods of poverty analysis), and Max Everest-Phillips (on the politics of aid). In Canada, working for the International Development Research Centre, I have benefited from the insights and friendship of Federico Burone, Fred Carden, Adrian Di Giovanni, Coleen Duggan, Tarik Khan, Kerry Max, Rohinton Medhora, Martha Melesse, and many others.

1

Why Is Aid Contested?

INTERNATIONAL DEVELOPMENT IS BIG BUSINESS. TOTAL GLOBAL OFFICIAL
aid flows from North to South are over $150 billion annually. In the
last decades, China, India, Turkey, Brazil, and other countries have
enhanced their roles as aid providers and, with that, introduced different approaches. International private philanthropies have become significant, with resources from the Bill & Melinda Gates Foundation, for
example, outstripping the annual budget of the World Health Organization. The Gates Foundation was also a major donor for the development of Covid-19 vaccines.

ıThe aid industry also is very complex. In 2007, the chair of the
Working Party on Aid Effectiveness of the Development Assistance
Committee (DAC), the body at the Organisation for Economic Cooperation and Development (OECD) that brings together dispersed aid
statistics and promotes coordination between donors, noted the following:

> A layperson observing today's aid industry might be understandably
> baffled by the sheer number of aid actors, funds and programmes. The
> last time the OECD counted, there were more than 200 bilateral and
> multilateral organisations channelling official development assistance.
> Many developing countries may have more than 40 donors financing
> more than 600 active projects, and may still not be on track to achieve
> the Millennium Development Goals. (Cedergren 2007)

That complexity refers to the "official" agencies only—each with
its own strategies and principles. Public–private partnerships have
added to the complexity, and the number of donors keeps increasing.

In developing countries, dozens of donors typically are in operation, financing hundreds of projects. Moreover, donors such as the United States have multiple agencies within the government responsible for various aid activities.

The policies of agencies, apparently always changing, tend to be inaccessible to outsiders, and procedures for project development are long and complicated. The language of the aid industry is often intractable, with many acronyms. The ambition of the aid industry is broad and has continued to expand: in 2015 at the United Nations, all countries agreed to the Sustainable Development Goals: 17 goals with 231 indicators.

Interest in development aid experiences surges. Disasters such as the Gujarat and Haiti earthquakes, the Asian tsunami, and the Ebola outbreak mobilize governments and constituencies of civil society, including of diaspora communities. The 2008 cyclone in Myanmar and the earthquake in China led to an increased role of the international community. In OECD countries, interest in international development is frequently fueled by celebrities who advocate for specific causes, such as Madonna, Angelina Jolie, Rihanna, Idris Alba, Oprah, Bono, and Bob Geldoff, or the Toronto-based WE Charity mobilizing young people in North America and the UK.[1]

The Jubilee 2000 coalition advocated successfully for debt relief for the poorest and most heavily indebted countries, and the Make Poverty History campaign of 2005 advocated for substantially increased aid commitments. This raised awareness and interest in the aid industry well beyond the earlier popular advocacy for relief, as seen during the Sahel emergency of the late 1970s. Anti-globalization and other similar types of protests frequently bring the World Bank and the International Monetary Fund (IMF) into the global public eye, and protests in 2007 contributed to the resignation of the World Bank president.

Alongside concerns about alleviating deprivation in the South, global security concerns focused renewed attention on global aid efforts. In the United States, after the 9/11 terrorist attacks, development was elevated after a decade of relative neglect and came to be seen as one of the pillars of national security next to defense and diplomacy (Brainard 2007a; Natsios 2006). The war in Iraq was important for aid programs. Afghanistan became an important recipient of many countries' aid; the US withdrawal from Afghanistan in 2021 was followed by debates about the impact that aid in this context had and can have (Shah 2021). Growing global interconnectedness has heightened concerns about the perceived spillover from underdevelopment, including in the form of migration and terrorism (Bermeo 2017).

Box 1.1   The Sustainable Development Goals

In 2015, United Nations member states adopted the 2030 Agenda for Sustainable Development, a "shared blueprint for peace and prosperity for people and the planet, now and into the future." This followed an extensive process of negotiation, including at the Rio+20 Summit (the United Nations Conference on Sustainable Development in 2012). The advocacy for this new framework, and how it was seen to differ from the preceding Millennium Development Goals (MDGs), including in terms of integrated approaches to economic, social, and environmental issues, is described in a detailed account by Colombian official Paula Caballero with Patti Londoño (2022).

At its heart are seventeen Sustainable Development Goals (SDGs), which—different from the MDGs—are a "call for action" for all countries, developed and developing, with a commitment to "Leave No One Behind" and concrete goals for global partnerships. Ending poverty and other deprivations is SDGs 1, and the development agenda stresses that this must go together with strategies that, for example, improve health and education (SDGs 3), spur economic growth (SDGs 8), reduce inequality (SDGs 10, SDGs 5 on gender), and tackle climate change and preserve oceans and forests (SDGs 13). The global framework includes 231 indicators that form the basis for regular national and global SDGs reporting.

Although the SDGs provide a unified framework for measurement of success of the international community in achieving the goals, and for calculations of amounts of aid needed, there are important differences in how agencies contribute to the goals. Similarly, how contributions are assessed is not uniformly agreed, for reasons documented in this chapter.

Sources: "Do You Know All 17 SDGs?" UN Department of Economic and Social Affairs, https://sdgs.un.org/goals; "SDG Indicators," Sustainable Development Goals, https://unstats.un.org/sdgs/indicators/indicators-list/; Caballero with Londoño (2022).

The growing populism in OECD countries has put aid programs under pressure.[2] Some countries reduced their aid commitments, and aid orientation changed. For example, in Europe, particularly since the rapid increase in the number of refugees arriving in 2015, deterring migration has become an increasingly important consideration of development aid—despite experts' warnings that such aid is unlikely to achieve that objective. The "EU Emergency Trust Fund for stability and addressing root causes of irregular migration and displaced persons in Africa" became a key policy instrument to integrate aid with foreign and immigration policies.[3]

Both the Covid-19 pandemic and the climate crisis have given debates about development aid, again, a different dimension. Both have highlighted the global nature of public policy challenges, with calls for unified global responses, but also stark North–South differences, including concerns around global vaccine inequality, lack of commitment by the countries in the North that are mostly responsible for climate change to fund the necessary investments in lower-income economies, and more broadly a weakening of multilateralism (Benner 2020) and "contested global governance" (Chaturvedi et al. 2020).

Aid has been studied from different theoretical angles, as described in Chapter 4, and these can be summarized as a series of opposites. Realist and Marxist perspectives focus on the role that aid plays in maintaining global power relations; scholars in a liberal tradition emphasize aid as a reflection of collaboration between states. Social democratic theories highlight that foreign aid is an expression of norms and ideas that assist in the improvement of quality of life; postmodernist approaches focus on aid practices as a discourse and way of exerting power. The entrance of new donors such as China has brought yet other perspectives. Finally, much of the literature places a strong emphasis on the management of aid, which has been criticized by commentators who emphasize the importance of personal relationships in aid. I agree with Carol Lancaster (2007) that none of these theories adequately explains the complexities of aid: its principles always reflect a combination of motives, and aid practices take on their own dynamics in the institutions responsible for their implementation, as all policies do. At the end of this book, following a discussion of how the impact of aid is measured, readers should be able to make their own judgments about these views.

The rest of this chapter highlights the main debates about aid: whether it should increase, whether the way aid is given is effective, and whether it is becoming irrelevant in the face of increasing private financial flows through trade and remittances. This does not cover all the arguments about aid. Notably, it does not cover the question of whether aid *can* reduce poverty—a question that runs throughout the book. I hope the book helps readers form their own opinion. This chapter finishes with a brief overview of the book.

International Commitment to Increase Aid

Many claim that not enough aid is given. Economist Jeffrey Sachs has forcefully advocated for more aid, including when he was adviser to Kofi Annan, former Secretary-General of the UN, and with regard to creating "Millennium Villages," in which over $100 million was invested (Sachs 2005; Munk 2013). In Canada, former political leader Stephen Lewis in nationally broadcasted lectures criticized rich countries for failing to live up to aid commitments (Lewis 2005). The Jubilee 2000 campaign advocated for debt relief, and similar arguments were made in the context of the growing debt crisis and global pandemic in 2020. Civil society organizations advocate for reversing the net financial flows from poorer to richer countries, including through multinationals' shifting profits to tax havens. Climate activists argue that the finance from rich countries to the South is insufficient, including in light of rich countries' responsibility for the growing climate damage.

Calls for increased aid have been common at least since World War II, and official aid has continued to be "a brand with value," thought to enhance national leaders' reputation of generosity (Kenny 2020). Although public interest surges and recedes, studies suggest that there is continued public support for providing aid. Political changes in donor countries, such as the rise of populism in the last two decades, of course can significantly change aid approaches, but these are balanced by advocates within countries as well as countries' participation in global forums.

The immediate post–World War II period witnessed large-scale funding through the Marshall Plan, which provided infrastructure support to Europe. Aid to developing countries that focused on technical assistance and cooperation was supported by development theory that identified finance gaps as a main obstacle to development. In 1951, a commission set up by the UN Secretary-General recommended an increase of aid to $5 billion a year to help countries increase economic growth to 2 percent (Riddell 2007, 27). Voluntary agencies started to expand work in developing countries.

In 1969, a commission set up by Robert McNamara, the newly appointed World Bank president, and chaired by Canada's prime minister Lester Pearson published *Partners in Development*, which became one of the most-quoted official reports arguing for an increase in aid. The report called on rich countries to devote 0.7 percent of their gross national income (GNI) to international development, and to reach this level of funding in 1975. It advocated for a simultaneous increase in the efficiency of aid. Its focus was development, with less explicit attention to poverty. The target was formally adopted by the United Nations in 1970 and has featured in international debates ever since. Aid levels did rise during the 1970s—but average spending did not come close to the target.

This optimism around 1970 was not to last long and was quickly followed by emphasis on "structural adjustment" and stabilization of economies. "Aid fatigue" arose based on perceptions that aid had failed to deliver results. Nevertheless, throughout the 1980s calls for increasing aid continued, for example, in response to the droughts and famines in the Sahel and Ethiopia, by the World Bank in reports on Africa, and through increasing involvement of NGOs. Levels of aid continued to increase.

The 1990s—at the end of the Cold War and with economic and budgetary problems in donor countries such as the United States and Japan—witnessed reductions in aid. The decline in aid to the poorest countries may have been even larger than the overall decline (Browne 2007). The amounts of aid to allied countries, including corrupt and repressive regimes, declined, but simultaneously the donors may have reduced their attention to conflicts and violence in developing countries. With the transition toward market economies, attention moved to the use of aid for governance reforms in the former USSR and for democratization processes in Africa.

From the late 1990s onward, civil society and international organizations' calls for increasing aid again became stronger and were accompanied by a sharpened focus on poverty reduction as the overarching goal for development. The change of government in the UK in 1997 led to the formation of a separate ministry and contributed to greater political interest in development aid, with stars such as Bob Geldof and Bono getting involved, and support from Prime Minister Tony Blair and Finance Minister Gordon Brown, who both continued advocacy for international development after their careers in government. The UN and World Bank highlighted the importance of and their commitment to poverty reduction and the Millennium Development Goals. In 2002, in Monterrey, Mexico, US president George W. Bush committed to enhancing international aid; Monterrey became the first "Finance for Development" conference, followed by Gleneagles in 2005, Doha in December 2008, and Addis Ababa in 2015.

Showing trust in the impact of aid, the UN Millennium Development project calculated the amount of aid that would be required to achieve the MDGs.[4] The UN stressed the lack of funding particularly in social sectors: according to the 2005 Human Development Report (UNDP 2005, 79), average health spending in sub-Saharan Africa was $3 to $10 per capita, while the cost of providing basic health care was estimated at $30 per capita. Similar calculations to achieve the much more ambitious SDGs estimate that $5 trillion to $7 trillion in annual investment would be needed.[5] With that much-higher figure has come growing recognition that official aid will not be sufficient and that leveraging private finance is critical.

During the pandemic of 2020–2022, aid advocates compared the small increase in aid to rich countries' governmental interventions. In some countries, international solidarity was posited as directly competing with needs at national levels.[6] Similarly, analysts and advocates have criticized developed countries' commitments to providing climate finance to developing countries (Bos and Thwaites 2021). More recently, calls for rich countries to fund the costs imposed by climate change have increased.

Official commitments have never been binding, and often have not materialized. In donor countries, political pressure is not strong enough, and aid is probably not sufficiently significant in national politics, for the commitments to materialize consistently. An exception to this is the UK's International Development (Reporting and Transparency) Act 2006, which committed the ministry to report annually on progress toward the UN aid target of 0.7 percent of GNI. This act was combined with commitments to enhance effectiveness and transparency, making the increase in allocation conditional. The UK did achieve the official target during 2013–2020, which was then followed by budget cuts.

The Arguments to Reduce and Abolish Aid

Public opinion often holds that too much money goes to foreign aid. It is often observed that the public suffers from aid fatigue. Right-wing political parties and populists often argue for reduction of aid and heavily criticize international institutions. In a US Senate confirmation hearing, Senator Rand Paul stated, "70 percent of [foreign aid] is stolen off the top" (in Kenny 2022). Such critiques are often based in lack of information; for example, in the United States, the public often greatly overestimates the amount given to aid.[7] Aid agencies have made efforts to counter these claims through "branding" of aid interventions and enhancing awareness of the SDGs (Laws 2016; OECD 2017).

**Box 1.2   Five Decades of Reports on Increasing
Development Aid**

Pearson Commission: Lester Pearson, *Partners in Development:
Report of the Commission on International Development* (1969)—
called for official development assistance (ODA) commitment of
0.7 percent of gross national income.

Brandt Commission: Willy Brandt, *North–South: A Programme for
Survival* (1980)—called for doubling of ODA by 1985.

World Bank, *Sub-Saharan Africa: From Crisis to Sustainable Growth*
(1989)—proposed a doubling of aid to Africa.

OECD DAC, *Shaping the 21st Century: The Contribution of Development Co-operation* (1996)—called for increasing aid, without
quantification, and focusing on enhancing the effectiveness of aid.

UN, *Monterrey Consensus on Financing for Development* (2002)—
urged developed countries to make concrete efforts toward the
0.7 percent target (and 0.15–0.20 percent to least developed
countries), while stressing the need for a "new partnership."

UN Millennium Project, *Investing in Development: A Practical Plan
to Achieve the Millennium Development Goals* (2005).

UN, *Framework Convention on Climate Change* (2009)—committed
developed countries to provide $100 billion annually in climate
finance for developing countries.

UN, *Addis Ababa Action Agenda of the Third International Conference on Financing for Development* (2015).

UN, *Inter-agency Taskforce on Financing for Development: Financing
for Sustainable Development Report 2021* (2021)—called for
meeting aid commitments and debt relief.

There is a common perception that aid has failed. A *New York Times*
article concluded that US$13 billion in aid to Haiti after the 2010 earth-
quake "seems only to have helped perpetuate some of the country's
biggest troubles" (Abi-Habib 2021). An article in the *Wall Street Journal*
(August 22, 2007) stated, "Despite star power, aid doesn't work," highlighting aid's potential damaging long-run effects on governance and economic competitiveness.[8] An article in the conservative US journal the
National Review in 2002 argued that "a strong case can be made that foreign aid has been the problem for many developing countries, rather than
the solution . . . [and] negative policies were perpetuated in the same way
that welfare perpetuated dependency" (quoted in Lancaster 2007, 96).

Graham Hancock, a British author and journalist, argued in a 1989 book that was reprinted several times and in various countries that the aid business should be abolished; in his view, countries that had not received aid had fared better than those that had, and the industry's history was littered with failures. To be sure, there is no doubt that many development projects have failed: a detailed analysis in Ghana suggests that one-third of projects started were not completed (Williams 2017).

Riding the wave of interest in aid in the early 2000s, Bill Easterly published his view on international development as "the white man's burden." Based on his experience as a World Bank economist, he highlighted the "tragedy in which the West spent $2.3 trillion on foreign aid over the last five decades and still had not managed to get twelve-cent medicines to prevent half of all malaria deaths" (Easterly 2006, 4).

Dambisa Moyo, a Zambian economist with a career at the World Bank and Goldman Sachs, in 2009 published *Dead Aid*, which became widely quoted and a *New York Times* bestseller. She concluded that Africa remains in dire economic straits despite having received more than $1 trillion from the West over the last half century, and she argued for building economic rather than aid relations, as well as deepening collaboration with China. She was heavily criticized by other scholars, but her arguments were supported by, for example, Rwanda's president Paul Kagame.

The arguments to reduce aid take different forms. First, there are concerns about aid dependency. In many countries, particularly in Africa, donor funding has formed significant shares of government budgets. New funding often leads governments to set up new agencies, which may not contribute to solving and may even worsen problems of existing public policy institutions. Equally, new loans are often thought to ensnare countries in debt traps; critiques of structural adjustment and debt relief campaigns, for example, have argued that poor countries have paid back far more in loans than they received. Aid can negatively impact governments' incentives to raise revenue and build state–society relations (Blair and Winters 2020).

A further argument against increasing aid makes reference to "absorptive capacity." It is argued that recipient governments may not have the administrative or policy capacity to effectively use increased aid flows, particularly when these are disbursed in a short period of time. Economists warn about the economic implications of large financial inflows: they can cause appreciation in the exchange rate and resulting decline in competitiveness of national industries. However, there is some agreement among economists that, for most aid-dependent countries, a foreign aid contribution to the national budget of about 20 percent does not lead to such negative effects. Jeffrey Sachs has argued against absorptive capacity concerns, highlighting, for example, that at current levels of funding it is impossible for health ministries in Africa to maintain a health-care system.

A third argument against increasing aid relates to the behavior of the donors. Though the history of the aid industry is full of donors' commitments to focusing on recipients' priorities, donors' motives and structures continue to drive the way aid is given. Aid is driven by foreign policy motives, which partly explains the great attention to aid during the Cold War and after 9/11. Commercial motives factor in as equally important in the way aid is provided. Much aid is provided as "tied aid," where the money given is required to be spent on goods and services of the donor country, as discussed below. Corruption in the aid industry exists but is hard to assess given the long channels through which aid is delivered.[9]

According to Easterly (2006), the main problem with aid was the emphasis on grand plans and the planners' limited ability to motivate people to carry out such plans. He stressed that development needs to be "home-grown." Michael Woolcock, a social scientist at the World Bank, and Chris Blattman, an economist and political scientist, highlight the need for aid practices informed by context-specific learning to build more strongly on local initiatives.[10] It is often argued that many aid recipients are not committed to development and poverty reduction and that aid may not be able to help improve governance.[11]

Donor procedures tend to be cumbersome, consuming valuable and often scarce governmental and administrative capacity, such as when donor projects and programs create parallel reporting structures, which is particularly problematic when large numbers of donors are present in countries with low administrative capacity. Mosse and Lewis (2006, 8) have argued that development policy is characterized by incongruence between a seductive mix of "development buzzwords" and "lack of progress in relation to a wide range of development indicators." Donor funding can undermine local accountability (Uvin 2004); donors' role vis-à-vis the accountability of national policies is discussed later in this book.

One strand of debate challenges the overall nature of the aid industry. Authors such as Escobar, Ferguson, and Ignacy Sachs have argued "that the entire development discourse is Western created and imbued with the usual dichotomies of Western superiority . . . [and] justifies the existence of an interventionist and disempowering bureaucracy . . . the entire development edifice—the concepts, the language, the institutions built up around it—*causes* the problems it supposedly seeks to solve."[12]

Over the last decade, calls for decolonizing aid have become more prominent,[13] with an increase in organizations such as No White Saviors. This argument was in part inspired by the Black Lives Matter movement and reinforced by critiques of the lack of global solidarity during the Covid-19 pandemic.[14] "Foreign aid is having a reckoning" read a headline in the *New York Times* in February 2021. Scholars have pointed at the discriminatory practices and attitudes in international development. Célestin Monga (2020) highlighted the prejudice he encountered as a Cameroonian World Bank economist, and the extent of racism in the aid industry was demonstrated in the UK's International Development Committee's (2022) report *Racism in the Aid Sector*. Analysis of public opinions in the United States have shown that negative views on foreign aid are linked to an underlying racial paternalism (Baker 2015). On the basis of conversations with 1,500 development practitioners, Clements and Sweetman (2020) concluded that the aid industry "relies on racialised, gendered relations of exploitation, extraction and inequality" and needs to change its focus from benevolence to solidarity.

The Case to Reform Aid

In the middle of the arguments for and against aid, there are those who focus on the ways in which aid is provided and the need for better assessment. The discussion above, about absorptive capacity and donor behavior, already moves us into the arguments about how aid is given rather than simply whether there should be more or less aid. Advocacy for more aid often goes together with calls for improving the quality of the aid system, for example, the Jubilee 2000 campaign, which argued that new resources should focus on poverty reduction; the Pearson Commission, which argued also for improvements in efficiency; and the Monterrey Consensus, which emphasized governance issues as central to delivering increased resources. The *2005 Human Development Report* argued:

> International aid is one of the most powerful weapons in the war against poverty. Today, that weapon is underused and badly targeted. There is too little aid and too much of what is provided is weakly linked to human development. Fixing the international aid system is one of the most urgent priorities facing governments at the start of the 10-year countdown to 2015. (UNDP 2005)

The difficult questions about the delivery of aid are central to this book, and this section lists the more pertinent ones. One argument emphasizes that aid is not well targeted, in that too much money is spent in countries that are not the poorest. Powerful historical, political, and strategic reasons determine why so much aid is given to countries that are not poor. Many bilateral organizations have tried to focus their aid on the poorest countries, and have set official targets for increasing the share of the total aid budget for the poorest countries, but the pull of other political considerations dominates their actions. Since 9/11, security concerns have led to an increasing—and often competing—focus on states that are thought to pose threats of violence to the North. The US aid program is particularly openly tied to foreign policy concerns; in fact, a former US Agency for International Development (USAID) administrator criticized the European aid programs for the failure to align their aid to foreign policy concerns (Natsios 2006).

A second and related argument has stressed that much aid—even if it does go to the poorest countries—does not reach the poorest people. The aid industry has increasingly focused on ensuring aid benefits poor people: the MDGs and SDGs are instruments to ensure targeting, and unconditional cash transfers are promoted as an effective mechanism to empower poor people. Since the 1980s, many development organizations, not least of which the World Bank, have been engaged in large-scale exercises to make sure that it is possible to know how many people are poor. Randomized controlled trials inspired by the scientific method have become popular over the last two decades in the hope of making aid donations more effective. But the ways in which aid benefits poor people can be manifold. Assessing whether aid succeeds in benefiting the poor remains a very difficult proposition, even within agreed-on frameworks such as the SDGs.

Third, even when it is agreed that the world's poorest people should be the prime beneficiaries of aid, controversy arises about whether it is desirable to provide these countries with large or increasing amounts of aid. The argument, put simply, is that many of the poorest countries are not able to use aid effectively. This can be for a range of reasons, but much of the focus has been on the "governance" in these countries, as discussed in Chapter 6 on aid approaches that emphasize administrative and public sector reforms. The agenda of good governance is broad, calling for improvements in political and economic institutions, administrative systems, and government bureaucracies.

An influential—and criticized, as we discuss in Chapter 8—World Bank paper from the late 1990s by Burnside and Dollar (2000) showed that aid was effective *if* its recipient government had the right policies in place, particularly good fiscal, monetary, and trade policies. Collier and Dollar (1999) used statistical analysis (cross-country regressions) to show that reallocating aid to the countries with the largest numbers of poor people—and that can use aid effectively—could increase the numbers of people lifted out of poverty from 30 million to 80 million per year. Paul Collier's publications *The Bottom Billion* (2007) and *Wars, Guns, and Votes* (2008) stressed the need to focus on countries where most poor people are (some forty countries) and the need to address the development "trap" of lack of governance.

A fourth concern about how aid is given revolves around the political nature of aid. As Chapter 4 describes, the perceived failure of the Washington Consensus that dominated in the 1980s (and the aid fatigue that blamed corrupt governments for the failure of aid) led to increased attention on the importance of governance for development and for poverty reduction and the emergence of Poverty Reduction Strategy Papers (PRSPs), which called for country-wide consultations to determine strategies for providing aid. Although these are less prominent issues in debates over the last decade, they continue to inform IMF lending. The attention to the institutional determinants of development led an increasing number of authors to argue that aid needs to be much more sensitive to political conditions and to call for political analysis to inform aid allocation and strategies.

A fifth question about how aid is given stresses donors' habits, the patterns of behavior and incentives that limit aid effectiveness. This involves a range of issues, many of which are discussed in the rest of the book. For example, current aid, with its longer-term nature and relatively small sums of development aid disbursed, is commonly compared with the Marshall Plan enacted directly after World War II, which disbursed large sums of money in a short period of time. Donors suffer from what is known as disbursement pressure: at the World Bank and bilateral donors, staff are incentivized for high and fast disbursement. The many donor agencies often work in uncoordinated ways and their procedures tend to be time-consuming. Aid flows are often unpredictable and follow donors' financial cycles and preferences rather than demand by recipients.[15]

Some argue that donors' attitudes can potentially undermine progress and increase the possibility of conflict. Autesserre (2021) described the "well intentioned but inherently flawed" and paternalistic operation of the "peace industry," emphasizing that local initiatives rather than billions in aid are key to success. Stephen Brown of the International Trade Centre concluded:

> The donor record [in fragile states] is patchy to say the least. And the closer you come, the worse it looks. Donors bear some responsibility for not being there, but that is not the worst accusation. Donors also appeared at the wrong times with the wrong attitudes. Working within their own scripted agendas, they succeeded in sometimes unpicking and undermining development progress. (Brown 2007, 32)

Finally, donor countries often use foreign aid for commercial purposes and set collaboration with or purchase from their national companies as a condition for the provision of aid.[16] This tied aid may restrict its efficiency, and civil society frequently argues for "untying" aid. According to the OECD's DAC, tied aid can increase the cost of development projects by 15 to 30 percent. Over the decades, and often following advocacy from within the development community, many countries have untied aid—for example, in the UK under the Labour government. According to the OECD, some 90 percent of aid is formally untied, but a difference between de jure and de facto untying remains.

During the 2010s, there was a growing pressure to use aid for donor countries' self-interests. Trends in the Principled Aid Index show a decline in public-spiritedness among most donors and a growing importance of short-term transactional benefits. The fall in average principled aid scores is driven by the highly ranked donors, including Sweden, Canada, Ireland, Iceland, Denmark, and Norway. In the index, the worst-performing countries lag significantly behind the best-performing ones, but some are becoming more principled.[17]

Foreign Policy, Trade, and Other Policies Can Matter More Than Aid

A further set of arguments emphasizes that aid is not as important as many of its supporters argue. There are at least three important considerations, related to the position of aid to donors' foreign policies, the importance of aid compared to private financial flows, and its importance vis-à-vis remittances that (unlike aid) have rapidly grown over the last decades.

First, as reflected strongly in writings originating in the United States, aid is an instrument of foreign policy and diplomacy. The resurgence of interest in aid in the United States in the early 2000s was closely related to the post-9/11 agenda and a "transformational diplomacy" (Natsios 2006). According to John Norris (2021), who credits USAID for contributing to successes in the Green Revolution, contraceptives, famine relief, progress against a range of diseases, and even economic transformation in South Korea: "We should recognize that USAID's most prominent failures have come in instances where the U.S. tried to use foreign assistance as a blunt strategic instrument."

Foreign policy considerations are important for all donor countries, even for those that have made development, poverty reduction, or humanitarian relief central to their policies. Foreign policy and strategic considerations (alongside economic needs and historical links) have had a big influence on which countries receive aid (Alesina and Dollar 2000). Donor countries' national policy institutions and ideologies influence how aid is given (Zimmerman 2007; Lancaster 2007).

A second question is: How important is aid in a world where private financial flows are so large, and constantly growing? It is often argued that broader international economic policies are more important than aid programs alone, and there are frequent calls to move "beyond aid" (Hulme 2016). Recipients of aid often emphasize that access to global economic cooperation is as important, if not more so, than aid. Civil society organizations have long emphasized that for global inequalities to be reduced, trade policies need to change, and advocates in aid ministries often try to influence other government departments. Donor countries are criticized when they provide aid while benefiting from, for example, import restrictions and subsidies to producers in the North, foreign investment that exploits countries in the South (with advice from donors helping to open up countries to global markets), interest payments on loans disbursed years if not decades ago, or the sale of arms by companies in the donor countries. As such, UK minister for international development Clare Short made globalization a core theme of the ministry's (second) white paper, responding to a felt need to "make globalization work for the poor" and arguing for the need for consistency in policies of all government departments.

Similarly, the financial contributions of migrants from the South outstrip development aid. Estimates put remittances at triple official aid flows. Although earlier writings emphasized the danger of "brain drain," that is, the loss of human capacity following moves by educated people to richer countries, analyses have emphasized the positive contributions of migrants, and some authors stress that remittances do not suffer from the problems of aid flows, such as difficulty in getting the money to the right people and corruption.

The Commitment to Development Index tracks a range of international policies on their commitment to supporting international development goals for a growing number of countries. The 2021 version lists eight indicators for forty countries. This shows that some countries that

are leading on development finance are also leading on the environment, and some countries' trade and investment policies support their
development finance commitments. But there are also large discrepan-
cies: notably many rich countries' migration policies are not supportive
of development.[18]

Thus, a development agenda is about much more than aid. But aid
does have its place. Wherever foreign policy considerations are dominant, constituencies for the use of aid for development purposes continue to exist. And private flows, through trade or migrants, cannot sub-
stitute for the essential role aid can play, providing countries with
essential preconditions for their development paths, including the ability to benefit from private flows, from which many of the poorest countries are still excluded. There may be too few success cases, but there
are enough of them to illustrate the point that aid does matter.

Why Are Views on the Aid Industry So Different?

The views on aid diverge for many reasons. In the first place, as highlighted, aid has been explicitly defined as fulfilling different purposes:
to support allies during the Cold War, to support countries and governments considered helpful in a global security agenda, to help countries
develop, to address global poverty, and so forth. Because there are
potentially many objectives of aid, of course, views on what it can
achieve differ too.

Second, and closely related, there are no agreed standards to measure whether aid works, which is discussed in Chapter 8. Even if we dis-
count the foreign policy and commercial purposes of aid, and focus on
the developmental aspects, an enormous variety of purposes can be categorized as development oriented: providing humanitarian relief, promoting economic transitions and reform, promoting democracy,
addressing conflict and postconflict situations—all can legitimately be
classified as aid. Poverty reduction can be achieved through a range of
instruments, including those that help create an environment for economic growth, policies that help provide services for the entire population (such as health and education), or programs that are targeted to the
poor (such as microfinance, cash transfers to the poor). Although the
SDGs provide a generally agreed-on framework of measuring progress,
there are still many questions about whether and how we can attribute
any of the progress or lack thereof to the aid industry.

Third, the differences can have deeper underlying reasons. Ideological differences between Right and Left have exercised a great influence

on framing aid debates (Thérien 2002). Political changes over the last several decades have impacted the shape of aid institutions. These differences often mirror differences in perceptions about responsibilities of the state, in terms of the state's duty to provide for its citizens and its ability to promote economic growth. US national public social policies, for example, are relatively ungenerous compared to their European counterparts, whereas private charities are larger in the United States than elsewhere. These differences are clearly reflected in patterns of aid, as we will see in Chapter 2. There are ideological differences in expectations about the extent to which governments can (or should) promote economic growth and how much of this should be left to the private sector; again, ideas about the ability of the state are reflected in ideas about what aid can contribute and how much should be given.

Overview of the Book

This book is neither a critique nor a praise of aid. It does not try to answer the questions "Does aid work?" and "Does foreign aid really work?" the titles of books by Robert Cassen and associates in 1994 and Roger Riddell in 2007, respectively, or why aid has done "so much ill," as in Easterly's book of the same title (2006), or whether aid is dead, as Dambisa Moyo (2009) argued. It will show that there are no easy solutions for "making aid work," as proposed by Abhijit Banerjee (2007). What is seen as aid's success differs among its many different protagonists and the people who criticize the industry. The key objective of this book is to help readers understand the different ways in which aid is provided, the varying objectives of aid, and the different ways in which it is assessed.

Chapter 2 provides insight into the institutions that form the aid industry: the United Nations, including the Bretton Woods institutions, the International Monetary Fund and World Bank; the main bilateral organizations—including relative newcomers, particularly China—and the various ways in which countries have shaped their aid programs; the role and importance of nongovernmental organizations (NGOs); and the newer private charities, of which the Gates Foundation is the largest and best known. The chapter ends with a description of the complexity of how donors allocate aid.

Although always common knowledge, during the late 1980s donors started to emphasize the need for country ownership for successful development. Chapter 3 describes country-led approaches and questions of, on the one hand, the capacity of aid recipients and, on the other hand, the perceived need for donors to harmonize their approaches.

This includes a discussion of Poverty Reduction Strategy Papers, program approaches, and country and vertical approaches and how each emerged, what they set out to achieve, how they worked, successes and failures in strengthening ownership, and whether donors can live up to the commitments this entails.

Chapter 4 describes the history of development studies, which established itself as a separate academic discipline in the early 1970s—more so in some countries than others—with a strong interdisciplinary and problem-oriented or applied focus. The description of the trends covers how aid approaches emerged out of late-colonial concerns, which were then followed by a focus on reconstruction after the war in Europe and support for newly independent nations. The optimism of the 1960s was followed by the period of adjustment, even though in the 1970s the aid agenda continued to expand and basic needs and human development became more central. The period of dominance of the Washington Consensus during the 1990s was followed by a new, or renewed, focus on poverty as the central object of development aid. In the chapter, I also describe the increasing attention paid to the role of governance and institutions in promoting development and how the global security agenda after 9/11 provided new directions.

Chapter 5 describes the implementation of development projects. Despite critique of the project approach, projects remain a key modality for donors, and the chapter highlights this rationale: A project framework allows donors to show results, enables projects to be flexible and demand-driven, and provides a potential for innovation. Projects are perceived to have disadvantages as well: overloading recipient governments, particularly but not only in aid-dependent countries; "fungibility" of funding, which points to the possibility that donor funding can lead to a reduction in recipient government funding in specific areas; and sustainability, whether projects initiated or funded by donors will be maintained. The chapter highlights microfinance and sustainable livelihoods projects, and describes logframes as a key planning tool for projects.

Whereas projects focus on one-off support to development, reforms, and sector-wide approaches (SWAPs)—the subject of Chapter 6—reforms focus on the broader administrative and policy systems in partner countries. Reforms have been a key element in the development debate since the 1980s. They are complex processes, often involving dozens of policy prescriptions imposed by donors on recipient governments. Sector reform and sector-wide approaches emerged as new instruments of the aid industry in a move away from project approaches to a focus on the policy environment; Chapter 6 illustrates this movement and provides examples from sector and budget support. These approaches have had notable successes, but practices varied. Often, progress is slow, and donors have continued to operate projects with sector approaches. Other issues relate to the importance of capacity for policymaking, the intensely political nature of aid and reforms, and how impact can be measured (which leads into the discussion of impact assessment in Chapter 8).

Chapter 7 discusses four themes that are integral to development but that have not always been central to the practices of the aid industry, with frequent calls to "mainstream" them: environment and climate, gender, participation, and rights-based approaches. Each of these themes has a substantial literature, and in Chapter 7 I place these in the context of development debates, how these approaches have or have not influenced mainstream debates, and how they have managed to obtain a central place in aid practices. Since 2010, the climate crisis has become central to aid debates, as has gender, notably with growing commitments for support. Participation became a central focus during the 1990s and 2000s, with seemingly less emphasis more recently, whereas rights-based approaches have remained much more at the margins.

How does the industry know what it has achieved? Government departments are under the influence of changing public service management practices and pressure by treasuries to show results. Add to that presumed or real aid fatigue and influential critiques on structural adjustment, and it has resulted in increasing attention devoted to measuring what aid has achieved. Chapter 8 describes the technical approaches to this, the information on which assessments are based, the advantages and disadvantages of different approaches, whether these assessments are taken seriously by organizations, and possible unintended impacts of the need to "show results."

The final chapter summarizes major challenges to the practices of international development. Has aid become irrelevant, with growing importance of international trade and remittances, global security concerns, and declining relative importance of aid budgets? What do the growing number of donors mean, and what are the prospects for harmonization of donors? How can the aid industry manage the dilemma of balancing the needs of many poor countries with their capacity to use aid effectively? Should aid programs be focused on ensuring aid reaches the poor directly or on supporting broader development processes and structures. If aid remains an instrument of international politics, how can the industry ensure this status complements its focus on development and poverty reduction, and what does this mean for advocacy to decolonize the aid industry?

Notes

1. The WE Charity was discredited in 2020, partly because of its role in Canada's internal pandemic responses (Findlay 2020). Martin (2016) describes the problems of "reductive seduction" in young people's commitment to help address poverty in developing countries.

2. Heinrich, Kobayashi, and Lawson (2021) provide an empirical analysis of foreign aid and populism, specifying the latter as anti-elitist and nativist sentiments.

3. EU Emergency Trust Fund for Africa, https://ec.europa.eu/trustfundforafrica /index_en; discussed in an Oxfam (2020b) Briefing Paper.

4. UN Millennium Development Project 2005. Jeffrey Sachs, adviser to the UN Secretary-General—accompanied by rock star Bob Geldof and featured in a 2005 MTV special *The Diary of Angelina Jolie & Dr. Jeffrey Sachs in Africa*—published with Penguin his call to increasing commitment to aid.

5. The Sustainable Development Agenda can be found here: https://www.un .org/sustainabledevelopment/development-agenda/; Vorisek and Yu (2020) discuss the calculations of the costs of SDGs.

6. Miller et al. (2021) calculate the 2020 increase in ODA of $8.4 billion is a mere 0.06 percent of the $13.7 trillion of national government fiscal measures.

7. Opinion polls show that US citizens overestimate the amount of aid given by their government by as much as fifteen times, according to one, and forty times, according to another poll (quoted in Bolton 2007, 154–155).

8. The *Wall Street Journal* article is by Arvind Subramanian. Subramanian with Raghuram G. Rajan wrote a 2005 IMF working paper titled *What Undermines Aid's Impact on Growth?*

9. For example, in 2010 the United Nations Ethics Committee upheld complaints by a former UNDP employee who had suffered retaliation from the UNDP for alleging corruption in its Somalia program.

10. Michael Woolcock writes for the World Bank blogs (https://blogs.worldbank .org/team/michael-woolcock); Chris Blattman's writings can be found here: https:// chrisblattman.com/about/. Stiglitz (2002) stressed the lack of adequate information for IMF prescriptions to be effective.

11. Documented, for example, in the 2022 book by former Department for International Development (DFID) chief economist Stefan Dercon, who concludes that countries' development depends on elites' "development bargains," and aid is likely to be ineffective if that commitment does not exist.

12. See Uvin (2004, 32). Many of the authors in this strand of "deconstructive" commentary have been anthropologists. Mosse and Lewis (2006, 5) focus on "the interaction of ideas and relationships in development arena." In "critical perspectives" on development, Kothari and Minogue (2002, 2), quoting Ignacy Sachs, have argued, "There has been a failure of the postwar development project."

13. There is a rapidly growing literature on decolonizing aid: for example, Peace Direct (2021); Gender and Development Network (2021), with a focus on the UK; and Patel (2021). In 2021, the new USAID administrator's "new vision" for development and her own agency listed staff diversity as the priority for change (Power 2021).

14. See, for example, comments by experts in *The Guardian*, February 5, 2021. Jonathan Glennie (2020) calls for a radical reform of aid, stressing its narrative is outdated and patronizing; he proposes "Global Public Investment" as an alternative concept to that of aid.

15. The AidData Listening to Leaders program surveys the perspective of leaders in low- and middle-income countries on development priorities and progress

(https://www.aiddata.org/ltl). Masaki et al. (2021) analyzes the views and preferences of recipient countries' public sector officials.

16. The OECD DAC statistics provide information about status of untied aid: https://www.oecd.org/dac/financing-sustainable-development/development-finance-standards/untied-aid.htm/.

17. Gulrajani and Silcock (2020, 7); the Principled Aid Index measures the balance twenty-nine bilateral donors strike between advancing the values of global solidarity and protecting their national interests, as revealed by their aid spending choices over the previous five years. Also, see Mawdsley et al. (2018).

18. The Center for Global Development (CGD) regularly publishes the Commitment to Development Index, which describes development commitments in eight policy domains (https://www.cgdev.org/project/commitment-development-index).

2

Defining the Aid Industry

OF THE MORE THAN $250 BILLION SPENT ANNUALLY ON INTERNATIONAL development, $150 billion is official development assistance, or ODA: resources from Organisation for Economic Co-operation and Development (OECD) member governments and international official agencies. ODA, partly as grants, partly through concessional loans and in "blended" form, and for a broad range of development purposes, is spent by a wide and ever-growing number of agencies and countries.

In the first section of this chapter, I describe what ODA is, how it is defined, and how it is allocated. I then discuss bilateral channels—programs between countries—administered by aid or foreign affairs departments and ministries that have large differences in orientation and implementation. Subsequent sections describe aid provided by UN agencies such as the World Health Organization (WHO) and by the World Bank and International Monetary Fund (IMF); by nongovernmental organizations (NGOs); and by private philanthropic organizations, notably the Bill & Melinda Gates Foundation.

Official Development Assistance: Definition and Trends

According to the OECD's Development Assistance Committee (DAC), ODA is

> defined as those flows to countries and territories on the DAC List of ODA Recipients and to multilateral development institutions which are: i. provided by official agencies, including state and local

23

governments, or by their executive agencies; and ii. each transaction
. . . [is] administered with the promotion of the economic development and welfare of developing countries as its main objective . . .
and is concessional in character.[1] (OECD DAC n.d.)

ODA is provided by over sixty bilateral agencies, of which twenty-
four were DAC members in 2021, twenty are international financial
institutions, and about fifteen are UN agencies. The purpose of ODA is
to promote economic development and welfare, which includes funding for both short-term emergency and longer-term development purposes. It is provided as concessional financial loans or as grants, or as
a combination of the two. Including loans as part of aid commitment
has been criticized by organizations such as Oxfam (2020a). Until
recently, ODA concessionality was defined as aid that contained a grant
element of at least 25 percent; more recently, different rates are applied,
varying from 45 percent for least developed countries (LDCs) to 10 percent for middle-income economies.[2]

The second largest funding share of aid is from non-OECD bilateral donors. China, India, the United Arab Emirates, and Turkey are
among the largest, and they reportedly spend perhaps $100 billion on
aid. These funds are increasingly documented and researched but generally less clear than those of the OECD donors, and the funding does
not necessarily follow the same reporting conventions. For the newer
bilateral donors, there tends to be a less clear distinction between aid
and commercial and diplomatic purposes.

Third, philanthropic organizations disburse some $20–$30 billion
annually; as for the newer donors, estimates of philanthropic donations
are less clear. Most of this type of aid comes from twenty major organizations, with the Bill & Melinda Gates Foundation being the single
largest and having multiplied its endowment over the last two decades.

Finally, there is a growing practice of "blending" ODA and private
finance (UNDESA 2021; Convergence 2021; Mawdsley 2018). Estimates indicate that ODA is insufficient to achieve the Sustainable
Development Goals (SDGs), for which some $2.5 trillion is needed. The
blending of private and public finance and new financial instruments
such as impact bonds creates additional resources for development,
even if this money is not called "aid." The rich countries' pledge to provide $100 billion a year to help lower-income economies adapt to cli-
mate change, for example, combines public and private funding.[3] Critical analysis stresses that blended aid is not simply additional funding
because the investment of official aid resources used in blended funding
comes with an opportunity cost. Questions of debt relief and invest-

ments in "global public goods" complicate the accounting and understanding of aid (Rogerson and Ritchie 2020).

Figure 2.1 shows the gradual increase in ODA since the 1960s. The
trends reflect periods of "aid fatigue" in the 1980s, the renewed advocacy in the late 1990s, and the growing importance given to aid following 9/11. During the pandemic year 2020, there was an increase in total
aid (OECD DAC 2021). The increases also reflect the growing number
of countries providing ODA—even though the largest share still comes
from the traditional G7 group. Table 2.1 shows this growing group of
funders, and how their contribution has evolved since 1960.

Since 1970, most countries have committed to provide 0.7 percent of
their gross national income (GNI) for development purposes.[4] Only a
few countries have reached this level of donation (see Table 2.2): in
2016, this was achieved by Norway, Luxembourg, Sweden, Turkey, Denmark, the UK, and Germany. The Netherlands, which had previously
achieved the 0.7 percent target, has fallen behind over the last decade.
The UK announced it will not be able to achieve—temporarily—the target following the Covid-19 pandemic.

Whereas ODA has continued to increase, its importance in relation
to overall financial and economic flows to developing countries has significantly decreased. Besides ODA, the OECD records "other official
flows." These have increased tenfold over the past six decades (World
Bank Development Finance 2021)—Figure 2.2 presents the figures for

Figure 2.1   Net ODA, 1960–2020 (constant 2020 US$ millions)

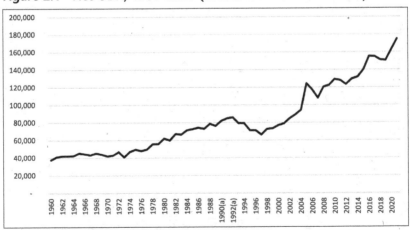

Source: OECD, "Official Development Assistance," https://www.oecd.org/dac
/financing-sustainable-development/development-finance-standards/official-development.
Note: a. Including debt forgiveness of non-ODA claims, except for total DAC.

Table 2.1 Countries' Contributions to Total ODA (net)

	1960		1980		2000		2019	
	US $	% Total ODA	US $	% Total ODA	US $	% Total ODA	US $	% Total ODA
United States	18,622	50	18,956	31	14,314	19	32,981	23
Germany	1,712	5	7,515	12	7,900	11	24,122	16
UK	3,952	11	3,663	6	5,579	7	19,354	13
France	7,144	19	5,579	9	6,422	9	11,984	8
Japan	1,367	4	7,422	12	12,095	16	11,720	8
Netherlands	487	1	3,422	6	5,248	7	5,292	4
Sweden	51	0	1,567	3	2,427	3	5,205	4
Canada	444	1	2,722	5	2,812	4	4,535	3
Norway	66	0	1,230	2	2,226	3	4,298	3
Italy	927	3	1,832	3	2,317	3	4,260	3
Switzerland	68	0	752	1	1,632	2	3,095	2
Australia	586	2	1,725	3	2,022	3	2,888	2
Spain	—	0	404	1	2,044	3	2,709	2
Denmark	84	0	1,151	2	2,766	4	2,541	2
Korea	—	0	—	0	296	0	2,517	2
Belgium	986	3	1,221	2	1,372	2	2,208	2
Austria	1	0	446	1	742	1	1,227	1
Finland	—	0	249	0	609	1	1,149	1
Ireland	—	0	85	0	393	1	973	1
Poland	—	0	94	0	50	0	761	1
New Zealand	—	0	235	0	252	0	555	0
Luxembourg	—	0	13	0	243	0	472	0

continues

Table 2.1 Continued

	1960		1980		2000		2019	
	US $	% Total ODA	US $	% Total ODA	US $	% Total ODA	US $	% Total ODA
Portugal	—	0	14	0	477	1	382	0
Greece	—	0	—	0	344	0	368	0
Hungary	—	0	156	0	—	0	312	0
Czech Republic	—	0	—	0	39	0	309	0
Slovak Republic	—	0	—	0	15	0	116	0
Slovenia	—	0	—	0	—	0	88	0
Iceland	—	0	—	0	13	0	61	0
Total DAC	36,498		60,453		74,651		146,482	

Source: Tabulated from "Financing for Sustainable Development," OECD, http://www.oecd.org/dac/financing-sustainable-development/.

Table 2.2   Net ODA Provided per Donor Country,
            as Percentage of GNI, 1970–2016

	1970	1990	2000	2010	2016
Norway	0.33	1.17	0.76	1.05	1.12
Luxembourg	—	0.21	0.70	1.05	1.00
Sweden	0.40	0.90	0.80	1.00	0.90
Turkey	—	—	0.04	0.13	0.76
Denmark	0.38	0.94	1.06	0.91	0.75
United Kingdom	0.39	0.27	0.32	0.57	0.70
Germany	0.32	0.42	0.27	0.39	0.70
Netherlands	0.62	0.92	0.84	0.82	0.65
Switzerland	0.14	0.30	0.32	0.39	0.53
Belgium	0.46	0.46	0.36	0.64	0.48
Finland	0.06	0.65	0.31	0.55	0.44
Austria	0.07	0.11	0.23	0.32	0.42
France	0.52	0.60	0.31	0.50	0.38
Spain	—	0.20	0.22	0.43	0.35
Ireland	—	0.16	0.30	0.52	0.32
Iceland	—	—	0.10	0.26	0.28
Italy	0.15	0.31	0.13	0.15	0.28
Australia	0.62	0.34	0.27	0.32	0.27
Canada	0.41	0.44	0.26	0.34	0.26
New Zealand	0.23	0.23	0.25	0.26	0.25
Japan	0.23	0.31	0.28	0.20	0.20
Greece	—	—	0.20	0.17	0.19
Slovenia	—	—	—	0.13	0.19
United States	0.32	0.21	0.10	0.20	0.19
Portugal	—	0.24	0.26	0.29	0.17
Hungary	—	—	—	0.09	0.17
Korea, Rep.	—	0.02	0.04	0.12	0.16
Poland	—	—	0.02	0.08	0.15
Czech Republic	—	—	0.03	0.13	0.14
Slovak Republic	—	—	0.03	0.09	0.12
Thailand	—	—	—	0.00	0.05

Source: Tabulated from "Net ODA Provided, Total (% of GNI)—OECD Members,"
World Bank, https://data.worldbank.org/indicator/DC.ODA.TOTL.GN.ZS?locations=OE.

the last two decades. Non-ODA flows provide a higher proportion of total flows in middle-income countries, and they tend to focus on infrastructure investments.

ODA is provided through various means. Table 2.3 shows that 72 percent was provided as grants by bilateral organizations, and about 28 percent by multilateral institutions (including the European Union). The proportion of grants has increased over the long run and forms almost

Figure 2.2   Types of Financial Flows from DAC Countries

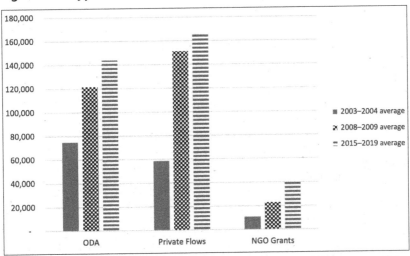

Source: "Statistics on Resource Flows to Developing Countries," OECD, accessed March 27, 2022, updated May 25, 2022, https://www.oecd.org/dac/financing -sustainable-development/development-finance-data/statisticsonresourceflowsto developingcountries.htm.
Note: In US$ constant prices.

90 percent of bilateral ODA. Recently, the proportion of loans has been increasing (Dodd, Knox, and Breed 2021). Grants come mostly from bilateral organizations, the UN, NGOs, and private charities. The World Bank and IMF, and some of the UN programs and foundations, provide loans: although the loans are concessional, this form of aid affects how donors organize themselves, and how recipients perceive the aid provided. Some of the aid is provided as a combination of grants and loans: for example, many bilateral organizations provide grants and so-called trust funds to the World Bank so that they can provide support that may not be feasible as a loan.

Table 2.4 shows sectors for which aid is provided. The largest category is social services including health, education, and government reforms and civil society support. In the data in the detailed DAC tables, basic health and education remain a small portion: $2.5 billion and $4.5 billion, respectively;[5] the total funding to basic services may be larger and included within other categories, such as support to civil society.

Humanitarian aid is among the most visible aspects of the aid industry. It forms about 10 percent of ODA, having increased during the

Table 2.3   ODA Flows by Donor Type, 2019 (US$ millions)

	Total	Percentage
Total	151,721	
Bilateral total	108,761	72
Bilateral grants	95,094	
Bilateral loans, grant equivalent	9,812	
Other bilateral	3,855	
Private sector instruments	3,762	
Multilateral total	42,959	28
Multilateral grants, capital subscriptions	42,116	
Multilateral loans	843	
Type of multilateral institution		
UN	7,565	
IDA	15,475	
Regional development banks	3,753	

Source: "Statistics on Resource Flows to Developing Countries," OECD, accessed March 27, 2022, updated May 25, 2022, https://www.oecd.org/dac/financing-sustainable-development/development-finance-data/statisticsonresourceflowstodevelopingcountries.htm.
    Note: IDA, International Development Association.

Table 2.4   ODA by Sector (US$ millions)

	2011		2019	
Sector	Total	Percentage	Total	Percentage
Social infrastructure and services	44,096	42	46,502	36
Economic infrastructure and services	14,778	14	21,729	17
Production sectors	7,561	7	9,016	7
Multisector/cross-cutting	10,132	10	11,370	9
Commodity aid/general program	3,572	3	2,327	2
Action relating to debt	4,102	4	43	0
Humanitarian aid	9,286	9	17,852	14
Unallocated/unspecified	11,543	11	18,577	15
Total	105,069	100	127,416	100

Source: "Statistics on Resource Flows to Developing Countries," OECD, accessed March 27, 2022, updated May 25, 2022, https://www.oecd.org/dac/financing-sustainable-development/development-finance-data/statisticsonresourceflowstodevelopingcountries.htm.

2010s. Many of the well-known NGOs, such as Oxfam, arose out of a history of humanitarian assistance. The category itself includes a wide range of aid agencies and activities, including in both natural and man-made disasters. It is sometimes disputed whether humanitarian aid should be classified as development aid, and in many organizations the implementation of emergency or humanitarian aid is institutionally separated from that of development aid. This book follows the practice of seeing humanitarian aid as an integral part of overall aid, on a continuum from emergencies and recovery to development.

Funding for production sectors has remained relatively low, some 7 percent during the 2010s. But over the last two decades, attention to economic infrastructure has increased, partly in response to critiques that it was underfunded. Infrastructure is financed by less concessional means. It is important to note that none of these purposes is necessarily better for poverty reduction than others: building roads can be as important as building hospitals or improving financial management for efficient service provision.

Finally, budget support and debt relief have been in decline—in Chapter 6 I discuss this. Technical cooperation (or assistance) formed about one-fifth to one-quarter of total aid; it is often questioned whether this form of aid provides as much benefit to recipient countries as other aid flows (Arndt 2000), and I discuss this topic in Chapter 5.

Official aid agencies engage private sector actors in various ways. I already mentioned blended funding and attempts to enhance private finance. Private companies operate as contractors for official aid. Most donors have throughout their histories supported, for example, small and medium enterprises, business environment reforms, and market systems development; the Donor Committee for Enterprise Development has consolidated lessons on supporting markets and opportunities that provide economic opportunities for poor people, including frameworks to measure results.[6] The Global Partnership for Effective Development Co-operation (2019), or GPEDC, reviewed a large number of private sector projects, highlighting the need for enhanced participation, for a focus on underserved areas, and for stronger monitoring.

The Allocation of Aid and Its Drivers

Motives for supporting countries through ODA vary, and donor responses are diverse and change over time. The aid industry's recipients, of course, are very diverse as well, and probably increasingly so.

ODA is support provided to countries classified as less developed. National income has been used as the main indicator of development level, though recently human assets and environmental vulnerability have been included in classifications (UNCTAD 2021). The category of less-developed countries includes a wide range of national income levels, which change over time as the Global South experiences varied economic performance. All poor countries have received some or another form of aid, including aid provided directly from other countries, such as China and India. In some recipient countries, aid forms a tiny fraction of public financial resources; but in many countries in Africa, aid can form over 20 percent of public finance. Countries in or emerging from conflict, such as Iraq, Afghanistan, and the Democratic Republic of Congo, have received large aid amounts.

Currently, almost half of ODA goes to forty-eight countries classified by the OECD as "least developed," meaning they had a per capita GNI of less than $1 per day in 2016. When countries "graduate" from the status of least developed (Yamey et al. 2018), they do not lose access to ODA, but the conditions of aid change, typically the aid becomes less conditional, and they can lose preferential trade arrangements.

The World Bank calculates that over the last two decades about 30 percent of ODA has gone to least developed and low-income countries (it used a shorter list than that of the OECD; World Bank Development Finance 2021). The share of ODA going to the poorest countries has fluctuated; it increased, for example, during the latter part of the 1990s and into the 2000s and then reversed again (OECD 2016). The share going to Africa has been roughly one-third of total ODA.

The extent to which ODA benefits poor people in poor countries varies (Briggs 2021). Many authors have argued for providing more aid to larger, less-poor countries—larger countries tend to receive relatively little aid per capita. Moreover, climate change is putting many countries at growing risk, even if they are not the poorest, leading to calls for new approaches to international funding.

Country need and poverty is only one of the drivers of aid allocation. Donors' choices of aid recipients and flow of money result from at least three other factors. First, colonial history has played and continues to play an important role, explaining, for example, the importance of British aid in India, French aid in Francophone Africa, Dutch aid in Indonesia (the Indonesian government suspended Dutch aid in 1992), and Belgian aid in Central Africa. The presence of significant numbers of immigrants can also influence aid giving, as we see in the case of migrants from Haiti in Canada.

Second, political and strategic considerations matter. They were central to aid relations during the Cold War and continue to partly explain the direction of aid. For example, aid to middle-income countries increased during the 1990s, as did the scale of aid provided to Turkey, Israel, Pakistan, and more recently Afghanistan and Iraq. Development aid can be used to enhance influence, and donor countries tend to provide more aid to recipients that support them in votes in the UN.

And third, aid flows partly follow "policy performance," the extent to which recipients' policies are in line with certain political and institutional conditions. Countries with democratic structures, for example, receive more aid from DAC donors. Policy improvements are important particularly in decisions of whether to provide program aid or budget support, a modality that for some time gained popularity with the heavily indebted poor countries (HIPC) initiative (see Chapter 6). The existence of a dedicated aid administration agency also can play a role, because receiving aid tends to be transaction-heavy and stretches over significant periods of time.

There are substantial variations across donors in terms of country focus, as Table 2.5 shows. Throughout the rest of this chapter, I describe how these various organizations operate.

Bilateral Aid Agencies

Bilateral aid is funding from national governments (mostly OECD countries) to partners in lower-income countries—governments and nongovernmental organizations—including aid provided through multilateral organizations. But that is where the commonalities end. The way that aid provision is organized, recipient countries' histories, perceptions of international roles, the focus of aid, the sectors to which it is provided, and partner countries all vary a great deal. Table 2.6 is a selective description of this diversity. It is organized around the "Three I's" framework developed by Carol Lancaster (2007, 18–22): donor countries' predominant ideas, institutions, and interests.[7] The table includes countries that have relatively dispersed aid provision agencies within their own government systems (as in the United States and China), countries where the provision of aid is managed within and coordinated by one government agency (as in the UK between 1997 and 2020 and Canada until 2013), and countries where aid provision is a program within other government ministries (Sweden, Netherlands).

Table 2.5 Main Donors' ODA Flow to Recipient Countries, by Economic Development Status

	Least Developed		Lower Middle-Income		Upper Middle-Income	
	2008–2009	2018–2019	2008–2009	2018–2019	2008–2009	2018–2019
Total DAC	43.8	47.8	33.1	35.8	22.1	15.4
Australia	34.3	36.2	49.6	51.6	14.8	12.0
Canada	57.0	56.6	30.3	30.4	11.7	12.3
France	36.6	35.5	39.3	42.4	23.8	21.7
Germany	36.1	32.4	31.4	39.9	32.0	27.1
Italy	42.8	43.5	28.5	35.1	28.2	20.9
Japan	40.8	65.9	39.9	42.8	19.1	−9.2
Korea	36.8	46.4	46.2	43.2	16.7	10.3
Netherlands	54.6	56.8	29.6	28.4	14.7	14.1
Slovenia	31.8	21.3	29.4	29.3	38.2	49.1
Spain	34.6	34.7	39.1	38.9	25.9	26.0
Sweden	54.0	58.0	31.6	26.8	12.9	13.1
Switzerland	47.5	49.2	33.0	32.9	18.4	16.6
United Kingdom	49.6	52.4	33.8	32.3	15.2	13.7
United States	43.5	52.9	28.8	32.3	26.1	13.4

Source: "Development Finance Data," OECD, https://www.oecd.org/dac/financing-sustainable-development/development-finance-data/.
Note: The negative figure for Japan in 2018–2019 indicates that loan repayments were higher than new ODA.

Table 2.6 Driving Forces of Bilateral Aid Programs

	Fragmented Aid Programs		Aid Program Within Other Ministries	Aid Managed by Own Ministry
	United States	China	Netherlands, Sweden	United Kingdom 1997–2020
Ideas	Tension liberalism—state as vehicle for redistribution. Role of United States as global leader in Western alliance	China is reemerging on global stage. Economic cooperation, not charity, South–South cooperation	Social democratic and consensus approach	Since 1997, dominance of New Labour and "Third Way"
Institutions	Presidential system. Influence Congress. Political autonomy of elements of government. Weak constituency within government	Aid is under the Ministry of Foreign Trade, Economic Cooperation CIDCA since 2018 is under State Council. Implementation is by multiple agencies	Coalition governments with sustained support for aid. Central role of "cofinancing organizations" (major Dutch NGOs). Strong cross-government support	Parliamentary system, since 1997 strong cross-party support for aid. PM and Chancellor influence benefits of aid
Interests	Aid lobby of NGOs, religious groups. Commercial: manufacture, agriculture, labor	Strong central control, little internal debate. Evolving under twin economic and diplomatic pressures	NGO cofinancing structure. Business community	Cross-party support. Strong advocacy-oriented NGOs. Business/consultancy community

Sources: Based on the framework in Lancaster (2007); references for country details are provided in text.
Notes: CIDCA, China International Development Cooperation Agency; NGO, nongovernmental organization.

Multiple Aid Entities: The United States

In Germany, Japan, France, the United States, and China, aid programs are carried out by multiple internal government entities. In the cases of Germany and Japan, compensation for the war and reestablishing their international reputations after the war, alongside economic motives, impacted the formation of aid programs. France's colonial past and desire to play a continued global role have played a central role in its provision of aid. In all cases, the multiplicity of agencies is accompanied by varied and relatively diffuse international development objectives.

The United States has been the world's largest donor but provides a low share of its GNI (0.2 percent or less) to international aid. It was the first donor in the modern era of international development: it provided aid to a Europe devastated by the war and to Asia in the wake of the Chinese revolution and outbreak of the Korean War (both the USSR and China soon started to provide aid to their allies), and it pressed other countries to establish their aid programs (Lancaster 2007, 28–29). As a major donor, the US Treasury directly influences international institutions, with a strong emphasis on fiscal responsibility.

The United States has been credited with major contributions in humanitarian intervention, health, and agriculture, including the Green Revolution. Its influence is perceived to have waned in the last decades, and its aid is often severely criticized. There is a perception "that USAID has . . . become excessively bogged down by rules, regulations, reporting, and earmarks imposed by Congress and its own bureaucracy" (Norris 2021).

US aid is shaped by conflicting trends in thinking (Lancaster 2007): classical liberalism, which argues for limiting the role of the state (which contributed to the Washington Consensus), and ideas about the state needing to play a key role in redistribution. The aid program has been shaped by the way the United States perceives itself as a world power and leader of the noncommunist world. Private charities play a key role, with an increasing number of very large private donors, which reflects a preference, relative to European traditions, for private over government-run support. For example, private charities provided more than three times the amount of aid provided by the US government in response to the Asian tsunami (Brainard 2007a).

The US aid program is fragmented, with at least twenty institutions involved in aid delivery alongside the US Agency for International Development (USAID), which often leads to calls for a clearer, unified framework. According to Kenny (2022), while only 9 percent of all US foreign assistance is implemented by the governments, firms, and nonprofit organizations in recipient countries, the Department of Defense allocated 23 percent of the budget in 2020 (31 percent went to multilateral organizations).[8] USAID is the "real" development agency, with about half of the total US budget, but it does not have cabinet-level status and is often excluded from high-level policy discussion (Lancaster 2007, 101).

Political and administrative institutions have been influential in shaping its aid program. The executive and legislative branches of government both play a role in shaping policies and deciding expenditure. Congress plays a direct role in funding and implementing decisions and imposing many of the congressional directives and special budget measures, called earmarks.[9]

As in other countries, there is an aid lobby in the United States. NGOs of varied backgrounds, including religious and labor organizations, universities, and think tanks, promote the use of aid for relief, development, environment, family planning, and gender equality. Commercial interests and lobbies include manufacturers and agricultural producers. The use of food aid has been an important and much criticized example of the commercial influences on aid, as it has helped to reduce the US food surplus with active support from Congress and the NGOs that have helped deliver this.[10] Whereas food aid may be important in some emergency situations, it is not an effective use of aid in normal situations.

Although support for aid with developmental objectives is not absent in the United States, other interests tend to have the upper hand. National security considerations have been a strong driver of the aid program, increasingly so since 9/11, with increased involvement of the Pentagon and frequent White House engagement in aid initiatives. The Department of State has been the main driver of the diplomatic motives behind the aid program, especially during the Cold War and in the post-9/11 period.[11]

Critiques have kept aid from being used entirely for diplomatic purposes; development has remained a core component of the aid program. Alongside initiatives on AIDS such as the President's Emergency Plan for AIDS Relief (PEPFAR; Lancaster 2008, 22–29), the Millennium Challenge Corporation (MCC) is an example of an initiative with good results and direct presidential support, as described in Chapter 6.

China's Growing Aid Program: ODA and Commercial Cooperation

China's growing aid program has received a lot of attention as a result of the country's jump into prominence as a global economic actor, its accession to the World Trade Organization (WTO) in 2001, and with much polarized debate,[12] particularly its role in Africa, and recently its role in the debt crisis in low-income countries.[13] China's aid program is often thought to be exceptional and very different from that of (older) OECD programs, but it can be described according to the framework used here.

Official estimates of Chinese aid remain unclear, but international research has now created a good overview of China's aid activities (Custer et al. 2021). Total "development finance" from China outgrew that from the United States during the 2010s. Whereas about three-quarters of US finance is ODA (grants and highly concessional loans), for China this is only 12 percent; its ODA remains smaller than that of the five major traditional donors.

China has provided aid for a much longer period than the last two decades, when it has received much attention. The Korean War motivated China to develop formal foreign and aid policies. It continued to provide substantial amounts of aid through the Great Famine and the Proletarian Revolution, with a strong ideological stance. There was a brief drop in aid post-1976, but since the early 1980s China has gradually built up its international development strategy, using aid as a tool alongside foreign policy and its economic development strategy. In 1982, the Ministry of Foreign Economics and Trade was established under the State Council. Policy statements signaled a greater emphasis on economic considerations, which became apparent a decade later after a period of sanctions following the 1989 crackdown.

In 1993, the new Ministry of Foreign Trade and Economic Cooperation (MOFCOM) and the Department of Foreign Aid became responsible for the aid program, alongside the State Council and Ministry of Commerce. In the second half of the 1990s, and with the "Going Out" Strategy of 1999, the China Exim Bank and China Development Bank became the main sources for official cooperation, providing concessional loans and export and import credits. During this period, China was both an aid recipient and a donor, and it used the experience of the former to build its own aid program. It played an important role in the creation of BRICS (Brazil, Russia, India, China, South Africa) instruments and institutions, such as the Contingent Reserve Arrangement and the New Development Bank.

China's international role continued to expand, and it became the largest creditor to developing countries, which led to critiques that it was creating a debt trap for lower-income economies (Chatzky and McBride 2020). China initiated the Belt and Road Initiative (BRI, formerly "One Belt One Road") as its diplomatic and economic cooperation strategy, focusing on major infrastructure and connectivity investment in some seventy countries. Although expected to have a major impact on global economic growth, some perceive it as a threat and an attempt to create China's economic dominance, and counterinitiatives have been formulated.

As Chinese aid itself and the international attention paid to it continued to grow, the need for a coordinating and distinct implementation agency became apparent, and Chinese officials studied OECD examples of aid agencies. In 2018, the government set up the China International Development Cooperation Agency (CIDCA), with some 100 staff. It is not an implementation agency but formulates strategic plans, taking over MOFCOM's responsibility. It is subsidiary to other ministries and reports directly to China's State Council. CIDCA oversees strategy, policy, project approval, and evaluation, working with about ten implementing agencies; concessional loans and multilateral finance remain the responsibility of Exim Bank and Ministry of Finance (Lynch, Andersen, and Zhu 2020).

CIDCA's white paper in 2021, which followed policy papers in 2011 and 2014,[14] reaffirms China's core principles of mutual benefit, non-interference, South–South cooperation, and a concept of development that includes trade and not just aid. It refers to aid effectiveness principles, somewhat aligning with other development agencies' debates. It shows a doubling of aid volumes over a five-year period, with a commitment to a focus on least developed countries.

Aid Programs as Part of Foreign Affairs

Within the aid industry, Nordic countries and the Netherlands generally have been seen to have progressive and relatively focused aid programs. In these countries, the departments for aid are implementing agencies or are merged into the ministries of foreign affairs. This group of donors, often referred to as "like-minded," show relative stability, both in terms of internal organization and public support—though neither is set in stone. Its embeddedness in foreign affairs has not stopped these like-minded donors from being a progressive force in the aid industry; the provision of aid for development purposes in these small countries is seen as an essential part of their foreign diplomacy.

The aid agencies were set up in the 1950s and 1960s, starting in Norway, where an aid program was established in 1952 with an objective of pacifying the Labour Party's opposition to Norway joining the North Atlantic Treaty Organization (Lancaster 2007, 30). Despite the early political origins during the Cold War, in these countries strong support for aid programs exists, and they have generally reached the 0.7 percent target, and Sweden even committed itself to a higher percentage (Lammers 2008). Social democratic orientations have exercised strong and stable influences over the aid programs.

In the case of the Netherlands the aid program also grew out of the colonial period. A tradition of coalition governments and consensus-style policy formulation sustained involvement of Dutch NGOs, and the business community contributed to a relatively stable aid policy environment. Dutch aid is an example of a program being housed within the Ministry of Foreign Affairs, with an integrated administrative structure and personnel policy. Although integrated, it maintains a clear development and poverty focus through a "two-headed" structure, with cabinet ministers for foreign affairs and development cooperation.

Dutch aid has had strong ministerial and parliamentarian support, and policymakers believe in the added value of a Dutch aid program, despite its relatively small size. Individual ministers have exercised much influence over the direction of and given visibility to the Dutch aid program, including Jan Pronk and Eveline Herfkens, both responding to international thinking and national constituencies, and, to a lesser extent, van Ardenne, who emphasized the role of the private sector.

The organization of Dutch aid has reflected the traditional organization of public and political life along religious and nonreligious backgrounds or pillars. "Cofinancing organizations" have had a central place in Dutch development cooperation. Although the percentage of aid to NGOs is not larger than the OECD average, Dutch aid has strongly emphasized working with NGOs in recipient countries. Following criticism and attention to quality, in the early 2000s the NGOs were made to compete for funding.

The Dutch program has been viewed as a front runner that adapts to new challenges and tests innovative operational approaches (DAC Peer Review, the Netherlands, 2006). It has interacted closely with multilateral institutions, highlighted, for example, in moves toward sector approaches, debt relief, and poverty reduction strategies. Dutch aid emphasized sectoral budget support to overcome the problem of project aid that had contributed to "islands of development." In the 1990s, Dutch policy started to emphasize "policy coherence," calling for collaboration between different government departments regarding policies that traditionally were not part of aid programs but that influence global development and poverty reduction.[15]

Dutch policy has continued to advocate for poverty reduction, human rights, and gender equality.[16] Dutch aid has been relatively well targeted to low-income countries, though attempts to focus aid on a smaller number of countries have not been successful—despite moves to concentrate efforts, in 2004–2005 Dutch funding could be found in 125 countries. Dutch aid appears to have a relatively strong tradition of independent evaluation and review, and over time demands for results have increased (Schulpen 2005).

The growing populism over the last two decades has challenged the traditional strong public support for aid in the Netherlands. The country maintained a target for ODA of 0.8 percent of its GNI, but this has declined since 2000. The aid program has become more closely tied to Dutch commercial and political interests and, as a 2018 policy paper shows, places a greater focus on "unstable regions . . . tackling the root causes of poverty, migration, terrorism and climate change" (Ministry of Foreign Affairs, the Netherlands 2018).

Aid Programs as a Ministry

In the UK and Canada, development programs have at times been their own ministry and part of ministries of foreign affairs, reflecting political priorities and with important implications for program implementation.

During the last decades, the UK has been perceived as one of the leading voices in aid driving a poverty orientation and improvements in the efficiency of aid. This push was initiated in 1997, under the stewardship of Clare Short, who held a cabinet seat, and with strong support from both the prime minister and chancellor. The UK gained a reputation as trailblazer in international development, having focused its development programs on the needs of the poorest countries and the most vulnerable within those countries.

The UK aid program also grew out of its colonial history. Provision of financial assistance was part of the late colonial administrations. Britain formulated the Colonial Development and Welfare Acts 1940 (replaced in 1945). Based on Fabian views of the state, and optimism about possible projects, it started, for example, a groundnut scheme in Tanganyika and the Gambia egg scheme. Historical links and approaches continued to play an important role. For example, the forced *ujamaa* villagization in Tanzania showed continuity with the former colonial policy in rural Tanzania.

Britain established development corporations in 1947. In 1958, it decided to extend aid to former colonies within the Commonwealth and some countries outside of it. In 1964, the incoming Labour government established the Ministry of Overseas Development. In 1967, it was demoted out of the cabinet, and in 1970 it was incorporated into the Foreign Office. It became a ministry again during the Labour government from 1974 to 1979, and the percentage of aid increased to 0.51 percent of national income, but commercial and other motives continued to exert their influence. Under the Conservative government during 1979–1997, aid again became part of the Foreign Office, and political, industrial, and commercial objectives obtained greater weight.

When the Labour Party came into power in 1997, it established the Department for International Development (DFID), and the aid budget started to rise. DFID increased the number of professional staff, and the number of overseas offices expanded significantly from a handful in the mid-1990s to over forty ten years later. The orientation of aid changed drastically, from a concern for promoting commercial and political interests toward a focus on reducing poverty in the poorest parts of the world. A crucial part of the new orientation was the decision to untie aid: whereas, previously, benefits to UK commercial interests were an integral part of the aid provided, according to the white paper of 2000 and enshrined in law in the International Development Act 2002, the purpose of aid became sustainable development, welfare promotion, and poverty reduction. The department adopted targets for the proportion of aid going to the poorest countries and developed criteria for poverty-focused allocations (DFID 2016). A strong policy drive was highlighted in a series of white papers, including reports on globalization and governance. As in the Netherlands, DFID promoted collaboration among government departments as a way to ensure foreign and commercial policy objectives contributed to global poverty reduction, and it developed shared objectives with other government departments.

The DFID started to focus on measuring the results of its aid efforts. New Labour's emphasis on modernization of government urged DFID to show how aid can work. Just as in all UK government departments, targets, ways of measuring achievements, and reports proliferated. The aid program is also extensively discussed and scrutinized through the parliamentary International Development Committee and the Independent Commission for Aid Impact.

The focus on showing achievements of its aid program has been accompanied by an explicit acknowledgment that DFID by itself cannot achieve stated development goals. Alongside European donors such as the Netherlands and Sweden, DFID strongly emphasized the importance of both partnership with recipient countries and harmonization among donors to reduce burdens on recipients. DFID emphasized the need for reform of the international system through strong advocacy at international meetings and by issuing "institutional strategy papers" that publicly set out the UK government's aim to initiate reforms.

The UK has a strong and issue-oriented civil society. Public support for aid remained strong, and several NGOs have continued to engage critically with the official aid program. The country probably has the world's strongest policy research community that supplies DFID with technical expertise and forms a critical voice, promoting broad public debate.

As it did elsewhere in Europe, during the 2010s the aid program shifted toward a stronger focus on the UK's national interests. In 2015, DFID stated: "We want to meet our promises to the world's poor and also put international development at the heart of our national security and foreign policy" (DFID 2015, 3). In 2020, the DFID was integrated into the Foreign, Commonwealth and Development Office (FCDO). Observers have raised concerns that this undermined the UK's reputation for poverty and development focus and represented a loss of expertise and transparency.[17] In that year, too, the aid budget was reduced from 0.7 to 0.5 percent of GNI.

Canada had a lead agency (rather than a ministry, with a minister of development) between 1968 and 2013. CIDA, the Canadian International Development Agency, was created under Liberal prime minister Pierre Trudeau, and it consolidated the dispersed functions under trade and external affairs ministries. CIDA succeeded the External Aid Office in line with the government's intentions to enhance its global role and presence.[18] CIDA administered most of the country's ODA, with mandates to reduce poverty, promote human rights, and support sustainable development.

In 2013, CIDA was dissolved and its responsibilities were absorbed by the Department of Foreign Affairs, Trade and Development (DFATD), though there was still a minister of international development. Under the Liberal government of Justin Trudeau, this became Global Affairs Canada (GAC). As in the UK, commentators have expressed concerns that this change might weaken the poverty objectives. An internal report commented on the difficulty of integrating departments that have very different approaches and work cultures.

Canadians are generally thought to be supportive of international development goals, an approach described as "humane internationalism," which enjoys strong civil society support (Black 2016). Canada sees itself as a progressive force and a medium power in international politics. It makes significant contributions to peacekeeping activities and actively supports, for example, the Mine Ban Treaty and the creation of the International Criminal Court. Lester B. Pearson, the former Canadian prime minister, was awarded the Nobel Peace Prize for his work on the Suez crisis in 1956 and the creation of modern peacekeeping. Since 2000, Canada has placed strong emphasis on aid to "fragile states," with major support sent to Afghanistan, Ethiopia, and Haiti.[19] Canada also supported the US-led Coalition and war in Afghanistan, which became the largest recipient of Canadian aid, with over CA$3.5 billion of aid given during 2001–2020, some 3 percent of overall Canadian aid. Canada provided aid to Afghanistan for a variety of purposes via NGOs and, for example, the 2006 Afghanistan Compact.[20]

Even though it was former prime minister Pearson who helped initiate the 0.7 percent target, Canada's aid has been around 0.3 percent since the mid-1990s, after a high of 0.58 during the "golden age" of the 1970s. Liberal governments generally are more supportive of the developmental and humanitarian objectives of aid, but this has not materialized as significant increases in aid commitments. Prime ministers tend to have significant impact on the country's aid program. In the 1990s, Jean Chrétien reversed a decline in aid and prioritized Africa. Under Paul Martin, in the mid-2000s, CIDA developed a "whole-of-government" approach (also known as a 3D approach of defense, diplomacy, and development), integrating aid more closely with foreign policy objectives. Under the Stephen Harper government, into the 2010s, Canada's interests became a more important driver of the aid program, and development-specific expertise and issues became less important. The integration of CIDA into DFATD further connected aid objectives to Canadian political and commercial interests.

Justin Trudeau's government revived the aid program's emphasis on humanitarian objectives and rejuvenated Canada's role in the international system with the motto "Canada is back." The prime minister has made efforts to gain a seat on the UN Security Council. Canada's signature policy emphasis became the Feminist International Assistance Policy (FIAP), led by Ministers Marie-Claude Bibeau and Karina Gould.[21] Canada continues to promote the private sector's role in international development.

Limits of Bilateral Aid

This brief description of a few bilateral aid programs shows that there are significant dissimilarities in the ways they structure their aid programs. The way aid is provided reflects a country's public policies and its respective history. The ways aid agencies are situated vary widely, and this affects the focus, implementation, and monitoring of aid programs. Humanitarian motives, such as seen in the 1970s and 1990s, have been superseded by economic and foreign policy objectives balanced by a continued advocacy to make aid work for development and justice. Some aid agencies can shelter themselves well from pressures on aid, but the national and political pressures never disappear.

Because of the complexity of bilateral aid agencies, some observers have argued for more multilateral and harmonized approaches, because the channeling of aid through agencies independent of national interests, pressures, and reporting requirements would allow a tighter focus on development purposes. We will come back to this in later chapters; here, it remains important to emphasize that the provision of aid is tied to national ideological, social, and political-administrative traditions.

World Bank and IMF

Like much of the aid industry, the origins of the World Bank and International Monetary Fund (IMF), also called the Bretton Woods institutions after the place in New Hampshire where they were created, lay in World War II. In July 1944, at the Bretton Woods Conference, forty-five governments discussed rebuilding Europe and the global economic system after a devastating war and how to avoid repeating the disastrous economic policies and nationalism of the 1930s. The Bretton Woods Conference led to the signing of the General Agreement on Tariffs and Trade (GATT) in October 1947, which later became the World Trade Organization (WTO). Although their role keeps evolving, and alternative and complementary institutions such as BRICS's New Development Bank and the China-led Asian Infrastructure Investment Bank (AIIB) have developed, and critique of voting shares and appointments of the heads of institutions remains, the World Bank and IMF continue to be central to the aid industry.

The IMF's main responsibilities are to promote international monetary cooperation, facilitate expansion of international trade, promote exchange stability, assist in the establishment of a multilateral system of payments, and provide resources to members experiencing balance-of-payments difficulties—all arguably essential conditions for economic growth and poverty alleviation. It employs three instruments: appraisals of member country's economic situation, which most countries publish; technical assistance and training for economic policies and systems; and financial assistance for balance-of-payments problems, conditional on a policy program designed and agreed between the IMF financing and national authorities.[22]

IMF's resources are provided by its 190 member countries, primarily through payments of quotas that reflect a country's economic size. The IMF has about 2,500 staff from 140 countries and is governed by and accountable to the governments of member countries. A board of governors represents member countries; they meet at the IMF–World Bank Annual Meetings. Twenty-four governors sit on the International Monetary and Finance Committee (IMFC), which meets twice each year. Day-to-day work is conducted by the twenty-four-member executive board, which is supported by IMF professional staff.

Over the last two decades, the number of alternative and complementary international financial institutions has grown. International reserves have grown rapidly, particularly since 2000 and through the financial crisis of 2008. Increasingly, and fueled by crises in 1997 and 2008, the IMF's role has been complemented by both regional and bilateral financial arrangements; for example, in Europe and Southeast Asia, by China, and the Banco del Sur in South America was set up in 2007 but has not been capitalized. The IMF's role was again enhanced, and criticized, during Greece's financial crisis in 2010 and with the 2020 European sovereign debt crisis (Masters, Chatzky, and Siripurapu 2021). For the lowest-income countries, as shown during the Covid-19 pandemic, the IMF's role has remained most important (Iancu, Kim, and Miksjuk 2021).

There have always been questions about the developmental role of the IMF and critique of its harsh lending conditions. The British delegation to Bretton Woods led by economist John Maynard Keynes proposed an international monetary fund as a cooperative fund that member states could draw upon to maintain economic activity and employment, but the US plan prevailed, and the IMF was set up like a bank that would ensure borrowing states could repay their debts on time and that was less focused on avoiding recession and unemployment. The IMF came to focus on fiscal stability, while the World Bank became the institution responsible for investment in development.

Over time, the IMF has successively incorporated development objectives into its policy, despite continued pushback. In the 1980s, IMF loans came to be known as structural adjustment loans (discussed in Chapter 6), and the IMF, working with the World Bank, added poverty reduction policies to its focus on economic stability. After the 2008 financial crisis, it created the Poverty Reduction and Growth

Trust (PRGT) to provide interest-free support loans to countries during crises, and this trust was expanded sixfold during the Covid-19 pandemic (IMF 2021). It has started to regard gender and environment as "macro-critical" and essential parts of its responsibilities.[23] It has produced analysis on fuel subsidies and cost of corruption (Wolf 2019). During the Covid-19 pandemic, the IMF enhanced its role for low-income countries by supporting debt relief and reallocation of resources through Special Drawing Rights (SDRs) and the use of the Catastrophe Containment and Relief Trust (CCRT), established during the 2015 Ebola outbreak.

The World Bank's initial focus was rebuilding postwar Europe. Its first loan, worth $250 million, was to France in 1947 for postwar reconstruction, followed by the much larger Marshall Plan. From the start, its organizational structure was unlike that of the other UN institutions. Founding governments have representatives on the World Bank board, but voting powers reflect the countries' financial contributions, and until today—despite gradual decline of relative US contribution—the United States has dominated in important decisions, including nominations for the World Bank president. There has been a slow movement toward more diverse representation in senior management in both Bretton Woods institutions.[24]

The World Bank is in fact a group of five associated institutions; their financial commitments and relative size are shown in Table 2.7. The International Bank for Reconstruction and Development (IBRD) is the oldest and focuses on poverty reduction in middle-income and "credit-worthy" poor countries. It has a board with twenty-five executive directors who jointly represent IBRD's 184 member countries. It provides loans, guarantees, risk management products, and analysis and advice. IBRD borrows in capital markets at low cost. It has provided over $500 billion in loans around the world since 1946, with its shareholder governments paying in about $14 billion in capital.

IDA, the International Development Association, provides financing to the world's eighty-one poorest countries that are unable to borrow on market terms. The funding is highly concessional through interest-free credits and grants financed by donor countries' contributions—which are "replenished" every three years—and IBRD's net income transfers. The resources support, for example, country-led poverty reduction strategies in a range of policy areas, including productivity, governance, investment climate, and access to basic services. Annual commitments have increased steadily to about $10 billion per year; since 1960, IDA has provided $458 billion to 114 countries.

Table 2.7   World Bank Group Institutions' Financing (commitments, US$ millions)

	2017	2018	2019	2020	2021
WBG (total)	68,274	74,265	68,105	83,547	98,830
IBRD	22,611	23,002	23,191	27,976	30,523
IDA	19,513	24,010	21,932	30,365	36,028
IFC	18,345	19,027	14,684	17,604	20,669
MIGA (gross issuance)	4,842	5,251	5,548	3,961	5,199
Recipient-Executed Trust Funds	2,962	2,976	2,749	3,641	6,411

Sources: "Fiscal Year Data," World Bank, https://www.worldbank.org/en/about/annual-report/fiscal-year-data; "International Bank for Reconstruction and Development," World Bank, https://www.worldbank.org/en/who-we-are/ibrd.

Notes: IBRD, International Bank for Reconstruction and Development; IDA, International Development Association; IFC, International Finance Corporation; MIGA, Multilateral Investment Guarantee Agency; WBG, World Bank Group.

The third institution in the group is the International Finance Corporation, established in 1956. It is the private sector investment entity of the group, providing support to businesses deemed too risky by commercial investors. The fourth, the Multilateral Investment Guarantee Agency, established in 1988, provides insurance for foreign direct investment in developing countries, providing both guarantees against noncommercial risks and advisory and mediating services. Fifth, the International Centre for Settlement of Investment Disputes focuses on settlement of investment disputes between foreign investors and host states, handling 210 cases since its foundation in 1966.

The World Bank has gradually broadened its mandate, and it has grown to about 10,000 professional staff, with capacity for development research that far outstrips any university department or think tank.[25] After shifting attention from the postwar reconstruction to development, its focus became infrastructure and "sound" projects that could be expected to generate financial returns—influenced by economic models that emphasized accumulation of physical capital. A focus on poor countries was formalized with the creation of IDA in 1960—in the middle of the Cold War, and a year after the Cuban revolution—which offers credit on much better conditions to the poorest countries.

A focus on poverty was intensified during the Vietnam War under Robert McNamara, who became World Bank president in 1968 after leaving the US Department of Defense. The World Bank started to pay attention to the question of whether economic growth did "trickle down" to poor people. McNamara created a range of new, specialized departments, for rural and urban development, health and nutrition, education, and so forth—thus creating a group that overlapped in function with the UN specialized agencies and, according to some, overextended itself and its mandate.[26] Much later, in 2013, this complexity was expressed in a reorganization that set up fourteen global practices and five cross-cutting solutions areas.

While the World Bank continued to see poverty reduction as its prime mandate, the second oil crisis in 1979 following the Iranian Revolution initiated a focus on "structural adjustment lending." The rise in energy prices hit many poor countries heavily. McNamara announced that countries would need to devalue their currencies to reduce trade imbalances and cut public spending to be able to pay back the loans, including those that countries had obtained in the preceding period when petrodollars were easily available. Structural adjustment lending was conceived as a form of support to reformers, to give them breathing space during a period of adjustment. It also meant a shift in development approach from projects toward programs, which I discuss in Chapters 5 and 6. In collaboration with the IMF, the World Bank's policy prescriptions for structural adjustment were broadened beyond the spheres of exchange rates and government budgets, and conditions around reducing trade barriers, free prices, and privatization were added. Although presidents after McNamara reduced the institution's attention on poverty reduction, and it took a long time for the World Bank to respond to calls to address the issues of debt relief, poverty did feature even during the years of adjustment. During the 1980s, the World Bank developed programs to monitor and analyze poverty that would prove to be influential despite criticisms, as I discuss in the next chapter.

No part of the aid industry has been under more criticism than the World Bank and IMF, including for their alignment with repressive regimes, and this gathered momentum during the 1990s. Sebastian Mallaby (2005, 7) highlighted the "alternating bouts of millenarianism and contempt" as well as the "cacophony of our advanced countries." At times (e.g., under the Reagan, George W. Bush, and Trump administrations), World Bank and IMF were undermined by the contempt and ignorance of its large shareholder, the United States. This was compounded by increased technical criticisms about the quality of projects. For example, member countries were critical of the manipulation of information in the "Doing Business Index" (which had been shown to have an impact on countries' foreign investment).[27]

The criticism covers a broad spectrum. International NGOs criticize the World Bank and IMF for aligning with global financial interests rather than the poor, for inappropriate advice regarding capital account liberalization, for the poverty impact of structural adjustments and neglect of basic services for health and education, for the environmental consequences of bank projects, and even for newer approaches such as the Comprehensive Development Framework and the Poverty Reduction Strategy Papers, which I discuss in later chapters. Some argue that the institutions should focus on providing support to the poorest countries and withdraw from lending to middle-income countries (for example, the Meltzer Commission established by the US Congress in 1998). Others criticize the World Bank for too strong a focus on poverty or they argue that it should shrink its range of activities and that it needs to focus on investing in the preconditions for economic growth. From the early 2000s, pressure increased for the World Bank to focus more on infrastructure and to listen more to its large borrowers.

James Wolfensohn's leadership (1995–2005) helped address some of the criticism the World Bank had been subjected to. Against resistance of many senior staff, he accepted that the organization needed to address debt relief. He broke an internal taboo and talked about corruption, particularly after reviewing the World Bank's approach in Indonesia. He strengthened the focus on governance, on countries' ownership of development, and on participation by beneficiaries of development projects and policies (which came to be seen as crucial to success of development projects). He brought in more informal leadership, tried to change the image of an arrogant institution, promoted decentralization of functions to country offices, sped up quality assurance, and improved relationships with international NGOs.

After Wolfensohn, appointments under Bush and Trump appeared to pull the World Bank back in a conservative direction. President Bush nominated Paul Wolfowitz, a former Pentagon official, as World Bank president. He was unpopular with many development advocates because of his background and personal style. He deepened the focus on corruption but had to resign because of the special considerations he gave to his girlfriend.

Bank presidents after Wolfowitz helped to modernize the institution and continued to expand its focus in line with the growing ambition of the SDGs and financing for development agendas. Robert Zoellick, a former US trade representative, restored calm after the unrest caused by Wolfowitz, increased lending significantly,[28] continued efforts to address corruption, and handled concerns about the World Bank's irrelevance with the growing role of China. Korean American Jim Kim was president for two terms until he resigned in 2019; he was unpopular because of internal reforms (mitigated by the appointment of Kristalina Georgieva, who later came to be the IMF managing director, as World Bank CEO) but was credited with managing difficult relations with President Trump.[29] He continued to promote a broad development orientation and innovative responses to the Ebola, refugee, and climate crises. Under the Trump administration, David Malpass, then undersecretary for international affairs with the US Treasury Department and critical of the World Bank, was appointed as president. Two years into the role, he is seen as playing an important, if sometimes controversial, role in addressing the growing climate crisis (Rappeport 2021).

Regional development banks exist in addition to the global financial institutions. Their governance and operations are similar to those of the World Bank, they play key roles in crisis responses, such as during the pandemic in 2020, and they also have seen their functions expanding over time. The "original" banks are the African Development Bank (AfDB), Asian Development Bank (AsDB), European Bank for Reconstruction and Development (EBRD), and the Inter-American Development Bank, or IADB (Ottenhof 2011; Clifton et al. 2021). The IADB was established first, in 1959, and provided loans and technical cooperation and became a model for the other regional institutions. It is owned by forty-seven member countries and is governed by boards of governors and of executive directors. Voting power is based on financial contributions, but the charter ensures the position of majority stockholder for the borrowing member countries as a group.

The group of regional development banks has expanded, first, with the Islamic Development Bank (IsDB) in 1975, which has provided loans worth $150 billion since and currently has fifty-seven member countries. The Asian Infrastructure Investment Bank was proposed and launched by China in 2013, with a starting capital of half that of the World Bank, high credit ratings, and over 100 members. The "BRICS Bank" or "New Development Bank" established in 2015 by Brazil, Russia, India, China, and South Africa has not generated the same amount of interest, though its membership started to grow in 2020.

Multilateral Agencies

The multilateral system of the United Nations is complex, so much so that the coordination among UN agencies, called "One UN," became a key focus. Unlike at the World Bank and IMF, UN decisionmaking operates on a one-member-one-vote principle. The UN is not just an aid agency but a political organization, with the Security Council as one of its main bodies. Its total revenue was over $60 billion in 2020, divided over forty-four organizations.[30] For the aid industry, it is the central convening power that can gather leaders who have committed themselves to international development, as seen in the 1995 Copenhagen, 2000 Millennium, and 2015 Sustainable Development summits. Its aid is provided mostly as grants, similar to many bilateral agencies, with a budget in 2019 of $7.5 billion (excluding World Bank and IMF), about 5 percent of total ODA.

The UN's forerunner was the League of Nations, established after the end of World War I, which aimed "to promote international cooperation and to achieve peace and security." The International Labour Organization (ILO), now a UN specialized agency, was created under the Treaty of Versailles. The name United Nations was coined by US president Franklin Roosevelt, and the body officially came into existence in 1945, after representatives of fifty countries met in San Francisco to draw up the United Nations Charter based on proposals from representatives of China, the Soviet Union, the United Kingdom, and the United States.

The image of the UN is strongly influenced by its Secretary-General. The UN was strengthened under the leadership of Kofi Annan, who served two terms, between 1997 and 2006, and who won the Nobel Peace Prize; he also faced criticism for the Oil-for-Food Programme in Iraq. Ban Ki-moon, the eighth Secretary-General, played important roles in the Darfur crisis and in helping to convince the government of Myanmar to open its door to international assistance and personnel. He faced criticism for the cholera crisis in 2010. He helped foster climate change agreements, including the 2015 Paris Agreement, which was carried forward by António Guterres, who became Secretary-General in 2017.

The work of the UN is carried out by and through its numerous agencies and funds, each devoted to a particular aspect of development, some of which I describe below. This decentralization implies the Secretary-General has relatively limited management power. There are about thirty UN specialized agencies plus several research institutes. As traditional sources of funding began to dry up, UN agencies looked for alternatives, including corporate sponsorship and organizations such as UNICEF (the United Nations Children's Fund), which have a record of raising private contributions.

The United Nations Development Programme (UNDP), founded in 1965, was set up to coordinate UN work in more than 160 developing countries, but in fact often operates as a technical agency itself. Its annual budget is about $5 billion to $6 billion, including noncore contributions. One of the best-known contributions has been its Human Development Report (HDR), which was started in 1990 and created under the leadership of Pakistani economist Mahbub ul Haq. The HDR provides major inputs to the international development debate, including the Human Development Index, and helped to broaden the understanding of development from a narrow perspective on and measure of economic growth (as described in Chapter 4).

UN agencies may be best known for humanitarian operations and the peacekeeping operations mandated by the Security Council. In the 1990s, and particularly after failures during the conflicts and genocides in Bosnia and Rwanda, the UN increased efforts in peacekeeping. Under the leadership of Kofi Annan, who accepted responsibility for the failures during the 1990s, a proactive approach to conflicts was promoted (UN 2004), involving major stakeholders, for example, in East Timor, which established independence in 1999. In 1998, the International Criminal Court was established, with member countries accepting the jurisdiction of a permanent international criminal court for the prosecution of the perpetrators of the most serious crimes.

The Office of the United Nations High Commissioner for Refugees (UNHCR) was established in 1950 to support World War II refugees. It aims to safeguard the rights and well-being of refugees and help them exercise the right to seek asylum and safe refuge. UNHCR estimates that since 1950 it has helped more than 50 million refugees, with over 6,000 staff in more than 100 countries. Its importance and budget increased during the 1990s as the number of conflicts rose after the end of the Cold War, with emergencies in former Yugoslavia and the Great Lakes region of Africa and elsewhere. Its budget increased steadily during the 2010s to almost $5 billion, mostly funded by direct, voluntary contributions from governments, nongovernmental organizations, and individuals.

In 2005, the UN Central Emergency Response Fund (CERF) was established by the General Assembly to "speed up relief operations for emergencies, make money available quickly after a disaster and help in financing underfunded emergencies." In 2020, it provided $848 million, supporting 70 million people with assistance and protection in fifty-nine countries.

The United Nations Children's Fund (originally called the United Nations International Children's Emergency Fund) is among the most visible of UN agencies, including in the vaccine distribution during the

Covid-19 pandemic (Glassman and Handa 2021). Many governments perceive it as an important partner for support during emergencies, and many celebrities act as "goodwill ambassadors" for it. UNICEF focuses on development and social protection of young children, basic education, and HIV/AIDS and children. It has a presence in many low-income countries and particularly in emergencies and humanitarian settings. It publishes its *State of the World's Children Report* annually, where it describes progress and challenges on these issues. It has a strong advocacy focus and bases its advocacy for children primarily on the 1989 Convention on the Rights of the Child (CRC).

The International Labour Organization (ILO) is a tripartite organization, the only one of its kind, that brings together government representatives, employers, and employees in its executive bodies. It was created in 1919, at the end of World War I, and under influence of industrialists Robert Owen and Daniel Legrand. ILO's charter was adopted during World War II. During the 1950s and 1960s, the number of member states doubled, industrialized countries became a minority, and its budget grew fivefold. The ILO received the Nobel Peace Prize in 1969 and has been lauded for its support of the Solidarność Union in Poland. The ILO faced politicization in the East–West conflict, and the United States withdrew from the organization in 1977.

The initial motivation for the ILO was humanitarian, focusing on workers' conditions and exploitation. Political and economic motivations played a role in its creation too: it was feared that social unrest or even revolution might occur if labor conditions were not addressed (the charter's Preamble notes that injustice produces "unrest so great that the peace and harmony of the world are imperiled"). International coordination was viewed as essential to ensure countries that implemented social reforms were not disadvantaged vis-à-vis their competitors. The governing body is the ILO executive council, which is elected by the conference, half of whose members are government representatives, one-fourth are workers' representatives, and one-fourth are employers' representatives.

The ILO supports technical cooperation projects for employment and personnel planning and provides labor market information through multi-expert, long-term projects and short-term consultancies. Regional employment teams provide technical advisory services and training courses in response to requests from countries. Technical missions for public works programs have helped governments define the scope of special public works programs, assess technical feasibility, and evaluate organizational and staffing needs.

One of the best-known ILO technical programs has been the World Employment Programme (WEP). Following a convention adopted in 1964 and inaugurated in 1969, this was perceived as the ILO's main contribution to the United Nations Second Development Decade. It focused on basic needs of the poor through advisory services, technical cooperation, and research. ILO initiatives have focused on the informal sector through the Regional Employment Program for Latin America and the Caribbean (its Spanish acronym is PREALC) and the Jobs and Skills Program for Africa (JASPA). These programs included data collection, training and technical cooperation, promotion of income-generating projects for specific vulnerable groups, apprenticeships and training for production, and case studies of regulatory barriers. In 1991, the ILO emphasized the "working poor," who work in jobs in the informal sector and on the fringes of the recognized labor market. It proposed that governments set and meet targets of creating sufficient jobs; in 2015, employment became part of the SDGs framework. In 1992, the ILO created IPEC, the International Programme on the Elimination of Child Labour, which I describe in Chapter 5 as an example of a technical assistance program.

The United Nations Conference on Trade and Development, or UNCTAD, is one of the lesser-known agencies. Created in 1964, its mandate is to promote the interests of the Global South in world trade. The idea for this agency originated in concerns that the WTO (then GATT, the General Agreement on Tariffs and Trade) and World Bank and IMF did not sufficiently represent the interests of low-income economies. It played a key role, alongside the Group of 77 and the Non-Aligned Movement, in the formulation of proposals for a New International Economic Order (NIEO). It focuses on supporting developing countries in accessing the benefits of economic integration through analysis, dialogue and technical assistance in trade, investment, finance, and technology—for example, the Digital Economy Report analyzes how data, a key strategic asset, can be managed to support achieving the SDGs (UNCTAD 2021).

WHO, the World Health Organization, is the United Nations specialized agency for health, established in 1948 following advocacy of physicians Szeming Sze of China, Karl Evang of Norway, and Geraldo de Paula Souza of Brazil. Governed by 193 member states through the World Health Assembly, WHO provides programs in health education, food, food safety, nutrition, safe water and basic sanitation, and immunization. Previous action plans focused on promotion of breastfeeding, production of foods to improve local diets, distribution of supplementary foods, and provision of health education. In 2018, its annual budget (revenue) was over US$2 billion; the United States, the Gates Foundation, and the UK are the main donors. Ninety percent of the WHO budget is funded by "voluntary" contributions of donors, which may hinder the organization's planning. The Covid-19 pandemic led to a call to significantly increase its resources.

WHO's global disease monitoring has been credited with helping to contain the spread of diseases. As the severe acute respiratory syndrome (SARS) broke out in China in 2002, some of the earliest alerts were provided by WHO's automated system that monitors electronic media, including discussion groups, for signs of disease outbreaks that could lead to epidemics. A global network links local networks that monitor and respond to outbreaks of infectious diseases, and WHO has a network of leading laboratories that can identify the cause of the disease and develop diagnostic tests.

WHO has been criticized for lack of effective responses. Research indicates that it did not provide an effective operational response to the 2013–2016 West Africa Ebola epidemic. There appears to be a discrepancy between what the global community expects the WHO to do and its financial and organizational constraints (Wenham 2017). Similar concerns were expressed during the Covid-19 pandemic, including regarding the lack of effectiveness of the COVAX initiative, which was set up to "guarantee fair and equitable access for every country in the world."[31]

The International Fund for Agricultural Development (IFAD) was established in 1978 with the mandate to increase food production in the poorest food-deficit countries. It finances agricultural development and food production projects with a combination of loans and grants. IFAD increasingly prioritized targeted poverty interventions by focusing aid in drylands regions and by concentrating on microfinance for landless and near landless people. In Chapter 5, I describe a program in Orissa in eastern India as an example of this approach, which evolved over the 1980s and 1990s, and one that encountered substantial and perhaps surprising criticism.

Concerns About the Future of Multilateralism

UN agencies usually do not come under the same kind of public criticism as the World Bank and IMF. But, like the aid industry more broadly, it has received critical attention, including for operational inefficiencies and lack of competency.[32] Emerging powers such as China criticize the UN for its lack of reform in governance to match changing global powers.[33]

The UN also remains subject to national politics. Criticism of the UN has been driven by growing populism and nationalism.[34] John Bolton, the US temporary ambassador to the UN during 2005–2006, was a strong opponent of multilateralism and wanted the UN to switch to voluntary contributions and make voting dependent on a country's financial contributions to the UN. President Trump pulled out of the Paris Climate Accord and threatened to pull out of WHO, too, which would have left the Gates Foundation as its largest contributor.

Despite criticism, the UN's humanitarian role and its role in the aid industry continue to expand as the need for global cooperation in health and the climate crisis expands. Emerging economies also see the UN as an important opportunity to have a presence in global forums.

Nongovernmental Organizations

Development-focused nongovernmental organizations, or NGOs, form a significant part of the aid industry. On average, about 15 percent of aid flows are spent through nongovernmental channels, with, for example, the United States having a high proportion of total aid flowing through its NGOs. The term NGO is applied to a diverse range of institutions, including the charities in OECD countries, similar organizations in the South (e.g., Oxfam India and Oxfam Hong Kong), small self-help and other organizations that often operate in one locality in very poor areas, and large organizations such as the Grameen Bank and BRAC in Bangladesh (discussed in Chapter 5).

The world of NGOs is vast, with a substantial literature, and I can only describe a small and selective portion of this variety (Banks 2021; Brass et al. 2018) and delineate it from the broader and partly overlapping concept of civil society.[35] Although there are no clear records, the number of NGOs has increased significantly since the 1980s. A count in 1989 showed 4,000 organizations devoted to international development existing in OECD countries alone. In Kenya in the late 1990s, over 500 development NGOs were operating, of which 40 percent were foreign (Desai 2002, 495; Manji 2003). GiveDirectly provides direct cash to poor people, a concept that is supported by evidence of the effectiveness of unconditional cash transfers. A number of organizations facilitate international volunteers (Sobocinska 2017; Tiessen, Cassin, and Lough 2021).

Charitable activities were significant during colonial rule; scholars have argued that the European colonial projects and humanitarian interventions were closely intertwined (Goris and Magendane 2021). NGOs came to play an increasingly important role in formulation of development policy in the 1950s, often working in close collaboration with bilateral or multilateral organizations. There is a view among the official aid agencies that nongovernmental partners have a key role to play in implementing aid programs because they have local knowledge and capacity. They are key during emergencies, often times when official aid channels cannot reach the populations affected by man-made or natural crises. (See Box 2.1.)

Box 2.1   Oxfam UK and Elsewhere—from Relief to Development to Advocacy

Oxfam is one of the best-known NGOs. It is now a confederation of independent charitable organizations led by Oxfam International. Though it has British roots and a nationwide network of shops in the UK, national Oxfam organizations have been set up in several other countries: for example, in India, Oxfam GB set up a registered society in 1978, which became independent in the mid-1990s.

Oxfam's origin lies in World War II. A national Famine Relief Committee in 1942 tried to persuade the British government to allow supplies through the blockade and raised funds for war refugees and displaced people. The Oxford Committee for Famine Relief, consisting of businessmen and church and university representatives, met for the first time in 1942. After the war, the committee continued and broadened its focus: to relief of suffering in wars by providing food, clothing, and grants, and to "other causes in any part of the world."

During the 1960s, Oxfam's resources expanded, reflecting the worldwide increase in attention to poverty. Oxfam presented a different picture of poverty: poor people were not perceived as passive victims but as human beings with dignity, and Oxfam provided education and information materials focused on causes of poverty and suffering. Oxfam's overseas operations focused on employing local staff and supported self-help schemes in water supplies, farming practices, and health. Relief work in the Sahel in the late 1970s stressed traditional ways in which communities survived and tried to ensure local people controlled development programs.

Over time, Oxfam increasingly focused on advocacy and lobbying at the global level and on providing research and analysis on issues

continues

Box 2.1 Continued

---

such as the causes of poverty, pesticides, food and others forms of aid, Third World debt, and more recently extreme global inequalities.

In 2018, Oxfam and the NGO sector was shocked by an investigation by *The Times* of London that showed gross misconduct of staff, sexual exploitation, the downloading of pornography, bullying and intimidation, and failure to make this public. The incident led the International Development Committee of the UK Parliament to issue a report about sexual harassment and abuse in the humanitarian sector. Oxfam has since reinforced a focus on decolonization.

Sources: "About Us," Oxfam, https://www.oxfam.org/en/our-history; Sriskandarajah (2020).

NGOs became more popular as the criticism of governments in developing countries was increasing and a (neoliberal) emphasis on the importance of the private sector and limits of the state's role became stronger (Veltmeyer 2012). Over time, the advocacy role of NGOs has become stronger, supported by availability of electronic media, and they advocate vis-à-vis the World Bank and IMF and contribute to global initiatives, such as the Extractive Industries Transparency Initiative (EITI).[36]

In the Global South, this has entailed advocacy for rights as well as the piloting of new approaches, and monitoring of government policy. For example, African NGOs developed a toolkit for policy monitoring (CAFOD, Trócaire, Christian Aid, 2006) in the areas of gender and the environment. Another example is in the context of a proposed $470 million in aid to Cambodia in 1999. This had a condition stipulated that tree log processing and export be independently monitored to ensure that the Cambodian government complied with the forestry reforms it had promised. With donor funding, the British environmental and human rights group Global Witness became the official independent monitor of Cambodia's forestry sector. The independent monitoring role complemented the new Forest Crime Monitoring Unit and inspection teams from the Forestry Department and the Ministry of Environment, both of which received donor funds to support monitoring. The Cambodian government terminated Global Witness's activities in 2003 and banned members of the organization from entering the country in 2005 (Global Witness 2007).

In the Global North, NGOs play a key role in development debates. They have formed powerful influences for large organizations such as the World Bank, particularly during the tenure of Wolfensohn, who cultivated relationships with a vocal NGO community. Influential issue-focused advocacy efforts of NGOs include the Make Poverty History campaign, the Jubilee Debt Campaign (now called Debt Justice), and Jubilee South. (See Box 2.2.)

Box 2.2   The Jubilee Debt Campaign and Its Impact

Since the mid-1990s, the Debt Crisis Network organized meetings on debt with African leaders, aid agencies, unions, and churches, raising the profile of the indebtedness of poor countries and the impact this has on poor people. This pressure contributed to the heavily indebted poor countries (HIPC) scheme launched by World Bank and IMF in 1996. The HIPC initiative was widely criticized for providing too little relief too late, and an international debt campaign continued to grow.

In 1997, the Debt Crisis Network transformed itself into the Jubilee 2000 Coalition. A broad-based campaign crystallized and began to mobilize under this banner, including Black refugee groups, trade unions, and organizations such as the Mothers Union and the British Medical Association. Well-established NGOs campaigned strongly behind the Jubilee 2000 campaign. Churches organized Jubilee 2000 meetings, and people chained themselves to railings, resulting in one of the largest demonstrations ever organized in the UK. It gathered about eighty-five groups as members in forty countries: "Jubilee South asserts that we—the peoples of the South—are the real creditors of a massive ecological, moral, social, financial, and historical debt," debt that was in their view imposed by international financial institutions (IFIs) and Northern governments to further their own profits and interests. Efforts to address debt and its impact on poverty gathered steam again around 2020, when low-income countries' public debt again had risen during the pandemic and under the growing climate crisis.

Sources: Debt Justice, "What We Do"; "No Climate Justice Without Debt Justice," https://debtjustice.org.uk/.

NGOs have also influenced large development projects. This has contributed to the withdrawal of some large and controversial World Bank projects, has increased surveillance over, for example, dam projects, and has led to the development of detailed environmental and social guidelines ("safeguards") in project preparation. In India, influential groups have vigorously opposed large projects such as the Narmada Dam and the influence of the World Bank in the country's policymaking. In September 2007, a group of organizations organized an "Independent People's Tribunal on the World Bank Group in India" that highlighted the fact that "local groups have been opposed to the often-disastrous intervention of multilateral agencies in India's economy and development. Specifically, the retrogressive impact . . . is being felt throughout the country by almost all marginal and impoverished sections of society."[37]

Although NGOs have been commended for the role they play within the aid industry because they are close to and able to reach poor people effectively, NGOs, too, come under regular criticism. NGOs' impact tends to remain limited, and smaller organizations tend to lack professional capacity.[38] NGOs also are scrutinized for their use of money. Coordinating bodies have been formed that help the public check the credibility of NGOs (e.g., GiveIndia), but publicized scandals do continue to highlight the importance of strengthening accountability and transparency. Relationships between governments and NGOs are not always collaborative, as the examples in Box 2.2 and Box 2.3 describe.[39]

The role of NGOs in social change is also debated. NGOs are not necessarily representative of marginalized groups. They are outsider organizations that work to help deprived groups, but they are not "membership-based organizations of the poor," like the Self-Employed Women's Association (SEWA) in India is (Chen et al. 2007). It is sometimes argued that NGOs working in the South are an invention of the aid industry. For example, in Vietnam the number of NGOs increased very rapidly in the 1990s, and in 2003 international NGOs were disbursing $90 million per year, but, partly because of its communist history, Vietnam did not have a concept that resembled NGOs or civil society, and the introduction of aid terms resulted in misunderstandings and disputes (Salemink 2006). Some argue that the work of NGOs, particularly as it is associated with a neoliberal development model, "contributes marginally to the relief of poverty, but significantly to undermining the struggle of African people to emancipate themselves from economic, social and political oppression" (Manji 2003).

Box 2.3   NGOs and Governments as Adversaries

Agragamee is an organization that was set up in 1981 in Odisha (formerly Orissa) and that is devoted to supporting tribal communities in the poorest parts of India. It has been heavily involved and often praised for its programs that reach the poorest, including watershed projects, and its support of grassroots organizations.

The organization resisted the exploitation of minerals by large companies, arguing this would be a looting of the tribal areas of Orissa. It withdrew from the collaboration in an IFAD project because it believed that the voices of project beneficiaries were not given sufficient attention.

The government revoked Agragamee's license in 1998 after a violent incident between villagers and companies (the nature of which remains disputed). For government officials, the organization and the incidents illustrated that NGOs can be "anti-developmental." The organization reobtained its license the next year, and after four decades has contributed to progress in livelihoods, representation, and rights.

Source: "Our Journey," Agragamee, https://agragamee.org/our_journey .php.

The Growth of Private Philanthropy

Over the last two to three decades, the aid industry has been expanded with new private philanthropic initiatives. The OECD has gathered statistics on private philanthropy for development (OECD DAC 2018b) that show a contribution of $8.8 billion in 2018–2019. Half of this was provided for health initiatives and half to Africa. The Gates Foundation contributed about half of the total ($4.1 billion), followed by the BBVA Microfinance Foundation ($1.2 billion), and thirteen other foundations with donations over $100 million each.[40]

These philanthropic efforts come in many forms, and here I discuss four overlapping categories: support for specific causes, foundations, companies, and public–private collaboration. First, private or charitable support often focuses on specific issues or events. There are charitable responses to large disasters such as the Asian tsunami and the Gujarat and Sichuan earthquakes, which generated huge support, including among diaspora communities and private companies (in China as well).

Hindu Aid coordinated development efforts of Hindu organizations in the UK and responded to disasters such as the tsunami by bringing together offers of support from the UK's South Asian population. In 2007, Dr. Kumar Bahuleyan, a Dalit or untouchable from Kerala who had made millions as a neurosurgeon in the United States, reportedly donated $20 million to his home village to establish a neurosurgery hospital and health clinic.

High-worth individuals have donated large amounts. Warren Buffett has donated $44 billion over his lifetime, about half his stake in Berkshire. McKenzie Scott donated over $8 billion to 800 organizations (in the Global North and the Global South) in 2020 alone, with a unique "no-strings attached" policy. And the importance of private donations could grow: for example, in 2021 Elon Musk promised the World Food Programme $6 billion if they could show how that would solve world hunger. US citizens donate over $400 billion per year, some 2 percent of the country's gross domestic product (GDP);[41] a small portion of this is for poverty or development purposes, either at home or abroad.

As mentioned, former politicians play a role. Although international development was not a priority for Bill Clinton's US presidency, he started the Clinton Foundation and the high-profile Clinton Global Initiative (CGI), following the example of previous US presidents starting with Jimmy Carter. CGI brings together global leaders, former heads of state, business executives, scholars, and representatives of nongovernmental organizations, a "Philanthropy Oscars" with 1,000 participants.[42]

Second, large foundations exert a growing influence over the aid industry. For a long time, the Rockefeller and Ford Foundations have made significant contributions to international development. In 2006, the Canada-based Mastercard Foundation was set up and became the second largest foundation, and in 2021 this foundation had the aim to "help 30 million young people to secure dignified and fulfilling work by 2030." The Bill & Melinda Gates Foundation has become particularly important. It has grown its endowment from $20 million in 2000 to $65 billion in 2021, outstripping the budgets of traditional agencies. The Gates Foundation's focus has been health, but it also invested in the agricultural sector, for example, with its $150 million donation to the Alliance for a Green Revolution in Africa alongside the Rockefeller Foundation.

Foundations are set up in the Global South too. The foundation set up by Mo Ibrahim, a Sudan-born businessman, aims to contribute to better governance, for example, through awarding a prize to good leaders after they step down from office, publishing an index of African governance ratings, and contributing money to address misinformation during the Covid-19 pandemic. In China, charitable donations have been rising fast, particularly those created by large companies (Chu and Wang 2018), and there are traditions and a growing philanthropic movement in Africa and other parts of Asia, such as the Tata Trust in India.

Third, during the 1980s, pharmaceutical companies started to donate drugs to eliminate diseases, which developed into successful collaboration among a range of agencies. In 1987, Merck & Co. announced it would donate the human formulation of its big-selling veterinary antiworm medicine ivermectin to combat river blindness (onchocerciasis). By 1998, nearly 25 million people were treated in thirty-one countries. In 1996, Glaxo Wellcome started donating its antimalaria drug. SmithKline Beecham, with the WHO, in 1998 launched a program with a twenty-year goal of eliminating the parasitic disease lymphatic filariasis, which can lead to disfiguring elephantiasis and male genital damage. In the same year, Pfizer announced it would donate its best-selling antibiotic as part of a large, integrated, five-country effort to control trachoma, a disease that typically affects the poor and can lead to blindness.

These initiatives, too, have been criticized. Companies have been criticized for using these programs as public relations exercises that possibly even undermine free trade in drugs. Some argue that the programs are not easy to administer in poor countries, and these initiatives may go ahead at the cost of other important programs (for example, meningitis and yellow fever control). But it is generally accepted that the initiatives have helped save millions of people from crippling diseases.

Fourth, public agencies and private companies have collaborated to promote the SDGs. Much more than the Millennium Development Goals (MDGs), the SDGs foreground the role of the private sector, and calculations of costs to achieve the SDGs emphasize that public funding must be complemented by private investment. New initiatives include public partnerships with large international companies, including through the UN Global Compact; the growing field of impact investment; corporate social responsibility initiatives; and public–private partnerships. In 2020, for example, private foundations provided over US$2 billion for climate action in developing countries (Ackva, Sandkühler, and Buxton-Walsh 2021).

These private philanthropies thus have added to the complexity and diversity of the world of aid in terms of backgrounds, motivations, ways of operating, and how these have evolved over time. Donor approaches change often, agencies frequently implement internal reforms and restructuring, and many agencies continue to expand their range of activities. New agencies emerge that may seem very distinct, but they also blend into the wide field of support for development and poverty reduction as part of the broader international role they envisage. The SDGs have encapsulated this continuously growing field to some extent by acting as a "coalition magnet" (Janus and Tang 2020); with the pandemic and the growing climate crisis, the field continues to expand. In the next chapter, I focus on the aid industry efforts to coordinate this complexity.

Notes

1. The DAC is the OECD's specialized committee on development cooperation. It collects data on aid flows of its members, which are available online and in the annual Development Cooperation Report (OECD 2022). Members periodically review amount and quality of aid programs (Bracho et al. 2021).

2. The definition excludes the concessional transfers to countries that are not low-income countries, such as Russia and Israel, but are often very important in countries' aid programs (Lancaster 2007).

3. According to OECD figures, of the $71 billion climate finance in 2017, $55 billion was bilateral and multilateral public funding, $2 billion was export credits, and $15 billion was private funding ("Financing for the Future: Climate Finance and the Role of ODA," Donor Tracker, https://donortracker.org/insights /financing-future-climate-finance-and-role-oda-0; see further Timperley 2021; Kenny 2020).

4. OECD DAC (2016). Clemens and Moss (2005) discussed the origin of the targets, assumptions behind the calculations, and declining relevance in terms of low-income countries' overall financial resources.

5. "Aid Spent on Health: ODA Data on Donors, Sectors, Recipients" (factsheet), Development Initiatives, https://reliefweb.int/sites/reliefweb.int/files/resources/Aid _spent_on_health.pdf.

6. Donor Committee for Enterprise Development, https://www.enterprise -development.org/.

7. The OECD's 2009 *Managing Aid: Practices of DAC Member Countries* is an excellent overview of bilateral agencies. Official definitions of aid can be found at https://data.oecd.org/oda/net-oda.htm. The edited book by Hoebink and Stokke (2005) includes chapters on the main characteristics of sixteen European donors.

8. Kenny's analysis is based on the official aid data available at https:// foreignassistance.gov/.

9. Flickner (2007) described the congressional restrictions on aid. Amsden (2007) highlighted the negative side effects of the way US foreign aid has been managed. Tendler (1975) described the early workings of USAID and the many restrictions on and unpopularity of aid.

10. Park (2019); Wahlberg (2008). In 2007, the US NGO CARE decided to forgo $45 million a year in federal financing for food aid because it believed the

system was inefficient and may hurt the people it aimed to support (Center for Global Development, www.cgdev.org).

11. Under President George W. Bush, "transformational diplomacy" became a prime principle of US foreign policy, also influencing other countries' approaches: "One of our best tools for supporting states in building democratic institutions and strengthening civil society is our foreign assistance. . . . One of the great advances . . . has been the creation of a bipartisan consensus for the more strategic use of foreign assistance" (Rice 2008, 11).

12. The work by Deborah Bräutigam (2011) includes attempts to dispel myths around China's aid and foreign investment, including on labour conditions and the idea of a debt trap of Chinese loans. Janus and Tang (2020) describes the convergence of China's aid approaches with that of older donors.

13. In 2022, China's ambassador to Kenya wrote a strong critique of perceptions of China's role in the debt crisis in the East African paper *Business Daily* (Zhou 2022).

14. "White Paper Highlights China's Progress in Int'l Development Cooperation," China International Development Cooperation Agency, January 12, 2021, http://en.cidca.gov.cn/2021-01/12/c_581653.htm; see also Cichocka, Mitchell, and Ritchie (2021).

15. Sweden passed a bill that commits all government departments to contribute to development in eleven policy areas; NGOs composed a "coherence barometer" and assessed the record as mixed (Lammers 2008).

16. The Borgen Project (2021) provides an overall positive view of Dutch aid (Eliza Browning, "The Importance of the Netherlands' Foreign Aid," Borgen Project, February 5, 2021, https://borgenproject.org/the-netherlands-foreign-aid/). This also provides assessment of the Danish and Swedish aid programs.

17. Calleja and Gavas (2021); Ritchie, Mitchell, and Hughes (2021) suggested declining aid focus on poorest countries and Africa.

18. Donaghy and Webster (2019), who added that the creation of IDRC, the International Development Research Centre, in 1970 underlined these intentions.

19. Described by Carment and Samy (2016), who highlighted that responses were unstructured and not informed by analytical tools. Baranyi and Khan (2016) analyzed the effectiveness of Canadian aid in five fragile contexts.

20. The independent Manley Commissions (Government of Canada 2008) concluded that there was a positive role to play for Canada in Afghanistan and the importance of integrating aid, defense, and diplomacy.

21. A Government of Canada (2019) note discusses the operationalizations and guidance of the FIAP. In 2021, it published an approach to support paid and unpaid care work. The OECD DAC (2018a) peer review highlighted the new civil society partnership policy, the untying of aid, competency-based workforce approaches, and strengthening of evaluation as key initiatives under the Liberal government.

22. In 2021, resources available to lend to member countries were $1 trillion, through quotas (including Special Drawing Rights, or SDRs), multilateral borrowing arrangements, and bilateral borrowing agreements ("At a Glance: The IMF's Firepower," International Monetary Fund, April 29, 2021, https://www.imf.org/en /About/infographics/imf-firepower-lending).

23. Sayeh (2021); see also the World Bank, *Gender Strategy: 2016–2023* (World Bank 2015).

24. Runde (2020); similar questions about appointments of senior leaders are asked about the other UN agencies, for example, the appointment of the UNICEF executive director, who has always been an American.

25. The World Bank's oral history project provides insights into its internal workings ("Oral History Program," World Bank, https://oralhistory.worldbank.org/).

26. Mallaby (2005, 35–36). It established a division for lending for health in 1979, and soon became the largest investor in health (Ruger 2005). Rogoff (2022) expressed a similar critique vis-à-vis the IMF.

27. Machen et al. (2021); Nicola (2021). This led to arguments for the bank to stop doing the survey and calls for resignations. A World Bank Independent Evaluation Group (2022) evaluation assesses the instrument's effectiveness.

28. Sandefur and Patel (2016) analyzed the growth in lending under different bank presidents; that growth was much higher under Zoellick (2007–2012) and Wolfowitz (2005–2007) than under Wolfensohn (1995–2005) and Kim (2012–2016).

29. Edwards (2019); this included managing difficult relationships with President Trump and setting up the Women Entrepreneurs Finance Initiative, or We-Fi, at the behest of President Trump's daughter, Ivanka.

30. "Total Revenue," UN System Chief Executives Board for Coordination, https://unsceb.org/fs-revenue. Linda Fasulo's (2004) "insider's guide to the UN" provides an overview of the wide range of responsibilities of the UN and its internal workings from a US perspective.

31. COVAX is co-led by the Coalition for Epidemic Preparedness Innovations (CEPI); Gavi, the Vaccine Alliance; and UNICEF and is part of the Access to Covid-19 Tools ACT-Accelerator. By the end of 2021, it had delivered some 700 million vaccines, much below set targets or needs (partly as the pandemic in India led to a decline of delivery by the Serum Institute of India).

32. According to Mark Malloch Brown (2007), the UN "was not corrupt but incompetent. Its failures were supervisory and operational. There was inadequate auditing and in many cases little-to-no attempt to rectify the faults that were found in audit." According to Sommerer et al. (2022), the UN "have principal decision-making bodies prone to deadlock and are best known for their failures to deliver."

33. Zhou (2019); Hallaert (2020). At Davos in 2017, General Secretary of the Chinese Communist Party Xi Jinping remarked: "The global economic landscape has changed profoundly in the past few decades. However, the global governance system has not embraced those new changes and is therefore inadequate in terms of representation and inclusiveness."

34. Evidence from the International Social Survey Programme's National Identity module in 1995, 2003, and 2013 shows that attitudes about international organizations have become less positive (Bearce and Scott 2019).

35. A good introduction to civil society organizations is Batliwala and Brown (2006); see also Michael Edwards (2020) and his writings on Future Positive (http://futurepositive.org/).

36. Batliwala and Brown (2006); Krawczyk (2019) stressed its limits to influence global policymaking; Davies (2014) described a longer history of transnational civil society.

37. Independent People's Tribunal, http://www.worldbanktribunal.org.

38. A literature review by Brass et al. (2018) indicates that the literature reports positive effects of NGO interventions in health and governance but also that there are significant geographical and methodological gaps in that knowledge.

39. DFID started a civil society program in Orissa, managed by a Delhi-based NGO. DFID found hundreds of NGOs in Orissa alone bidding for funds and rumors that individuals were offering services to write proposals.

40. Global estimates of charitable donations are uncertain. The CAF World Giving Index provides an overview of the charitable activities by individuals across the world (based on World Gallup data in 128 countries): its most recent data show Indonesia as the most generous country.

41. Charity Navigator, "Giving Statistics," https://www.charitynavigator.org/.

42. *The Economist,* "The Brand of Clinton." September 22, 2007, 69.

3

Can the Aid Industry
Let Go?

THE COMPLEXITY OF THE AID INDUSTRY, THE DIVERSITY IN INSTITUTIONS and their incentives, as described in the previous chapter, is a common concern within the industry. As many have argued, it can undermine country "ownership," which is seen as an essential precondition for aid to effectively contribute to development. Even though aid is gradually becoming less important in countries' finances and policies, these aid relationships remain important.[1] Countries' leaders want aid they receive to support their own reform efforts and not impose undue burdens on their systems (AidData 2021).

In this chapter, I describe initiatives within the aid industry that promote ownership and coordination. First, the World Bank introduced the Comprehensive Development Framework as a unified framework to improve the effectiveness of aid, with country-led partnership. The UN developed an assistance framework that stressed similar principles as a foundation for coordination across UN agencies. Second, Poverty Reduction Strategy Papers (PRSPs) became the way debt relief and aid was meant to be delivered and to create coordination and ownership. Third, concern about coordination of activities has prompted actors in the aid industry to create agreements to coordinate donor countries' aid delivery, but challenges imposed by the political and administrative imperatives of each aid agency remain. Fourth, program and sector approaches focus on supporting aid recipients' administrative and policy systems rather than providing aid projects that focus on one-off and clearly traceable support. Fifth, global partnerships have emerged in education, health, and climate to galvanize donor commitments in specific sectors.

Comprehensive Frameworks at World Bank and the UN

One of the changes James Wolfensohn made at the World Bank was the introduction of the Comprehensive Development Framework (CDF). He announced this in early 1999 with much fanfare, though few people around him saw it as pathbreaking, and some argued it would mean increased conditionalities. It was piloted in thirteen countries and presented as "a means by which countries can manage knowledge and resources to design and implement effective strategies for economic development and poverty reduction. It . . . is centered on a long-term vision—prepared by the country through a participatory national consultation process—that balances good macroeconomic and financial management with sound social, structural and human policies."[2]

Referring to the World Bank's emphasis on short-term macroeconomic stabilization, the CDF stressed the need for considering longer-term structural and social considerations, including in education, health, infrastructure, and training. Development strategies, Wolfensohn thought, should have a long-term vision, be comprehensive or holistic, and embrace social and structural issues alongside concerns about stabilizing the economy. The CDF stressed the need to measure the impacts of investments on people and their needs and the idea that development performance should not be measured by inputs and outputs but by results on the ground—which mirrored a broader move of the industry toward "results-based management" (see Box 3.1).

Although he defended structural adjustment, saying that some of the donor-driven aid delivered under it had been effective, Wolfensohn accepted the critique that many of the difficult adjustment measures had not been sustained, and sometimes they even were undone. This brought to the fore the idea that if recipient countries have greater say in shaping reforms, governments are more likely to commit to seeing them through. Therefore, the CDF stressed that goals and strategies needed to be "owned" by recipient countries, and the goals and strategies needed to be shaped through a process that included broad citizen participation. To ensure effective use of human and financial resources, the CDF emphasized partnerships between government, civil society, the private sector, and external assistance agencies. It emphasized that recipient countries should be in the lead of aid relationships, be in charge of coor-

Box 3.1   Results-Based Management and Programming

Although many different interpretations and perceptions exist, results-based management (RBM) is generally seen as a management strategy that focuses on outcomes and impacts, and how an organization's human and financial resources can be best used to optimize outcomes. Different terms mean roughly the same thing, such as "management for results" and "performance management." The logframe discussed in Chapter 5 is a common management tool used for this purpose, though its use, or at least the term itself, precedes that of RBM. The use of RBM in the aid industry followed the popularity it gained as part of the "new public management" reforms of the early 1990s, which brought market strategies into public management.

RBM has become a central theme of the aid effectiveness agenda and emphasizes engaging all stakeholders in the process. More recently, instruments have been introduced to align financing and programming with results. In 2012, the World Bank introduced a lending instrument called Program-for-Results, alongside investment projects and development policy financing. It links disbursement of funds directly to the achievement of specific program results.

Sources: Binnendijk (2001); Hatton and Schroeder (2007); "Program-for-Results Financing (PforR)," World Bank, October 5, 2021, https://www.worldbank.org/en/programs/program-for-results-financing.

dination, and actively manage aid rather than be led by donor preferences. The framework encouraged coordination to improve efficiency and coherence in the use of financial flows and services and to take advantage of synergies among development partners.

While Wolfensohn was pushing for changes at the World Bank, UN Secretary-General Kofi Annan equally tried to make the UN a more effective and efficient institution. In a letter to Wolfensohn, Kofi Annan stressed: "It is the responsibility of governments to be at the centre of all coordination efforts on assistance. Too often a bewildering surfeit of diagnoses and programming modalities has strait-jacketed national responses and imposed high transaction costs . . . the task now is to ensure consistent quality country-level partnership that reduces costs and overlap and boosts our overall impact."[3]

Annan called for the UN to develop a unified approach to the development goals that included an emphasis on the interlinkages of peace and security, poverty reduction and human development, and respect for human rights. Apart from developing a Common Country Assessment, this push resulted, in 1999, in the development of the United Nations Development Assistance Framework (UNDAF), a collective UN response to national priorities and needs. When the PRSPs became the most common instrument or plan used by recipient countries, the UNDAF was presented as the UN's business plan in support of the PRSPs. An example of the UNDAF for Uganda, a country seen as a leader in new aid approaches, is described in Box 3.2.

Box 3.2   Donor Frameworks and the Uganda Experience

Much writing on the new approaches at the end of the 1990s came from donors' experiences in Uganda. Uganda, during the 1990s, in the eyes of many donors, underwent successful stabilization and adjustment, and in the middle of the 1990s the country was seen as a model of success in development, a model for effective aid relationships, with strong and development-oriented leadership. In the 2010s, these relationships and donors' assessments of progress on issues of corruption, for example, worsened, as described by Habraken, Schulpen, and Hoebink (2017).

The government of Uganda and donors actively coordinated to improve aid effectiveness. The country's Poverty Eradication Action Plan (PEAP) became an overarching strategy for poverty eradication. Donors were asked to commit to supporting only programs in this plan, and the plan described preferred aid modalities. Agencies providing budget support used the policy matrix as a framework for funding and the Medium-Term Expenditure Framework for monitoring and implementation. Progress was assessed through one annual government–donor review.

The UN framework for cooperation in Uganda was set against the development challenges of rapid population growth and poverty. Civil war had uprooted more than a million people. Corruption and human rights violations were still big concerns, but improvements were in progress, according to the aid community, and would be felt

continues

Box 3.2 Continued

into the early 2000s. The UN declared itself in support of the government to achieve the Millennium Development Goals (MDGs) and the PEAP, and the UNDAF was intended to support decisionmaking, enhance collaboration, and reduce transaction costs. It focused on a multidimensional approach to address development challenges; on equal opportunities, empowerment, sustainability, human rights, and governance; on minimizing the impact and halting the spread of HIV/AIDS; and on resettlement and reducing the regional disparities.

The UNDAF committed the UN to "multidimensional" partnerships with the Ugandan government, NGOs, the private sector, bilateral donors, and UN agencies. The strategy revolved around dialogue and collaboration linking aid coordination to ongoing reforms, and regional cooperation with other countries and international agencies in the context of security challenges in Uganda. The resources available to implement the UNDAF included allocations by each participating UN organization and the resources that organizations expected to mobilize. Coordination and "harmonization" among UN agencies were key to the UNDAF, alongside the PEAP. Working groups were created to oversee implementation of the UNDAF, and the government and development partners completed joint evaluations.

Although the terms UNDAF and CDF have not maintained currency, the principles have remained important in aid organization goals and became central to the PRSP, which I describe below. Findings from a Word Bank evaluation in 2003 are worth highlighting here.[4] Progress in the World Bank's country-led approach, giving recipient countries the leading voice in aid management, was found to be far from even. Some donors did better than others, and it worked better in some countries and in some sectors than in others. Long-term and comprehensive development frameworks often ended up as long wish lists. Objectives were often not translated into affordable priorities and proper budgets, and hence their operational use and ability to define clear policy choices remained limited. The evaluation highlighted a need for capacity building to enable formulation and implementation of development plans.

The evaluation found that the country-led principle was overly demanding and many recipient countries lacked technical capacity.

Measures of impact on people rather than inputs and disbursement were found to be "the most elusive" among the CDF principles. It also found that there were inadequate incentives to follow a results-oriented approach and a lack of demand for monitoring and evaluation results. The specific aid projects and programs continued to drive monitoring rather than the requirements of governments' regular functions and service delivery. Finally, the evaluation noted that public consultation about aid-related activities had expanded and promoted ownership of reforms, but the consultations were found to be limited and were often confined to the executive branch of government and organizations chosen by donors and governments.

Poverty Reduction Strategy Papers

In 1999, the World Bank and International Monetary Fund (IMF), prompted by two developments, endorsed the framework of Poverty Reduction Strategy Papers. First, in 1996, the World Bank and IMF launched the heavily indebted poor countries (HIPC) scheme to reduce the external debt of eligible countries and achieve debt sustainability— this was not the first effort to reschedule debt, but the first one involving the World Bank and IMF. A broad movement, encapsulated in Jubilee 2000, argued for further debt relief and increased pressure on the World Bank and IMF to make this debt relief pro-poor and to address the negative consequences of structural adjustment. The international financial crisis in East Asia increased the pressure on the World Bank and IMF to review their policies and their effects on poverty.

Second, the changes happened against the background of an intensive debate about the effectiveness of aid. The World Bank's 1998 *Assessing Aid* report emphasized the need for good economic management for aid to be effective while acknowledging problems with traditional lending conditionalities that directly informed the CDF and PRSP approaches. The IMF responded to criticism about the inflexibility in its macroeconomic and fiscal options and the need for better prioritization of policy measures and division of labor among international institutions. It increasingly focused on the quality of budgets and sectoral spending, including how additional funding through debt relief could be used for, among other things, funding health and education.

Initially, PRSPs were an instrument for borrower countries seeking to benefit from HIPC, and they were seen as an effort to make debt relief integral to wider poverty reduction strategies. Over time, this PRSP model was broadened to include policy dialogue in all countries receiving concessional funding, and this had significant implications for national poverty strategy formulation and the way donors engaged with it. By 2005, about forty countries had a poverty reduction strategy, and a few had gone on to a second-generation strategy (Driscoll and Evans 2005).

Countries qualified for HIPC assistance if they faced an unsustainable debt burden and established a track record of reform and sound policies. To qualify for debt relief, countries needed to demonstrate capacity to use assistance prudently and to establish a further track record of agreed structural policy reforms, maintenance of macroeconomic stability, and adoption and implementation of the PRSP. Similar to the CDF approach, PRSPs were based on principles of ownership and partnership between donors and recipients, encouraged national-level participation in strategy formulation, and had a results-oriented approach, including regarding debt relief and poverty impact.

Financial support for PRSPs implementation was to be provided through the World Bank's Poverty Reduction Support Credit and the IMF's Poverty Reduction Growth Facility (PRGF), the successor of the Enhanced Structural Adjustment Facility (ESAF). Targets and policies in PRGF programs were to emerge directly from PRSP or similar frameworks. This was meant to integrate poverty reduction with macroeconomic policies. Discussions on the macroeconomic framework were made subject to public consultation. Key programs and structural reforms for poverty reduction and growth had to be identified, prioritized, and budgeted in the PRSP. In 2021, the IMF reported that $76 billion in debt relief had been provided to thirty-seven countries (thirty-one in Africa), with another three countries eligible for HIPC initiative assistance.[5]

As with the CDF, countries had diverse experiences, but there are few doubts that the debate brought in a much stronger focus on poverty reduction, discussions across government ministries, and poverty analyses. Preparation of PRSPs involved clear costing of the PRSP, which linked it to medium-term expenditure frameworks, the key instrument for policy dialogue between borrowers and lenders. Pressure on the World Bank and IMF forced them to review the impact of aid on poverty much more carefully; the development of the Poverty and Social Impact Analysis (PSIA), described in Chapter 8, is an example of how external (and internal) pressure can force new instruments to be introduced.

At the same time, observers concluded there was "no fundamental departure from the kind of policy advice provided under earlier structural adjustment programmes" (Stewart and Wang 2003, 19), for example, related to the role of the market, fiscal and monetary matters, inflation, and privatization.[6] Observers noted gaps between poverty profiles and proposed policies and that the poverty analysis, in some cases, insufficiently informed the development strategy. Observers questioned whether donor lending sufficiently addressed the priorities in PRSPs, which often included "wish lists," without prioritization and clear budgets.

The PRSP approach made a difference in the way donors approached the aid relationship—though challenges remained substantial, experiences varied, and the tendency to deal with the aid relationship in a bureaucratic manner continued. Observers regularly emphasized that the approach "is no panacea," highlighting the high expectations that the approach would resolve problems in the aid relationship. Booth, Grigsby, and Toranzo (2006) concluded that donors tended to get closely tied to paths set out through the PRSP process, and that disarray would set in when the partner government's policies did not follow plans set out earlier. Donors in many cases appeared unequipped to deal with the politics of public policymaking.

It became clear that promoting comprehensive and long-term planning through this aid modality was challenging. PRSPs covered most if not all areas or sectors relevant to development—even though there was much discussion whether particular sectors or issues received sufficient attention. The approach broadened the policy dialogue with donors beyond finance ministries to include a larger number of sectoral organizations and line ministries.[7]

The PRSP approach promoted stakeholder participation in the formulation of national plans for poverty reduction. Significant technical support emerged that built on, for example, poverty assessments and community participation and tried to move this "upstream" to influence the macropolicy discussions. Civil society organizations engaged in the donor dialogue and perceived the process as an opportunity to open up the space for political engagement.

Critiques of the participation practices emerged as well, and the term *participation* was used to mean different things.[8] Some believed participation remained ritualistic and that the macroeconomic framework did not change following even good processes of participation. Sometimes, processes of participation remained outside mainstream politics, for example, they excluded parliaments, trade unions, the private sector, women, and marginalized groups. Participation was not institutionalized but remained restricted to the processes related to aid disbursement. Where the donors did intensively engage with political leaders, as in Bolivia, subsequent political dynamics challenged the implementation of PRSPs (Booth, Grigsby, and Toranzo 2006).

Questions emerged of whether PRSPs contributed to comprehensive and cross-sectoral policymaking and about potential trade-offs. Critiques stressed the gaps in comprehensiveness in the development plans, the limited capacity for comprehensive planning, and the time that such planning required.[9] Differences over where aid efforts should focus continued in PRSP discussions: some NGOs saw PRSPs as a venue to emphasize social sectors, others argued that the big gap was in so-called productive sectors. Booth and colleagues (2006) reviewed PRSPs in Bolivia, Honduras, and Nicaragua and concluded that comprehensiveness could conflict with ownership.[10] Leaders often did not feel committed to such comprehensive plans and argued that donors should be more pragmatic in supporting initiatives that arose from the leaders of the day.

The critiques show that there is no magic bullet to solve the challenges of the relationships between donors and recipients. Views on the effectiveness of these new approaches—as with all approaches—differed among the official donors, NGOs, and Southern voices. The new approach came, as often in the aid community, with high expectations; and the aid industry again showed a tendency to move on to the next approach. As countries' debt levels declined over the 2000s and early 2010s, this aid modality received less attention.

In the late 2010s debt levels again were increasing, and debt sustainability and need for relief became key questions during the pandemic. This has led to initiatives for debt relief, including the Debt Service Suspension Initiative and the allocation of Special Drawing Rights. The latter has renewed interest in how debt relief can be used and how debt can be managed to support development goals and climate action (which was less central in the late 1990s), though these efforts are complicated by the significant role of private lenders. This led to a World Bank and IMF proposal to set up a Resilience and Sustainability Trust (RST) to provide affordable long-term financing to support countries tackling structural challenges. The proposal raised concerns, alongside fears of renewed austerity, that the scale is insufficient about the continued use of conditionalities (Ahmed, Bárcena, and Titelman 2021), and led to discussion about the need for national level reforms to make external support effective (Economic Research Forum and Finance for Development Lab 2022).

Aid Effectiveness and Paris Consensus

Coordination of aid agencies has generated much attention, particularly at the time of implementation of Poverty Reduction Strategy Papers and as the amount of aid and numbers of agencies increased. As highlighted above, the need for donors to coordinate behind development approaches led by recipient countries emerged as a key concern, and debates on aid effectiveness have focused on the need for donors to harmonize their procedures in support of recipient countries' priorities.

The Organisation for Economic Co-operation and Development (OECD) Development Assistance Committee (DAC) is the main forum for discussions on aid effectiveness and "harmonization." Following the Monterrey Declaration on financing, in 2003 a Rome Declaration on Harmonisation was endorsed by ministers and top officials of aid recipient countries and donors agencies.[11] This declaration was informed by documented recipient country concerns about donor practices and requests to simplify donor procedures and reduce transaction costs: donors should collaborate and agree to common sets of procedures, they should synchronize their procedures with those of recipient countries, they should increasingly rely on recipient countries' systems and budgets, and they should become more transparent and share more information with recipients.

The Rome process was followed by the Paris Declaration on aid effectiveness (summarized in Figure 3.1) and in a series of high-level forums on aid effectiveness that focused on reducing the fragmentation of the aid industry and ensuring aid is better at supporting country-led development. The declaration was agreed on by sixty-one bilateral and multilateral donors and fifty-six aid recipient countries, while fourteen civil society organizations acted as observers. Specific indicators for progress were agreed on, and a Working Party on Aid Effectiveness was made responsible for monitoring the declaration.

The Paris Declaration aims to increase aid effectiveness by folding results-based management into the aid industry and to urge increased spending. The declaration highlights the need for mutual accountability, for performance assessment frameworks to be shared between donors and recipients, and for incentive systems to align. Within the framework, *ownership* (or partners and recipient countries setting the agenda) was seen as a key ingredient for success; with the development of PRSPs and national plans, many countries had already developed frameworks that set out plans that donors could support jointly. *Alignment* refers to the way the donors should engage with such national plans and priorities. Alignment called for making the priorities of donors and those of recipients more consistent and aligning donors' procedures with the processes of national institutions. Aid instruments should become better at relying on national budgetary systems, complement existing systems, and strengthen good

Figure 3.1 Paris Declaration Pyramid

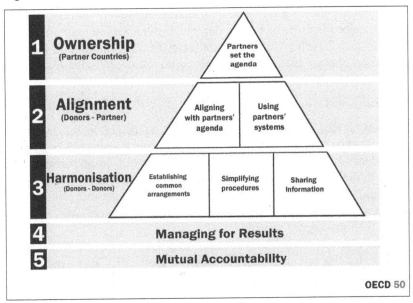

Source: OECD DAC (2006).

practices.[12] *Harmonization* focused on how donors work together and called for donors to establish common arrangements, share information, and simplify their procedures.

Challenges in implementing this declaration remain. A DAC survey in 2006 (OECD 2007) with thirty-four recipients and sixty donors highlighted the fact that there were too many actors with competing objectives, especially in the poorest and most aid-dependent countries, which led to high transaction costs. Technical cooperation remained donor-driven, in-country practices did not always reflect the commitment from agencies at headquarters, and it was concluded that donors needed to provide more assistance so recipients could develop capacity. Civil society organizations voiced related criticisms: a Eurodad (2008) report, *Turning the Tables*, emphasized similar points and highlighted that support still came with too many conditionalities.

Over the last decade, the number of donors has increased, and they have focused on and adopted these principles to different extents, partly because of political motivations to distinguish themselves. Some argue that the "old donors" also did not sufficiently embrace the principles

(Brown 2020; Habraken, Schulpen, and Hoebink 2017, on Uganda), and political changes in (old) donor countries have reemphasized the need for branding of aid for home constituencies. However, donors continue to emphasize the principles, for example, through the Global Partnership for Effective Development Co-operation (GPEDC), initiated in 2014 as a multistakeholder platform with a proposed stronger Southern lead.

Program and Sector Approaches

Aid is typically provided through projects, as described in Chapter 5. The existence of too many projects by too many donors has been seen to hinder aid effectiveness and recipient ownership. In response to this concern, the aid industry tried to move from a project approach to a program and sector approach, which aligned aid with recipient government programs and reforms and disbursed funds to government budgets rather than to specific projects.

The central idea behind the sector approach is this: "all significant funding for the sector supports a single sector policy and expenditure programme, under government leadership, adopting common approaches across the sector and progressing towards relying on Government procedures for all funds."[13] Sector approaches included the existence or development of a comprehensive sector policy and strategy and expenditure frameworks. It implied donor coordination, steered by recipient governments. Under sector approaches, donors provided joint support within an agreed framework and were committed to increasing reliance on government financial and accountability systems.

The term "program-based approach" has been used as an extension of the concept of sector-wide approaches: "A program is an integrated set of activities designed to achieve a related set of outcomes in a relatively comprehensive way [mostly health, education] . . . a way of engaging in development cooperation based on the principle of coordinated support for a locally owned program of development" (Lavergne and Alba 2003).

Some eighty sector programs were thought to exist around 2000. Most of the sector programs were in Africa, reflecting the greater need for donor coordination in aid-dependent African countries. The approach was implemented elsewhere, too, including in India, where the government was proactive in reducing the numbers of and ensuring the coordination of donors, and the government applied principles of multi-donor sector support for the national primary education and health programs.

Sector approaches often focused on support for health and education, but there are examples in other sectors. In Kenya, the principles of joint-donor support to the agriculture sector continue in the form of the National Agriculture Investment Plan (FAO 2019). In the area of social security, support for Ethiopia's Productive Safety Nets Program started in 2005, providing multiyear support and longer-term and predictable financial resources. In Uganda, there were attempts to develop a sector approach to support the justice sector.[14]

This aid modality was a response to a number of issues. First, it addressed concerns about lack of funding for social sectors, particularly primary health and education. Second, it was described as a shift from "conditionality" to "ownership." Donors found that conditionalities— requirements that recipients comply with conditions for aid, as I describe in detail in Chapter 6—did not work well, and sector approaches became a way of providing support to governments on the basis of their commitment to and track record in providing services for poverty reduction. Third, sector approaches focused on creating and supporting a sound policy environment. Rather than donors directly funding services, sector approaches provided funding to promote changes in policies and institutions, including budgeting, which form the preconditions for nationwide services.[15]

Questions of budgeting were central to sector-wide and program approaches. The projects provided by donors, often many at the same time, led to fragmentation of recipient governments' budgeting processes. Much aid was, and is, provided outside the regular government budgets, and financial oversight focused on accountability to donors rather than to finance ministries and parliaments. The proposed solution was that "government and donors should work together to implement a single, coherent expenditure programme which prioritises the use of all sources of public funding" (Foster 2000, 8).

Program approaches highlighted the need to promote recipient country leadership and the use of local procedures, which supported coordination of aid and reduced transaction costs for recipients. A program implies a single budget framework is used, not a range of projects financed outside countries' regular budgets but integrated into common budget processes and supported by pooled donor funding. This was seen as particularly important in aid-dependent countries, where policymakers were busy servicing the requirements of donors. Whereas projects have clearly defined time spans and outputs, program approaches recognized that support was likely to take a long time to develop and that the direction of change mattered more than particular levels of achievement. Aid programs intended to support locally owned development programs, but donors emphasized that this did not mean following a blueprint; programs needed to be dynamic and needed to take into account country specificity, for example, in fragile and post-conflict countries.[16]

The program approach recorded successes because it addressed problems created through project support and improved services and development outcomes. An evaluation of general budget support to seven countries by the OECD DAC Network on Development Evaluation (2006) found that this form of support was ambitious and practices differed across the countries, but it contributed to better donor coordination and alignment with government policy. It also helped strengthen public financial management. In Uganda and Ghana, program approaches facilitated overarching agreements between governments and donors and sector approaches behind government programs, for universal primary education, for example. Sector support may have helped to enhance political commitment, efficiency in resource use, and capacity for policy formulation and implementation while promoting donor aid coordination. Research has shown that donors can indeed more effectively shape reform priorities if aid is channeled through public financial management systems rather than provided as technical assistance that bypasses government systems (Parks et al. 2016).[17]

However, a number of concerns emerged. Donor coordination remained challenging, and it became clear that the processes of establishing joint-donor support were very time-consuming. Program design and monitoring frameworks tended to be complex and costly, and limited capacity in many countries hindered effective implementation. The number of qualifying criteria remained large: even though these focused on ongoing and completed actions and reforms, a large number of policy intentions and plans remained central to qualifying for support. Some recipient governments believed that joint-donor responses were a potential disadvantage because they risked a complete halt to support.

Measuring success or progress became more difficult compared to using the straightforward indicators common in project approaches. Showing the links of program aid to development outcomes and impacts on poverty proved to be challenging. It was also noted that sector approaches did not easily allow for strengthening decentralized governance structures (Land and Hauck 2003). Concerns about corruption and fiduciary risk remained and even increased because donors had less control over money flows and relied on recipient government systems.

Budget support remained a small proportion of the aid from bilateral donors and has been declining since the early 2000s (Dreher, Langlotz, and Marchesi 2016; Swedlund and Lierl 2020). "Newer" donors on the whole did not adopt this approach. The incentives for donors—to spend money, to show results in their organization, and to show achievements to the taxpayers—often were believed to conflict with the aim of enhancing ownership. Discrete projects and emphasis on particular donors' preferences continued to thrive, including with a growing number of new and often private donor agencies. New global partnerships were created, as I discuss next.

Global Partnerships and Vertical Initiatives

Along with sector approaches, "vertical initiatives" have flourished. The MDGs and Sustainable Development Goals (SDGs) frameworks have brought donors—official and private—further together behind specific sets of issues, such as primary education or specific diseases. The Global Financing Facility, created in 2015 by a range of donors, is managed as a trust fund by the World Bank and supports government health and nutrition policies and leverages significant amounts of funding for priority health investments (Keller et al. 2021). With the growth in finance for climate action, reportedly twenty-seven climate funds were created (Kharas, McArthur, and Snower 2022); the Green Climate Fund is described in Chapter 7.

In 2002, the Global Partnership for Education (formerly called the Education for All Initiative) was created to promote the MDGs for universal primary education by 2015. It had an annual budget of $7 billion at the end of the 2010s and works with seventy countries. It is a platform managed by the World Bank that brings together developing countries, donors, civil society, foundations, and the private sector. It put in place specific indicators for alignment with national systems and harmonized modalities for grants (GPE 2021, 87–89).[18]

Health has a number of global partnerships that aim to streamline donor efforts. In 2005, some seventy partnerships were recorded. The World Health Organization (WHO) from the time of its creation developed partnerships with other organizations, and from the mid-1990s increasingly so with the World Bank. The Bill & Melinda Gates Foundation has played an important role in promoting and funding the partnership. One important partnership is Gavi, the Vaccine Alliance, Roll Back Malaria, and the International Finance Facility for Immunisation. The Global Fund to Fight AIDS, Tuberculosis and Malaria is thought to be very effective, with a minimal bureaucracy and high impact, such as the initiative to distribute 30 million anti-malaria bed nets. CEPI, the

Coalition for Epidemic Preparedness Innovations, was launched in 2017 to develop vaccines to stop future epidemics. COVAX is co-led by CEPI, Gavi, and the United Nations Children's Fund (UNICEF).

The impacts of such "vertical" and sector-specific initiatives on the country leadership discussed above, to which sector programs are meant to be a response, are as yet unclear. A review (supported by the Gates Foundation) of the health partnerships, viewed as the dominant modality for health support, showed that they have had successes, including increased funding and policy improvement. At the same time, these commitments for increasing aid are made in the face of doubts about government capacity. Some countries struggle to absorb the health resources provided. Despite alignment intentions, countries continue to be burdened with parallel and duplicative processes arising out of multiple health partnerships that bypass country systems. Vertical initiatives may imply a move away from the state as the central actor in providing legislative frameworks and standards toward "a multiplicity of new—and largely unaccountable—actors in the health arena," with public–private partnerships "as potentially radical new systems of global governance" (Poku and Whiteside 2002, 192).

Dilemmas and Trade-Offs in Aid Delivery

The aid industry is deeply involved in the design and appraisal of projects, as I will describe further in Chapter 5, and staff spend considerable time working directly to promote these activities. This close involvement in itself is not problematic. In the case of aid to China, government officials often showed much appreciation for the engagement and the technical expertise brought in, and the collaboration fitted within a strategy that the government set out.

But in the case of aid-dependent countries, this can be different, and donor projects can operate outside government priorities and be a drain on an administration rather than strengthening it. Approaches such as CDF, UNDAF, PRSPs, the Paris Declaration, and global partnerships have tried to change aid relationships, but have not been as successful as was intended. For some observers, these approaches manifested as signs of further domination of global institutions, whereas for others, agencies simply failed to implement the approach they advocated. Sector reform and sector-wide approaches that implied a focus on the policy environment have had notable successes, but practice remained varied, and their popularity has declined.

These shifts demonstrate significant trade-offs. The focus on aid coordination by some has been regarded as key to the survival of the industry, whereas others believe that it puts "Paris before poverty" and that aid coordination neglects considering what aid can achieve on the ground. Capacity needs to be strengthened in countries that are dependent on aid, but building up capacity and the will to use aid most effectively are also difficult in those countries.

From the start, these approaches were donor-driven and did not fundamentally change relationships between donors and recipients. Donor efforts to align support have been only partly successful, and though the principles of these approaches were sound, progress in implementation remained limited and project funding remained dominant. Finally, the aid industry's urge to show results persists, and in many cases has intensified, which does not make leaving ownership to recipients easy, and neither does it help to make the case for program and budget support.

I discuss the way donors implement development projects in Chapter 5, but first we'll turn to the field of development studies, which has provided much of the scholarly input for and critique of the aid industry.

Notes

1. As interviews carried out by AidData (2021) demonstrate. Heinzel and Liese (2021) analyzed how the way World Bank staff operate impacts project results. See Chwieroth (2013) for analysis of IMF staff practices.

2. "The Comprehensive Development Framework (CDF) and Poverty Reduction Strategy Papers (PRSP)," Joint Note by James D. Wolfensohn and Stanley Fischer, International Monetary Fund, April 5, 2000, https://www.imf.org/external/np/prsp/pdf/cdfprsp.pdf.

3. Extract from Mr. Kofi Annan's letter to Mr. James Wolfensohn, May 11, 2001. The World Bank and IMF also were quick to emphasize the complementarity of the CDF and PRSP approaches, though institutionally there was some competition between the initiatives.

4. World Bank Operations Evaluation Department (2003); a management response was published that supported many of the conclusions and recommendations made.

5. "Debt Relief Under the Heavily Indebted Poor Countries (HIPC) Initiative," International Monetary Fund, March 23, 2021, https://www.imf.org/en/About/Factsheets/Sheets/2016/08/01/16/11/Debt-Relief-Under-the-Heavily-Indebted-Poor-Countries-Initiative; "Poverty Reduction Strategy Papers (PRSP)," International Monetary Fund, December 28, 2016, https://www.imf.org/external/np/prsp/prsp.aspx.

6. A similar criticism has been expressed vis-à-vis the CDF: Owusu (2003) argued that this approach settled a long-standing debate over development strategies in favor of neoliberalism and global integration.

7. The IMF and World Bank review of PRSP progress in 2005 highlighted that "comprehensiveness is important in order to capture the complementary nature of

public actions across sectors." In Tanzania, "a comprehensive strategy does not mean sacrificing priority setting. In fact, the more comprehensive the strategy, the more important it is to identify its main priorities" (IMF and World Bank 2005, 16).

8. Stewart and Wang (2003) have provided a good discussion and emphasize that the process of participation was strongly led by government.

9. Cheru (2006, 369) emphasized the weak state capacity in Africa was a hindrance: "Co-ordination of economic policy formulation and implementation has been hampered by constant inter-ministerial infighting, as well as by the disconnect between key sector ministries and ministries of finance."

10. Some observers of Latin America (Dijkstra 2005) argued that the PRSP approach should be abandoned; in the view of Booth, Grigsby, and Toranzo (2006), emphasis should be on harmonization that allows strategic support to specific initiatives.

11. These guidelines, approved in the Rome Declaration, suggest good practices for donor–government engagement, interdonor coordination, intradonor reform, and simplification of procedures to reduce costs and enhance efficiency ("The High Level Fora on Aid Effectiveness: A History," OECD, https://www.oecd.org/dac/effectiveness/thehighlevelforaonaideffectivenessahistory.htm).

12. An example from the World Bank on how this should be implemented in the health sector is available in this document: https://tinyurl.com/3zvcuamb.

13. Foster (2000, 9); Walford (2003). Bilateral donors, World Bank, and UN specialized agencies all use slightly different definitions (Riddell 2002, 2008). Lucas (2013) described sector approaches in the context of fragile states.

14. Sserumaga (2002); Asiimwe et al. (2004); UNICEF (2021).

15. For the health sector, the need for aid to be channeled through the national systems, "following the government playbook," is described in a 2021 World Bank publication (Piattifuenfkirchen et al. 2021).

16. Foster and Leavy (2001); Collier and Okonjo-Iweala (2002); Manor (2007). Chandy (2011) gave a more optimistic view of aid to fragile states, with specific recommendations on ensuring ways in which aid is provided is suited to specific conditions.

17. An IMF paper by Cordella and Dell'Ariccia (2003) used an econometric model to show that program aid is more effective than project aid because governments can reallocate money when receiving support, for example, to build schools.

18. Its impact has been described here: https://www.globalpartnership.org/results/gpe-impact and here: https://www.globalpartnership.org/content/results-report-2021.

4

The Evolution of Development Studies

THE AID BUSINESS IS MARKED BY VERY RAPID CHANGES AND TRENDS driven by political considerations of donors that are sometimes short term, sometimes long term, such as during the Cold War or following the security agenda of the 2000s. Different approaches to aid also are the outcome of meetings of often quite radically different views, theories, and thoughts about development. In this chapter, I present an account of approaches to international development with an overview of the main issues as they have evolved over the last six decades.[1] It is important to keep in mind that such periodization—as with any categorization—implies simplifications. While some approaches can be characterized as dominant, different views of course continue to exist, diverging strands of thought exist, and different donors draw on different ideas and traditions. I first discuss the location of development studies, which has been mainly in the Global North.

Where Are Aid and International Development Studied?

The annual *Global Go To Think Tank Index Report* of the University of Pennsylvania lists 128 international development policy think tanks. This is a small proportion of all think tanks, a listing of the ones that mostly focus on domestic issues. Most of them are based in the Global North: only 3 of the top 20 are based outside Organisation for Economic Co-operation and Development (OECD) countries, and only 6 of the 128 are based in Africa.

Influential think tanks that make direct contributions to the aid industry include the Institute of Development Studies and the Overseas Development Institute in the UK, the German Development Institute, and the Brookings Institution and the Center for Global Development based in Washington, DC (the last publishes the Commitment to Development Index). Other scholars position themselves more remotely from the aid business and study development processes more broadly. Research on development and aid also happens at institutes that focus on training professionals and at a range of institutions focusing on development practices. With the growth in nongovernmental organizations (NGOs) and transnational civil society, their role in development research has been increasing as well, and these organizations often offer insights critical of or alternative to those put forward by organizations such as the World Bank.

Although large development studies think tanks play an important role in donor countries, few have sprung up in the South. But they are not absent, and strong development studies institutes exist in, for example, Thailand, the Philippines, Zimbabwe, India, and Bangladesh. The Institute for Development Studies (IDS) at the University of Nairobi, established in 1965, is possibly the world's oldest development institute. Also, emerging economies have created new research institutions, such as China's Belt and Road Initiative International think tank, though there is little tradition of development studies in these areas of the world. Some Southern NGOs, such as BRAC in Bangladesh, have created their own research capacity in a growing number of countries.

The African Economic Research Consortium (AERC) was established in 1988 to strengthen research capacity related to the management of economies in sub-Saharan Africa. It was supported by bilateral and multilateral donors, private foundations, and African organizations and created under the assumption that good economic policy requires locally based professional economists to conduct policy-relevant research and that research agenda must be determined locally rather than by donors. Collaborative research projects on poverty, for example, contributed to the preparation of Poverty Reduction Strategy Papers (PRSPs), and a network of universities facilitates information sharing and access to world resource centers.

The World Bank houses the single largest group of development economists, publishes a large number of publications, including the much-cited journal *World Bank Research Observer*, and receives regular criticism about the independence of its research.[2] Similarly, regional development banks contribute to the study of development, including through the Asian Development Bank Institute.

Other research organizations in the UN system operate autonomously and with limited core funding. For example, UNRISD, the United Nations Research Institute for Social Development, was set up in 1963 with a grant from the Netherlands. It has had a modest budget, and it has depended on core funding mainly from bilateral donors and grants for specific projects. Similar institutions are WIDER (World Institute for Development Economics Research), based in Helsinki, which, for example, conducts major research projects on economic inequality, and the IILS (International Institute for Labour Studies), which is closely linked to the International Labour Organization (ILO) and which was among the first to bring a focus on social exclusion to the development studies debate in the mid-1990s.

One of the important scientific organizations supported by the aid industry is CGIAR, the Consultative Group on International Agricultural Research. Created in 1971, with 8,000 staff in over 100 countries, it focuses on promotion of sustainable production, supports national agricultural research systems, promotes research on policy that impacts agriculture, and works directly on germplasm collection and improvements.

Over the years, significant efforts have been made to strengthen research capacity in the South. Canada's International Development Research Centre (IDRC), created in 1970, focuses on supporting applied research, gathering expert advice, and building local capacity in developing countries so they can undertake research and innovate. The Department for Research Cooperation at Sida (Swedish International Development Cooperation Agency) has supported partner country development research as well as Swedish research activities relevant to developing countries.

Despite capacity-building support, development studies continue to be concentrated in the North. Studies suggest that Southern researchers continue to be marginalized (Amarante et al. 2021). While aid agencies have continued to strengthen their own think tanks' capacities, think tanks in many countries in the South have not developed at the same pace. The growing emphasis on national interest in aid programs may have reinforced a North–South imbalance. Innovations in development research, such as use of randomized controlled trials, tend to originate at and attract financial resources for Northern institutions. It has also been argued that aid agencies' funding for primary education has tended to neglect higher education and research. Aid agencies have often been ambivalent about supporting research capacity, believing that it is diffi-cult to identify the impact of support on research capacity.

Aid and Development: Theoretical and Disciplinary Perspectives

Aid has been studied from varying theoretical angles (Lancaster 2007; Eyben 2008; Gulrajani 2011), and the emergence of new global powers and actors in the aid industry has contributed even more different per-spectives (Chaturvedi et al. 2020). Realist perspectives highlight the role of foreign aid as an instrument of political power. Marxist or "depen-dency" scholars see aid as an instrument for maintaining positions of control in world capitalism. Scholars in a liberal tradition emphasize aid as a reflection of collaboration between states. A "constructivist" lens and social democratic theories highlight that foreign aid is an expression of norms and ideas that can assist in the improvement of quality of life, whereas "deconstructivist" approaches focus on aid practices as dis-course and ways of exerting power.

Carol Lancaster stresses that none of these theories adequately explains the complexities of aid. Its principles almost always reflect a combination of motivations, as discussed in Chapter 2. Aid practices tend to take on their own dynamics, as all policies do, while working their way through the institutions responsible for their implementation. The inter-action of development analysts or students with "practitioners," similarly, is not straightforward. In fact, the industry continues to struggle with the question of how research influences policymaking, while it is equally possible that policy influences research, particularly when much of the development research is directly funded by the aid industry itself.

The aid industry originated in the colonial period, and there has been a degree of continuity from the colonial to the postcolonial period. Early development projects were set up by colonial administrations, and academic research and training informed and supported the colonial administration. There was continuity in terms of personnel, with former colonial officers staying on after independence to work in universities, government departments, and the new aid industry (Kothari 2006). Eco-nomic theories that emphasized dualism between modern and traditional sectors were first articulated during the colonial period, for example, by the Dutch economist Julius Herman Boeke with reference to Indonesia.

Academic approaches to aid in the two decades after World War II were dominated by economic theories of "modernization," as described below. From the late 1960s onward, particularly in the UK, the subject of "development studies" started to grow, with IDS Sussex, to my knowledge, the first that focused explicitly on "development" as a subject; it remains one of the largest institutes in its field. Since then, the number of institutes and research centers on development has continued to increase. At many places, development is studied as part of other fields, notably international relations, public administration, and (mainstream) economics.

A problem-oriented nature has been a defining feature of development studies. The field of development studies, at its beginnings, was seen as the science or discipline that would help with the most urgent problems of poverty in the South. At present, too, students of development are motivated by concerns about deprivation and look for ways to assist in solving problems, usually in other countries that are shown in the press and public campaigns.

From its origin in economics, development studies has been interdisciplinary because of its problem-oriented nature: development problems are recognized as multifaceted and multisectoral, and therefore multi- or interdisciplinary approaches are required. That interdisciplinarity, though, is contested. Among World Bank researchers, by far the largest proportion is economists. Among its social scientists, researchers at the International Food Policy Research Institute (IFPRI) also tend to be economists, though they, too, have increasingly adopted multidisciplinary approaches. Poverty analysis, developed since the 1980s, and use of randomized controlled trials have been dominated by economists; the contest this implies is described in Box 4.1.

Box 4.1   The Debate on Poverty Analysis and Development Studies Disciplines

---

Poverty analysis gained importance during the 1980s, when the World Bank came under criticism for aid not helping the poor and it responded with efforts to assess the scale of poverty, particularly in Africa. The main form of poverty analysis used large-scale representative household surveys, and donor agencies invested in implementing surveys and building capacity. The main indicator of poverty became the poverty headcount, a measure of the number of people living below a poverty line (national or international, such as dollar-a-day). A second measure that was used is the so-called poverty gap,

continues

Box 4.1   Continued

---

which describes how far people are below the poverty line, which measures the extent of their poverty (this measure is used in assessing the impact of microfinance projects, for example).

The poverty analysis that started to dominate the debate was criticized heavily because of its focus on the income dimensions of poverty and on the use of quantitative analysis of poverty based on household surveys. For development studies, the critique highlighted the need for study of health and education and access to assets as central components of poor people's well-being and, some argue, even preconditions for economic growth. Measuring people's income neglected dimensions of vulnerability, the risks that many households were exposed to, which might make them fall back into poverty (or move in and out of poverty), and the need for participatory poverty analysis. Finally, scholars promoted the integration of qualitative and quantitative analysis, for example, in the World Bank's *World Development Report 2000/2001* (see also Shaffer 2013).

The poverty analysis that has been so important within development studies remained dominated by economists, much more so than the poverty analysis in Europe, where sociologists played a more important role. By focusing heavily on measurement and indicators rather than explanations, poverty analysis suffered from the lack of attention paid to the societal and political influences on poverty.

Political science has had less influence over the development debate than economics has, as demonstrated in the book by former Department for International Development (DFID) chief economist Stefan Dercon (2022). As described later in this chapter, during the 1990s, development theories started to pay more attention to institutions, though economic methods continued to shape the approach to institutions and politics.

Anthropologists have engaged relatively little with development studies, including poverty analysis, and have instead focused on critical analysis of aid discourse and power relations. "The relationship between anthropology and development has always been difficult," wrote Ralph Grillo (2002, 54). Influential anthropologists such as E. E. Evans-Pritchard distanced themselves from applied study after World War II, so no anthropologist was involved in setting up the UK's official development assistance (ODA) in the mid-1960s, for example. It was not till 1978 that an anthropologist joined the World Bank.[3] The last decades have seen a shift toward ethnographies of organizational and knowledge practices and a growing literature that analyzes the daily practices of aid providers and recipients (Mosse 2013; Sou 2021).

Development Studies in the 1950s and 1960s: Optimism, Kick-Starting Economies

With countries' independence, development became the core objective of newly established governments, and development studies became a growing discipline initially dominated by US scholarship. The study of poorer or developing countries became a separate subject after World War II. William Arthur Lewis (1954), winner of the Nobel Prize in Economics in 1979, highlighted this by arguing that standard economic models are less relevant to poor countries, and he defined a distinct role for development economics. Dudley Seers (1967) emphasized the role of development studies as distinct from colonial economics.

The early period of independence was one of optimism, even though many economists did not believe economic growth rates could achieve levels much above 1–2 percent. New governments expected to be able to modernize their economy, while simultaneously addressing historical injustices of the colonial era. The optimism of the 1950s and 1960s was fueled by a growing world economy, booming export markets for primary commodities, and low energy prices. Although aid was heavily determined by donors' security concerns in the context of spreading communism, donors looked favorably on newly established countries, where elites took proactive roles in modernizing economies.[4]

With socialism experiencing popularity across the former colonial world, and the international community heavily influenced by the experience of the 1930s Depression, economic policies emphasized planning. Five-year plans became common across the South, with industrialization through import substitution central to many countries' objectives. Economic models provided the necessary theoretical support, while food aid contributed to keeping agricultural prices low and thus shaped favorable conditions for economic development. Until the late 1970s, international development thinking assigned a primary and entrepreneurial role to government, and models that are now often seen as failures—such as the socialist model promoted by Julius Nyerere in Tanzania—found widespread acceptance.

The development model that dominated during this period emphasized economic growth. Social objectives were seen as complementary to or resulting from increasing national products. Poverty reduction seldom emerged as a specific priority and was assumed or expected to emerge from better infrastructure and employment-intensive growth. The path of development was seen as linear, such as in Walter Rostow's 1960 book *The Stages of Economic Growth*, which used a metaphor of an airplane taking off. With little development aid to the agricultural sector—the US Alliance for Progress in support of Latin American land reform in the 1960s being a short-lived exception—modernization was thought to start in the industrial sector, which would pull the agricultural sector along, and thinking was accordingly strongly focused on urban areas.

The main economic framework emphasized the role of investment, as highlighted in the one-sector economic Harrod-Domar model. In the absence of sufficiently high savings rates, foreign aid was seen as providing countries the necessary capital to kick-start their economies through a "big push," including funding for infrastructure projects. As OECD countries established bilateral aid programs with a focus on "productive sectors," economic frameworks were expected to predict the amount of aid and investment needed.

Economic thinking during the colonial period had emphasized dualism between a modern and a traditional sector. This became deeply ingrained in the thinking of the 1950s and 1960s and is still influential today. Statistical systems started to record economic activity and employment in the modern (large-scale) sector, and expanding social security remained limited to that sector too. Thinking about employment and migration was dominated by dual models (such as that of William Arthur Lewis) and the idea that modernization involved transfer of labor from a traditional agricultural sector, with an unlimited supply of labor, to a modern sector.

As in other periods, development thinking in the 1950s and 1960s was not undisputed. In the 1960s, notably through the work of Theodore Schultz, human capital was perceived as important in addition to physical capital, and issues of education and fertility were on the agenda. From the early postwar period onward, despite aid's emphasis on large infrastructure projects, community development models were popular among the international community, for example, in India, where the modernization view promoted by Jawaharlal Nehru was balanced by Gandhian traditional and village-oriented views.

Marxist-oriented authors, and mostly Latin American social scientists, formulated a more radical critique of modernization theories, such as W. W. Rostow's. This way of thinking came to be known as dependency theory, with an important root in the United Nations Commission for Latin America. For dependency theorists, underdevelopment was not just the result of failure to modernize, or identical with a traditional state, but also the result of the expansion of global capitalism and colonialism, through which the South became underdeveloped. Dependency theory made little impact on mainstream thinking within the aid industry, but its ideas are reflected in the movements that view the World Bank and International Monetary Fund (IMF) as instruments to maintain global capitalism and injustice.

Thus, development thinking in the early postwar period was already a mixture of various ideas. Emphasis on growth and modernization was combined with thinking about the need for supporting human capital and education. Models of planning and socialism, in line with the Keynesian economics of the time, were well accepted and promoted, but the push toward modernization was also informed by the felt need to contain communism: Rostow's book about modernization is subtitled "An Anti-communist Manifesto," and Rostow was an adviser on US national security affairs.

The 1970s: The Short Era of Redistribution

Levels of aid, which had remained constant since the mid-1950s, increased during the second half of the 1970s. In terms of development thinking, the 1970s were a period of opposing directions. Whereas the 1960s was a period of great optimism, cracks appeared in the early 1970s, at the start of the period of adjustment and with the processes of global liberalization that followed the collapse of the economic regulation that had dominated. In 1973, both the first oil crisis, though not as severe as the crisis in 1979, and the fall of Chile's president Salvador Allende took place. This was the year many regard as the advent of the classic form of neoliberal structural adjustment under an authoritarian regime.

In the same year as that of Chile's political crisis, Robert McNamara explicitly committed the World Bank to a focus on poverty reduction. In a famous speech at the Bank–Fund meeting in Nairobi in 1973, he emphasized the extent and persistence of rural poverty in particular and pledged to increase and transform aid. Thinking at the World Bank in the 1970s was influenced by Hollis Chenery, who as chief economist under Robert McNamara put inequality and redistribution on the agenda and questioned the ideas of "trickle down"—the assumption that economic growth would automatically benefit the poor—that had dominated the earlier thinking. The early 1970s was also the period of radical debate about the New International Economic Order (NIEO) and the "right to development."[5]

Other players in the aid industry also started to emphasize poverty, sharing doubts about modernization and trickle-down paradigms. The late 1960s and 1970s saw experiments with targeted interventions, reflecting the growing poverty focus among more and more donors. "Reconstruction Bangladesh" in the early 1970s challenged the predominant aid strategies as doing far too little for the poor. Canada's Pearson Commission and Dutch and Scandinavian donors expressed worries that growth from aid was inadequately translated into poverty reduction, and these countries focused on rural, decentralized, and small-scale projects. Britain's first white paper on aid in 1964 had prioritized poverty, as did its chief economist, Dudley Seers (1967), who in an IDS article argued that development was about much more than national income and should include normative concerns around basic needs and distribution.

Food aid became less important as a donor instrument, and the aid industry started to pay more attention to agriculture, increase lending, and help remove technical constraints to redress its relative neglect during the 1950 and 1960s. Debates started to see agriculture as productive, as part of economic growth strategies, rather than just the traditional sector that would shrink with modernization. As the aid industry reflected on failures of large projects, participatory approaches to agricultural development became more popular. Development economics promoted an understanding of the interaction between traditional and modern, rural and urban sectors, and ideas of balanced growth and intersectoral linkages came to the forefront of debates. A much-cited publication that contributed to a shift of focus toward agriculture was Michael Lipton's (1977) on "urban bias," in which he argued that development was designed by and for people in urban areas. He estimated that, although most poor people lived in rural areas and depended on agriculture, they received no more than 20 percent of development spending.

The 1970s was also the period when employment became central to development debate. The ILO's World Employment Programme, founded by Ajit Bhalla, focused on the creation of productive employment and provision of public services, partly as a response to the authoritarian turn that the process of modernization had taken in many postcolonial and Cold War contexts. The 1976 ILO conference emphasized that strategies and national development plans and policies should prioritize employment promotion.

An important contribution during this period was the introduction of the term *informal sector*. The term was coined by an anthropologist, Keith Hart, in 1971 (published in 1973), and the ILO adopted it in a report on employment in Kenya in 1972. It highlighted that the problem in less-developed countries was not one of unemployment but one of the "working poor," people in occupations that offered them only a low income and precarious labor relations. During the 1980s and onward, research came to focus on the growth of the informal sector, including related to globalization and liberalization, which were thought to increase the size of the informal sector and undermine the rights and entitlements of people in the formal sector (though in many poor countries the formal sector had never been larger than 15 percent of the labor force). Hernando de Soto, a Peruvian lawyer, contributed to the debate from a liberal economic perspective. His 1986 book *El Otro Sendero* (*The Other Path*, with reference to the extremist group Sendero Luminoso) described people in the informal sector as a group of entrepreneurs who were hindered from making economic contributions by government rules and regulations.

Questions of migration occupied a central part in debates on employment. Migration was viewed simply as a part of the transition from the traditional to the modern sector, by and large a positive phenomenon, but views and approaches differed. There has been a long-standing concern among policymakers and academics that migrants from rural areas congest cities and drain urban resources, and many rural development programs have attempted to reduce out-migration—usually with little success. The most important model of rural–urban migration became the Harris-Todaro model, which describes migrants as economic agents who weigh the difference between the expected earnings from formal sector urban employment and the expected earnings in the village.

A "basic needs" approach was central to the 1970s focus at the ILO and elsewhere: an emphasis on satisfaction of basic needs and inclusion of people in decisionmaking processes. Nobel Prize winner Amartya Sen's book *Poverty and Famines* (1981), written for the World Employment Programme, stressed that starvation did not happen because food was unavailable but because people did not have access to food. Sen presented four case studies of famines—Bengal in 1943, and Ethiopia, the Sahel, and Bangladesh in the early 1970s—and concluded that these famines happened not only because of a lack of food but also because of inequalities in distribution of food. Sen emphasized the role of democracy and the free press in averting large-scale starvation. His later work (*Development as Freedom*; Sen 1999) has been interpreted as one of the theoretical foundations of rights-based approaches.

Thus, during the 1970s, the international development debate moved from a focus on growth to a more explicit focus on poverty, redistribution, basic needs, direct anti-poverty interventions, and partic-ipatory approaches to rural development. Yet there were trends that con-flicted with this increased poverty focus. First, donors and recipients faced financial constraints owing to oil price rises and increasing balance of payments pressures. They cut back on long-term or "soft" projects, including anti-poverty programs. Second, a growing part of aid came from new donors (Japan, Organization of the Petroleum Exporting Coun-tries [OPEC] members) who, like the United States, World Bank, and western Europe earlier, focused on heavy infrastructure projects. Third, although debate and donor policy in the 1970s continued to view the state as the key actor in development, a reaction against state interven-tion began. For example, reviews showed that massive state-subsidized credit labeled "for the poor" failed to reach the poor or stimulate agri-cultural growth. The backlash against support for state intervention came to full force in the 1980s.

Washington Consensus and the Lost Development Decade

Mexico defaulted on its external debt in 1982, starting the debt crisis. As financial crises hit, the Bretton Woods institutions designed pack-ages to enable countries in the short run to stabilize and address balance of payments problems, and in the longer term to liberalize and to restore economic growth. The 1980s were dominated by structural adjustment programs, and donor approaches shifted attention to program lending and targeted interventions to ameliorate the effects of financial crises. Many see it as a lost decade for development, and structural adjustment came to be a major rallying advocacy point, for example, in the Jubilee 2000 coalition.

Whereas the 1970s were characterized by a basic-needs focus, a key development of the 1980s was the emergence of the Washington Con-sensus—even though it never formed a full consensus and opinions remained diverse (Stern 2002; Archibong, Coulibaly, and Okonjo-Iweala 2021). The "consensus" highlighted the need for policies of fis-cal discipline, market-determined exchange and interest rates, protec-tion of property rights, liberalization, privatization, and openness to trade. During the period, an increasing proportion of aid came to be given as program aid (discussed in Chapter 3) and was provided with a large number of "conditionalities" regarding adjustment of the economy and state intervention.

Contrasting with earlier optimism about the state as a key agent for development, the state came to be associated with many development problems, ranging from low economic growth to continued and sometimes even increasing poverty. It was argued that the state should focus on its minimum functions, including "getting prices right." The "state . . . was charged with intellectual responsibility for whatever had gone wrong," concluded Albert Hirschman in 1981 (in Fritz and Rocha Menocal 2007, 540). During this period, studies of the East Asian economic successes showed how important state intervention was for development, but these studies did not receive as much attention as the studies of failures in Africa. The development debate became increasingly influenced by policy research at the World Bank. Controversies over structural adjustment came to dominate the debate, including regarding user fees, as Box 4.2 describes.

Box 4.2 User Fees, Social Spending

In the 1980s, under the influence of the fiscal crisis in Africa and elsewhere, affordability of services became an increasingly important concern. A World Bank paper by Thobani in 1983 argued that charges in education were necessary because governments could not afford the total subsidy required. Concerns for poverty were not absent in the paper. It argued that, with fiscal constraints, governments would ration services, which would hurt the poor, and that introduction of user fees would help expand access for the poor. The conclusion about the positive impact of user fees, particularly in primary health and education, was strongly challenged in a major critique of the social and economic policies under structural adjustment. The report by Cornia, Jolly, and Stewart (1987) on the "human face of adjustment," commissioned by the United Nations Children's Fund (UNICEF), describes how adverse economic developments and consequent stabilization and adjustment policies affected vulnerable groups, especially children.

The question of social spending is still debated in development studies. On one side, and particularly influenced by NGOs, there is the view that the World Bank and IMF have forced government spending in poor countries on social sectors to remain low. On the

continues

Box 4.2   Continued

---

other side, the IMF and World Bank have argued that under fiscal crises governments need to address their spending but that the World Bank and IMF have not forced governments to reduce spending on education and health more than in other sectors. The World Bank produced research showing that a large percentage of the additional donor funding available for debt relief has been spent on social sectors, and research showed that investments in agriculture had suffered more than that in social sectors.

Many observers have proclaimed the failure of the Washington Consensus and of the economic policy prescriptions, including those related to capital controls. The growth performance has not been uniformly favorable, and "supply responses" to adjustment measures have been weak. Studies indicate adjustment policies have increased inequalities (Lang 2021) and impacted bureaucratic capabilities in developing countries (Reinsberg et al. 2019). Moreover, the development in fast-growing economies of East Asia, including China, did not follow the path of the Washington Consensus.[6]

That assessment of failure is not uniformly accepted. The range of policy issues encapsulated under the Washington Consensus is probably too complex to have one summary assessment. Many countries did move to fiscal and monetary stability during the 1990s, and it has been pointed out that this shift was as much generated by national policymakers as imposed from the North. Although the evidence of the impact of adjustment on development and poverty was mixed, the critique of adjustment did lead to a renewed focus on (and measurement of) poverty.

Ensuring that the poor benefit from health and education services became an increasingly important concern. In the context of crisis and adjustment, the World Bank and regional development banks turned their attention to "add-ons" designed to mitigate the impact of adjustment in the poor. This started with the Bolivia Emergency Social Fund and the Program of Action to Mitigate the Social Cost of Adjustment in Ghana; both schemes were set up in decentralized and participatory ways and were designed primarily for the people who had lost jobs and livelihoods as a result of retrenchment. Also, donor attention was shifting toward innovative targeted projects, as with the World Bank support for the Tamil Nadu Integrated Nutrition Programme and the International Fund for Agricultural Development (IFAD) support for Grameen in Bangladesh.

The study of development thus expanded during the 1980s, fueled by both structural adjustment policies and development and poverty becoming more central to the various motives of aid agencies. A proliferation of statistical information allowed economists to develop increasingly sophisticated ("general equilibrium") models of national economies and to compare achievements across an ever-larger number of countries (using cross-country regressions). Development economics got a better understanding of the role of human capital in economic growth, and "new institutional economics" emerged. The development debate became increasingly heated, while the numbers of NGOs continued to grow, and the field of development studies was enriched by the annual *Human Development Report* in 1990, challenging the World Bank's *World Development Report*.

1990s: Poverty and Governance Take Center Stage

Although the period after the end of the Cold War led to a decline in interest in development at higher political levels, the 1990s ended with increased attention paid to aid and poverty reduction—this culminated with the Millennium Develop Goals (MDGs) in 2000 and the Sustainable Development Goals (SDGs) in 2015. The Washington Consensus continued to be criticized, even though many of its basic principles have not been abandoned.[7] The World Bank and IMF were increasingly pressed to respond to the critique. The financial crisis in Asia in 1997, followed by radical political changes in Indonesia, for example, provided an impetus to focus the development debate on poverty, and the study of development was broadened, with an emphasis on institutions and governance.

Among the World Bank's annual *World Development Reports*—a major research exercise that brings together evidence from across the world without describing World Bank policy—*World Development Report 1990: Poverty* is often viewed as one of the most important ones. It proposed a two-part strategy for tackling poverty: promoting labor-intensive economic growth and investing in health and education. The report added a leg that some saw as only half a leg: it noted that people who were vulnerable to shocks and unable to benefit from growth required protection in the form of "safety nets"—the latter would grow rapidly in importance over the next decades (Gill, Revenga, and Zeballos 2016).

In the same year, the first Human Development Report (HDR) was published under the leadership of Pakistani finance minister Mahbub ul Haq and Amartya Sen. They were motivated by the common preoccupation with the growth of real income per capita as the measure of well-being. Expansion of an economy, measured as such, does not necessarily mean that people are better off in terms of health, freedom, education, meaningful work, and leisure time. According to the 1990 HDR: "People are the real wealth of a nation. The basic objective of development is to create an enabling environment for people to enjoy long, healthy and creative lives. . . . [This] is often forgotten in the immediate concern with the accumulation of commodities and financial wealth." The Human Development Index (HDI) was introduced, as described in Box 4.3.

Development economics became increasingly sophisticated. From the mid-1990s onward, it became possible to relate data on growth to

---

Box 4.3   Human Development Index

In a push to broaden the development debate beyond a focus on income poverty, the Human Development Report introduced the Human Development Index (HDI). This is a summary measure of human development that provides an alternative to the common practice of evaluating a country's progress in development based on per capita GDP. It measures countries' achievements in three dimensions: a long and healthy life, measured by life expectancy at birth; knowledge, measured by the adult literacy rate and combined primary, secondary, and tertiary gross enrollment ratio; a decent standard of living, measured by GDP per capita in purchasing power parity (PPP) terms in US dollars. The HDI is a composite index, calculated as the average of the indices for each of these dimensions, expressed as a value between 0 and 1. HDI tables comparing countries' performance have helped draw the attention of governments and international organizations to improvements in services in health and education. Since the first report, new composite indices for human development have been developed—the Gender-Related Development Index, the Gender Empowerment Measure, the Human Poverty Index, and measures of happiness.

data on income poverty, health, and education. This was made possible by the increasing number of surveys on income, education, and health that became available, particularly in Africa and often supported by donors. Even social relations and connections were considered sources of economic growth. A concept of social capital was introduced that measured these social relations—though the concept was also heavily criticized.[8] When an internationally comparable set of prices became available, it was possible to compare data on poverty. A measure of $1-per-day poverty was the result, later revised to $1.25 and $1.90. This does not represent an actual dollar converted with normal exchange rates; it represents a consumption bundle that includes the minimum necessities in different parts of the world.[9]

There has been a tendency to equate poverty reduction as the focus of international development efforts with development itself. Much poverty analysis has focused on identifying the characteristics of the poor and less on the causes of and particularly the policies that lead to or sustain poverty. It remains challenging to conceptualize the politics of public policymaking and how the international community relates to these politics. Debates on scaling up aid indicate that even if the analysis is restricted to questions around economic growth, questions about politics are pertinent.[10]

A major change in development thinking during the 1990s was the increasing attention paid to the role of institutions, or "governance," in development thinking and practice, which contributed to new approaches of sector support and PRSPs, as described earlier. Writings on the "post–Washington Consensus" show approaches to economic policies that define a wider role for public policies. Stern (2002), who did not disagree with the principles of the Washington Consensus, concluded that it

> said nothing about governance and institutions, the role of empowerment and democratic representation, the importance of country ownership, or the social costs and the pace of transformation. The development community has learned the hard way, through the setbacks of the structural adjustment programs in developing countries of the 1980s, and the transition of the 1990s in eastern Europe and the former Soviet Union, that these elements are at the heart of the development challenge.

This new approach took into account earlier critiques, concluding that the policy prescriptions were not wrong, certainly not regarding the need for macroeconomic stability, but that the prescriptions were insufficient. It stressed the complementary role of the state vis-à-vis the market and was hopeful that processes of democratization would support a vibrant market economy.[11] The approach recognized the key role of economic growth, the role of the private sector and trade, and the importance of national ownership of the development agenda, empowerment of people, and basic health and education. I discuss the importance of governance in aid approaches further in Chapter 6.

The IMF response to the 1997 Asian financial crisis was heavily criticized by authors such as Joseph Stiglitz, who has continued to be critical of policies related to abolishing capital controls, for example. But 1997 also was a turning point from aid fatigue and declining levels of aid. Rather than merely emphasizing short-term stabilization after the crisis, the response implied a strengthened emphasis on poverty reduction and protecting the poor from the effects of crises.

A new consensus around the role of human development and participation and empowerment was illustrated in *World Development Report 2000/2001: Attacking Poverty*—even though the report's publication was surrounded by the controversy of the resignation of the lead author, Ravi Kanbur. The report highlighted that economic development was central for reducing poverty but that poverty was also an outcome of economic, social, and political processes, which interact and can reinforce each other. The report used a new three-part framework for analyzing and addressing poverty: expanding poor people's opportunities, empowerment, and security. It was influenced by participatory poverty analysis; Deepa Narayan's (1997) study in Tanzania, *Voices of the Poor,* established within the World Bank the utility of participatory methods in development.

The MDGs and SDGs Period: Convergence in Development Studies?

In the last two decades, development studies have continued to expand rapidly. Attention to poverty and multidisciplinary perspectives on development, energized by the global development goals, continue to be central. This has accompanied growing attention on measuring the success of aid, as I discuss in Chapter 8, and on the development success of China (and discussions of a "Beijing Consensus"). Here, I discuss four dominant themes since 2000: the links between poverty and growth, the rise of randomized controlled trials, the importance of governance, and climate and development.

First, studies of and debates about economic growth and its relationship to poverty flourished. As mentioned, the publication of *World*

Development Report 2000/2001 was marked by controversy, and the authors were pressured to put more emphasis on economic growth and change the order of the chapters on the three main themes of opportunities, empowerment, and security. The World Bank and US Treasury officials believed that analysis of growth had to be the most important business of the World Bank and that a chapter focusing on growth should come first. Subsequent World Bank publications highlighted how growth did benefit the poor.[12] Dollar and Kraay's (2002) "Growth *Is* Good for the Poor" responded to concerns within the development community about the importance of growth; in 2013, Dollar, Kleineberg, and Kraay (2013) reinforced this with the working paper *Growth Still Is Good for the Poor.* Taking the question whether growth was good for the poor a step further, research started to explore the extent to which this was the case, through concepts of "pro-poor growth," "inclusive growth," and "growth that works for everyone."

Although questions of rising inequality did not receive much attention in the late 1990s, they became the central subject of *Human Development Report 2005, World Development Report 2006,* in World Development Reports on gender quality (2012) and jobs (2013), and in the growth of data through, for example, the World Inequality Database. As the understanding of the links between growth and poverty reduction and inequality evolved, agreement emerged that policies needed to be multifaceted. The growing attention to inequalities contributed to expansion of programming in social protection, a "development revolution from the Global South" (Hanlon, Hulme, and Barrientos 2010), with participation of many development agencies, including the World Bank, and through the United Nation's Social Protection Floor Initiative, launched in 2009.

Findings on the importance of growth—including China's success in rapidly reducing poverty despite growing inequalities (OECD 2019)—also reinforced calls for growth-promoting policies. This included emphasis on supporting infrastructure and the role of technologies, particularly information and communication technologies, and regarding the need for industrial policies (OECD 2013; Lauridsen 2018; Chang and Andreoni 2020). The thinking about agriculture and how it is related to development more broadly also continued to change. In the mid-1990s, a "sustainable livelihoods" approach (Chambers and Conway 1992; Scoones 1998) had been adopted by a number of agencies, emphasizing participatory approaches and highlighting the ways in which poor communities manage their relationship with environmental change, but its popularity appears to have diminished; it cannot be found in the World Development Report for 2008 on agriculture.

There was a growing interest in understanding and debate about the role of the private sector in development (Kindornay and Reilly-King 2013), entrepreneurship, public–private partnerships, and blended finance. This was accompanied by optimistic writings about the microfinance revolution following the success of the Grameen Bank and about the potential for growth at the "bottom of the pyramid" (Pralahad 2004). Others criticized such an approach as potentially reinforcing inequalities in aid relations (Hart, Russon, and Sklair 2021) and as an effort to reorganize aid around partnerships with global finance (Gabor 2020). Although varying views remained, there was some convergence in thinking on creating the institutions to make markets work, supporting "inclusive growth," and improving investment climates.

Second, development economics took a distinct turn with the growth in use of randomized controlled trials (RCTs), as recognized by the 2019 Nobel Prize in Economics awarded to Michael Kremer, Abhijit Banerjee, and Esther Duflo.[13] Concerns about the inability to establish causal relations led to an interest in experimental approaches. Researchers began to use "natural experiments" comparing outcomes for groups that were randomly assigned to a certain treatment as part of a policy, such as draft lotteries (the 2021 Nobel Prize was awarded for this innovation). RCTs focused on microquestions, and researchers designed and implemented experiments—often in areas outside the field of economics, such as in textbook provision, nurse attendance, and forms of microcredit. The method became very popular at major development agencies but also received much criticism related to its methodological rigor, ethics, and relevance, or lack thereof, for many development questions (Muller, Chelwa, and Hoffman 2019; Drèze 2022).

Third, the focus on institutions and governance continued and broadened to include studies of law. The list of necessary reforms had grown exponentially and included participation, accountability, predictability of government action, transparency, free information flow, and rule of law, among others. It had become clear that the donor literature on good governance produced too many requirements to be practical. Optimism in the early 1990s about implementing good governance gave way to an understanding of the influences of the local context on how reforms were implemented, as I discuss further in Chapter 6. This included emphasis on better understanding of local politics. Agencies introduced forms of political analysis, for example, "power analysis" at Sida (the Swedish International Development Cooperation Agency), the World Bank's Institutional and Governance Reviews; and DFID's Drivers of Change. A "political economy" approach highlighted that politics and power could not be separated from economics. Politics also entered the development debate, and the idea that governments in developed and developing countries needed to build public support to translate development aspiration into action was emphasized, as was the need for political leadership, in the South for undertaking institutional and policy reform and in the North for strengthening solidarity with poverty reduction efforts in the South.

The terrorist attacks in the United States and the subsequent War on Terror of course influenced development studies, and attention on conflict and security and "failed states" grew.[14] Some scholars and practitioners criticized the categorical distinction and argued that the aid industry should consider a conflict–development continuum and a security–development nexus,[15] while Hill (2005) provided a postcolonial critique of the concept. Analysis has shown that specific interventions—such as "democracy aid" (Mross 2021)—can have positive impacts.

Development studies have generally been skeptical about the impact of aid in fragile contexts. Duffield (2007) questioned the possibility of bringing prosperity to unstable regions. Anderson (1999) highlighted the risks of international engagement contributing to conflict as much as reducing it. Woodward (2017) assessed experience with two decades of "statebuilding" and found it can reinforce the problems it tries to address. Although aid interventions started to include efforts to reduce migration, addressing its "root causes," studies showed doubts about the possibility of doing so (Clemens and Mendola 2020). While some described the continued validity of peacekeeping operations (Paris 2010), Autesserre's (2014) ethnographic *Peaceland* focused on the habits and practices of foreign peacebuilders and their unintended consequences in sites of international intervention.

Fourth, the growing climate crisis has increasingly become central to development studies. International attention on the impact of climate change increased with the efforts of US vice president Al Gore, the "Stern Report" in the UK, and reports of the Intergovernmental Panel on Climate Change (IPCC). Development reports, such as the 2007 Human Development Report, examined links between poverty and climatic conditions, and a Sustainable Development Index analogous to the Human Development Index was introduced.[16] The relationship between climate and development became the main theme, for example, of a new journal in 2009, *Climate and Development*, and emphasis was renewed on "sustainable development" (Parry 2009), a concept launched in the 1987 Brundtland Report. A growing literature has contributed to the understanding of the unequal impacts of climate change on poorer countries, from which calls for compensation for "loss and damage" have arisen. A large literature has emerged on communities', rural and urban, strategies to adapt to climate change impacts and on how adaptation needs to become part of national policymaking.

Continued Questions and Challenges for Development Studies

The thinking about aid and international development continues to evolve and broaden alongside growing development agendas such as the SDGs. Sometimes ideas converge, but they are continuously heavily debated. Development studies as a field of research has been very closely linked to development practice, though many researchers remain critical and at a distance. When aid organizations increasingly focused on poverty in the 1990s, development studies evolved by and large in parallel. It has also been at the forefront of highlighting the multidimensionality of poverty and has paid increased attention to issues of empowerment, governance, security, and responses to climate change. Its multidisciplinarity has contributed to an improved understanding of economic development and how this can be promoted as well as the role of governance and institutions.

The field remains divided on many fronts. For example, the importance and role of the state vis-à-vis the private sector remains heavily contested, which reflects broader differences in public policy scholarship. Till the 1970s, the state was seen as a key agent of development, but during the 1980s "rolling back" of the state became a predominant theme. PRSP approaches implied some return to state-led development, and lessons from East Asia challenged conventional wisdom. The debate on investment in social sectors continues to be divided between those who stress the need for increasing investment in health, education, and social security, on the one hand, and those who emphasize the limited resources available nationally or the need to invest in infrastructure and agriculture, on the other hand. Such differences can be technical but are also informed by different values, different national histories and traditions of public interventions, and different ideas about what the core of development is and ought to be.

Development studies as a field has continued to be dominated by academic institutions and think tanks in the Global North, partly because it must inform donor organizations. Studies show that three-quarters or more of publications about the Global South are written by scholars based in the Global North (even though many of these scholars are originally from the Global South), and similarly, editorial boards of journals are dominated by Northern scholars.[17] Over time, there has been a small shift in favor of Southern-based researchers, but this shift is heavily concentrated in large emerging economies such as China. The aid industry has supported research capacity in the South, but this is outweighed by the investments in development research among and within Northern institutions. The expansion of donors such as China, India, Brazil, and South Africa and the emphasis on South–South cooperation may change this, but capacity in the poorest countries and researcher access to international funding and publication continue to be major challenges.

Notes

1. Overviews of development thinking can be found in many places: in the chapters by Erik Thorbecke tracing five decades of development thinking, Irma Adelman on the role of government in economic development, Hjertholm and White in the volume edited by Finn Tarp (2000), and Simon's (2019) "key thinkers" in development.

2. An independent evaluation of World Bank research highlighted "substantial criticisms of the way . . . research was used to proselytize on behalf of Bank policy, often without taking a balanced view of the evidence, and without expressing appropriate skepticism. Internal research that was favorable to Bank positions was given great prominence, and unfavorable research ignored" (Banerjee et al. 2006, 6). Examples discussed in the report (p. 52 ff.) include research on globalization and growth and on aid effectiveness.

3. This was Gloria Davis, who described the history of social development in a 2004 World Bank paper. The first sociologist hired by the World Bank was Michael Cernea. Michael Woolcock has been an influential non-economist social scientist at the bank; his blog is a helpful source: https://blogs.worldbank.org/team /michael-woolcock.

4. Amsden (2007, chap. 3) described the period 1950–1980 as the First American Empire, which favored "trade, not aid," with flexibility in allowing deviations from free trade and in the promotion of alternative development models.

5. The New International Economic Order was finally adopted as a UN General Assembly resolution in 1986 (Uvin 2007, 598). Approaches to rights are further discussed in Chapter 7.

6. Discussed, for example, in the *Marshall Lectures* by World Bank chief economist Justin Lin (2007) and articulated as "New Structural Economics." Ang (2016) provided a detailed analysis of China's development path, highlighting adaptive governance and government-led piloting as key ingredients for success.

7. Ha-Joon Chang (2007) emphasized that the northern "Bad Samaritans" continue to provide simplistic and ideological advice, which often also serves donor countries' interests; and see Babb and Kentikelenis (2021).

8. The edited book by Bebbington et al. (2006) describes the use of the social capital concept in the World Bank and how this helped to form a bridge for its social scientists with other staff. Many critiques of the concept and its use have been written, for example, Harriss (2002).

9. This international comparison is difficult to make. One of the critical factors is the availability of comparable price data, which have undergone major revisions, leading to big changes in estimates of numbers of poor people (Chen, Mu, and Ravallion [2008] discussed this for China).

10. The research program Effective States and Inclusive Development focused on the role of politics in inclusive development ("Findings Summary," Effective States and Inclusive Development, https://www.effective-states.org/findings-summary/).

11. Eyoh and Sandbrook (2003, 228) labeled the new approach a "pragmatic neo-liberal development model" and highlighted its similarities with the "Third Way" promoted by Tony Blair and Bill Clinton; the approach found expression in the Comprehensive Development Framework promoted by the World Bank's President Wolfensohn.

12. Martin Ravallion at an IFPRI conference in Beijing in 2007 highlighted that "growth is not an anti-poverty policy."

13. According to the committee that awarded the 2019 Nobel Prize in Economics to Esther Duflo, Abijit Banerjee, and Michael Kremer, randomized controlled trials improved the world's ability to fight global poverty. The 2021 prize was awarded for innovation in methods with natural experiments.

14. Ghani and Lockhart (2008); World Bank, *World Development Report 2011*. A growing number of studies have analyzed the links between (civil) wars and development (Collier et al. 2003).

15. OECD (2007); Hettne (2010); Bush and Duggan (2015) focused on research in contexts of violence.

16. Sustainable Development Index, https://www.sustainabledevelopmentindex.org.

17. Demeter (2021) analyzed the changes in development studies articles; over six decades, publication remains dominated by the Global North, and the main shift has been between US and European scholarship. See also Cummings and Hoebink (2017), Amarante et al. (2021).

5

Implementing
Development Projects

THE PREVIOUS CHAPTERS HAVE REFERRED TO DEVELOPMENT "PROJECTS"
and intentions to move away from a focus on projects to "program" aid
and "sector approaches." These terms are important to an understanding
of the ways aid is provided by different agencies in different periods of
time. In this chapter, my objective is to provide an understanding—
through examples—of project approaches, their characteristics, whether
and how they "target" the poor or development in a broader sense, and
advantages, disadvantages, and critiques of these approaches.

Projects are the original way aid was provided, by assisting countries
that were short of savings and technological capabilities. Late-colonial
authorities developed projects, and the World Bank started to develop
infrastructure projects that could be expected to generate financial
returns, and this moved into integrated rural development projects. More
recent project approaches include sustainable livelihoods approaches,
microfinance projects, and social funds. As described in Chapter 4,
during the 1950s and 1960s economic theories emphasized the low
savings rates in developing countries and viewed foreign aid as the
means to kick-start economies. Funding of projects was a way the new
aid industry tried to promote developing countries' "take-off." Most aid
is still delivered as projects across a range of sectors, is provided by
nongovernmental organizations (NGOs) and large organizations such
as development banks, and ranges from thousands to hundreds of millions of dollars.

Although design and implementation of projects are now common
and well-established practices of development agencies, the aid industry

first had to find ways of institutionalizing these activities in the newly established bureaucracies. Judith Tendler (1975) described the workings in the US Agency for International Development (USAID) and the World Bank in the early years of the industry. Infrastructure projects became popular for two reasons: a belief that accumulation of fixed assets was the key to development, and officers in these relatively small and new development bureaucracies experiencing a pressure to spend large amounts of money in short periods of time.

These projects were not generated automatically. "The initial position of the Bank was that preparation of a project was the responsibility of the borrower; if the Bank became involved, it could not thereafter be sufficiently objective in appraising the project. Though buttressed by logic, this position soon gave way to the pressure of events. Experience has demonstrated that we do not get enough good projects to appraise unless we are involved intimately in their identification and preparation" (Tendler 1975, 87). Over time, this became common practice. Development practitioners do not simply respond to demands from partners for loans or grants but actively engage— supported by bureaucracies that encourage disbursement of loans or grants—in discussions about possible new projects.

Projects exist in a wide range of areas, not all of which may appear related to poverty reduction. Not all aid agencies have had a narrow focus on poverty reduction; much assistance is provided for development more generally, and as described earlier the focus on poverty is a relatively recent phenomenon. Even if agencies have a strong focus on poverty, they emphasize that poverty reduction can be achieved in different ways and that the preconditions for sustainable poverty reduction are broad. For example, the Department for International Development (DFID) in the UK distinguished three types of activities: *enabling* actions that support, for example, economic growth or more effective governments; *inclusive* or broad-based actions that benefit the entire population, for example, in health and education sectors; and *targeted* interventions, of which the benefits go directly to poor people.

Project Management

A project approach involves donor involvement in a specific area or intervention. It targets the use of funds for specific activities, for which objectives and the outputs and inputs required to achieve them have been defined. Aid projects are defined as specific and distinct activities, with concrete outputs. Goals, results, and measurement of success are specific to the project. The activities include tangible objectives, such as the building of schools, water tanks, or roads. Projects can consist of "gap filling," delivering technical expertise, skills, or "capacity development" more generally.

Projects have a clear, distinct, and time-bound rationale, which is often described in a "project cycle," from identification to implementation to evaluation (see Figure 5.1).

In the 1970s and 1980s, with increasingly professionalized aid agencies, it became common to describe and report project objectives in the form of "logical frameworks," or "logframes," an example of which is provided in the next section. A logframe usually consists of a matrix with rows describing inputs, outputs, outcomes, and impacts (the development goal); columns describing objectives, measurement indicators, ways of measuring these; and assumptions or conditions influencing success and failure. The logframe's systematic approach is meant to facilitate planning, execution, and evaluation of a project, with periodic reviews that highlight performance against a specific level of the logframe. The tool has been criticized for its mechanistic character, for not allowing complex policy processes and indirect consequences to be

Figure 5.1   Project Cycle

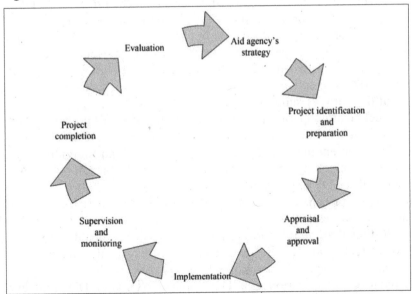

Source: Graphics based on World Bank, reproduced by Arjan Rai Randhawa.

described, and for neglecting personal relationships, cultural sensitivity, and potential conflicts.[1]

An alternative or complementary tool that emerged in the late 1990s is the "theory of change," or "ToC" (Prinsen and Nijhof 2015). This emphasizes that interventions can be expressed as sequences of causes and effects and are a description (and illustration) of how a desired change is expected to happen. Interventions typically use an "outcomes framework" to identify the desired goals, and assumptions, conditions, or outcomes that must be in place to achieve these goals.

Though international agencies have emphasized the need for projects to be "owned" and implemented by local agencies—government or otherwise—in practice the form of management has varied a great deal. At one end of the spectrum, special implementing agencies, often staffed with international personnel, have been responsible for the direct management of projects. At the other end, projects are undertaken by government or other local agencies, and the role of international staff is restricted to supervision and evaluation—the rural development project described in Box 5.3 is an example.

Technical Cooperation and Capacity Development

Technical assistance and technical cooperation, or TA and TC for short, form about one-quarter of total official development assistance (ODA). TA or TC is one form of a project approach but also usually part of program approaches, as discussed in Chapter 3. While most agencies see TC as an integral part of their work, Germany has set up a separate but government-owned agency for technical cooperation, GTZ, now called GIZ.[2] Consultants and NGOs often play a key role in the delivery of this form of support.

Technical cooperation focuses on the transfer of knowledge and skills, which can be technical, economic, organizational, or otherwise. It aims to strengthen capacities of organizations and individuals for development and poverty reduction. Such cooperation can be directly with civil society or grassroots organizations, promoting, for example, livelihoods or enhancing the status of women or organizing and training communities.

Rather than simply providing money or other benefits to poor people, technical cooperation focuses on strengthening people's or organizations' ability to promote development. The Organisation for Economic Co-operation and Development (OECD) Development Assistance Committee (DAC) defines *capacity development* as follows:

"Capacity development can be understood as a process whereby people, organizations and society as a whole strengthen, create, adapt and maintain capacity over time. Promoting capacity development refers to what outside agencies do to facilitate or catalyze capacity development. Not all TC or TA . . . in donor statistics is capacity development, and there are other parts of aid that do qualify as capacity development."[3]

Much TC does not work directly with poor communities and focuses on broader development objectives. For example, donors have supported reform and strengthening of capacity of finance ministries (through secondment and technical training), of offices of personnel or human resources, and of public utilities responsible for infrastructure (see the example in Box 5.1).

The International Programme on the Elimination of Child Labour (IPEC)—within the International Labour Organization (ILO)—was

---

Box 5.1   Technical Assistance for the Electricity Industry—Example of Orissa, India

In the first half of the 1990s, the government of Orissa, with support from the World Bank and TA grants from the Department for International Development (DFID), started to reform its electricity industry. The objectives of the reform included reducing the industry's losses, rationalizing generation and supply of electricity, enhancing the industry's competitiveness and participation of private entrepreneurs and investment, and improving the quality of services. For DFID, whose overarching objective had become poverty, this TA did have a poverty reduction objective: with pre-reform losses, it was difficult for the government to make any policies benefiting the poor, and better electricity provision would benefit the entire population, including the poor.

Substantial amounts of money were spent on consultancy, both local and "highly rated consulting firms of international repute." This form of TA was thought essential to preparing the blueprint reform (Orissa was among the first states in India to undertake this) and to developing systems of operation management, financial control, and contract management. Official government reports and various external critiques emphasized that the utilities were unable to fully absorb the advice and remained dependent on the international consultants, possibly weakening more than strengthening the organizations themselves.

created in 1992 with the goal of progressive elimination of child labor. It is another example of TC. The ILO supports countries' capacity to address problems of child labor, and in this case promoted a worldwide movement to do so. IPEC has operated in more than 100 countries, with an expenditure on TC projects of over US$70 million in the middle of the 2000s. IPEC's partners include employers' and workers' organizations, other international and government agencies, private businesses, and a wide range of civil society organizations. It estimates it has contributed to helping a million children escape child labor and to enacting labor laws in more than fifty countries. An example of the program in China is provided in Box 5.2.

Box 5.2   ILO Project to Prevent Trafficking in Girls and Young Women for Labour Exploitation Within China (CP-TING Project)

As part of IPEC, CP-TING was an ILO program in China (2004–2012, funded by the UK and Canada) that focused on eliminating labor exploitation of children and women, particularly the trafficking of girls and young women. It built on China's ratification of ILO Convention 182, which addresses the worst forms of child labor, including trafficking, and the UN Convention on the Rights of the Child (CRC).

The project started with the observation that, although migration has helped many people escape poverty, it also poses risks and that women and girls are particularly vulnerable. The ILO worked with the All China Women's Federation on a range of practical activities to address these risks and helped vulnerable groups prepare for the process of migration (rather than trying to stop people from migrating). CP-TING operated in three sending provinces (Anhui, Henan, Hunan) and two receiving provinces (Guangdong, Jiangsu) and developed information campaigns that reached over a million women and girls. It helped to establish a network of female employers who had committed to following good labor practices. Women's Homes provided training and referral services. Further, the project helped inform national policymaking, for example, by contributing to the drafting process of the National Plan for Action on Anti-trafficking. A post-project evaluation in 2013 found that the project overall had been successful (ILO 2013).

Infrastructure Projects

Infrastructure projects were a main modality of the early aid industry, often with the involvement of state-owned enterprises. They are regarded as key to reconstruction efforts after disasters, to kick-starting economies, and to promoting trade, for example, in the African Continental Free Trade Area. For many, including international donors, investment in infrastructure is not merely about roads but is a precondition for poverty reduction and economic growth.

Infrastructure projects are ideally suited for large-scale investments, with distinct outcomes and relatively easily calculated rates of return. Despite the risks and long pay-off periods, they have attracted increasing amounts of foreign capital. Most of the aid and investment for physical infrastructure (transport, communication, energy) comes from the World Bank, regional development banks, China, the EU, and Japan.

Infrastructure projects have been large and small. An example of a large infrastructure project is the World Bank's highway projects in Morocco, which is generally viewed as successful. Donor support gradually moved toward national rural roads programs that constructed and improved thousands of kilometers of roads and that had a stronger poverty focus, and more recently have also begun to support climate action.[4] While overall ODA financing or infrastructure has decreased, infrastructure and transport, in particular, have remained among the largest sectors within the World Bank (perhaps 15 percent of all lending, with 20 percent of that in Africa).

Donors have also supported much of the infrastructure implemented in smaller projects. Village roads have gained attention because they are more directly relevant to helping the poor (as mentioned for Morocco, above) and because they tend to receive less emphasis in existing national government priorities. In smaller-scale infrastructure projects, community participation tends to be greatly emphasized, and as such often forms part of wider rural development projects, social funds, and community-driven development (CDD), which I describe later.

Infrastructure provision has been criticized often for being overly focused on technical goals and operational efficiency. Over time, approaches have become more sensitive to questions of economic development, poverty reduction (with much analysis highlighting the importance of the preconditions people need to get out of poverty, such as roads), and the need to adapt approaches to different conditions in developing countries, including addressing the growing impacts of climate change. The demand for infrastructure, community willingness to contribute, decentralization in implementation and management, and forms of ownership and financing are now gaining attention.

Critiques of international development tend to focus on the failures in large infrastructure projects, and highlighting the failures informed the aid fatigue of the 1980s and 1990s and contributed to the relative decline in ODA since the late 1980s.[5] Large failed projects—"white elephants," wide roads that were not used, inappropriate blueprint approaches, and lack of maintenance—have characterized much of this negative image. NGOs heavily criticize support for dam building, and this has led to a withdrawal from these forms of funding. Infrastructure came to symbolize the lack of attention paid to the poor and even the anti-poor nature of development. With the 1980s focus on markets, the failure of state and public sector units to build and run utilities was increasingly highlighted. The urge toward privatization of government services and cost recovery was indirectly responsible; as described by Kessler (2005), expected private finance was not forthcoming. With the onset of the debt crisis, long-term investment also declined.

After declining attention in the 1990s, infrastructure projects have found renewed prominence. Recipient countries have focused on the need for infrastructure, particularly in Africa, where investments have suffered most as a result of the debt crisis. Growing amounts of private foreign capital have materialized to finance infrastructure projects. Delivery models for infrastructure projects changed: away from government-managed projects toward more private sector participation and public–private partnerships, with the International Finance Corporation (IFC), for example, playing an increasingly important role. China—with its Belt and Road Initiative—India, and Persian Gulf nations have significantly increased funding for infrastructure.

Integrated Rural Development, Sustainable Livelihoods, and Productivity

Approaches to rural development have been as diverse as any in the other development fields. An International Food Policy Research Institute (IFPRI) article in 1997 identified nine different agricultural paradigms since the 1960s, including commercialization via cash cropping, community development, basic human needs, national food self-sufficiency, structural adjustment, and sustainable development (Delgado 1997). The aid industry has witnessed the rapid rise and subsequent decline in popularity of the sustainable livelihoods approach, and then renewed attention on agriculture as part of a broader economic growth agenda. This section focuses on two of the major project approaches: integrated rural development and sustainable rural livelihoods.

The Green Revolution, with significant contributions from agencies such as the US Agency for International Development (USAID), exerted a significant impact on approaches to rural development. Between the mid-1960s and the mid-1970s, agriculture in parts of Asia and South America rapidly modernized. The period witnessed massive adoptions of improved cereals, mainly wheat and rice, and adoption of improved crop technologies, including use of fertilizers, irrigation, and management practices. Asian countries doubled their rice production per capita. Yet, it also became clear that despite successes in increasing food supply, Green Revolution progress did not necessarily translate into benefits for the poor. It was the better-off in rural society that gained access to improved technology and enhanced incomes. Women often lost jobs as a result of modernization. Moreover, the Green Revolution has been criticized for reducing genetic diversity, increasing vulnerability to pests, increasing soil erosion, and causing water shortages.[6]

During the 1970s, the goals of equity and poverty alleviation entered explicitly into thinking on agriculture, which previously had focused on commercialization that benefited both poor and rich. The World Bank focused concern on poor farmers and started an approach called Integrated Rural Development (IRD) that aimed to address their multiple problems simultaneously. This move highlighted rural poverty as part of wider socioeconomic development and implied it was the result of limited access to resources. The World Bank defined the development problem as integrated and multisectoral, highlighting the multiple functions of agriculture in the development process and the need for simultaneous development in different sectors and areas, for example, technology, training, research, and marketing. IRD projects addressed issues of rural food production and distribution, nutrition, health and child welfare, off-farm employment opportunities, and rural enterprise initiatives. Planning units to coordinate multisectoral projects were set up in government ministries that were often linked to a national board. NGOs played an increasingly important role, but planning tended to be top-down.

This approach, too, came under fire, partly because emerging financial crises challenged its possibilities. The institutions created by the projects were often very complex, and coordination was very difficult and time-consuming. Expectations regarding planning capacity were overly optimistic, and the need and potentials for local planning were underestimated—an issue that became core to participatory approaches developed later.

A new project approach to rural development appeared in the 1990s. The sustainable livelihoods approach that emerged in the Department for International Development (DFID), United Nations Development Programme (UNDP), and International Fund for Agricultural Development (IFAD) was portrayed by some as a radical departure from past practices, although others described it as a revitalized version of the IRD approaches of the 1970s. (An example is described in Box 5.3.) The term *livelihood* was popularized by the advisory panel of the World Commission on Environment and Development and by Robert Chambers and Gordon Conway in a paper in 1992. *Livelihood* was defined as people's capabilities, social and material assets, and activities needed to make a living. *Sustainability* was seen as a key addition and was defined as the capacity to cope with and recover from shocks while maintaining capabilities and assets as well as the natural resource base. The sustainable livelihoods approach was presented as a new way to analyze rural life and poverty, and its framework put people at the center of development.

Box 5.3   IFAD Focus on the Poorest and Criticism of This Approach: Orissa Tribal Empowerment and Livelihoods Programme

In the 1980s and 1990s, southwestern Orissa (now Odisha) was one of the most deprived regions of India, with about two-thirds of the population living below the poverty line and active insurgency movements (Naxalites). Fifty percent of the population belonged to so-called tribal groups, or *adivasis*. The area has been in the public debate in India for decades, with prime ministers regularly visiting and announcing large programs with vast sums of money, which often remained unspent.

IFAD started working in this area in the mid-1980s, after Prime Minister Rajiv Gandhi made a widely publicized visit to Kashipur, an area that more than any other symbolizes deep poverty. The Orissa Tribal Development Project, the first of its kind financed by IFAD in India, with a value of over US$20 million, aimed at improving the livelihoods of tribal people. It was followed by the Orissa Tribal Empowerment and Livelihoods Programme, with a total value of

continues

Box 5.3   Continued

US\$90 million, including cofinancing by DFID and the World Food Programme (WFP). Whereas the first project emphasized physical infrastructure and technologies, the second focused more on building the capacity of poor people and their institutions to enable vulnerable groups, particularly women, to manage their own development. The project aimed to provide access to and management of natural resources, improved access to financial services and markets, and the development of nonfarm enterprises. It was multifaceted, including wage employment, microfinance services, investments in agriculture, and funds for creating community infrastructure.

Although a DFID evaluation was positive overall (ICAI 2013), the projects have been criticized. It is often asserted that decades of development projects and millions of dollars of government and aid money made no difference to the area; the area continued to suffer from deep poverty, health epidemics, and perennial starvation deaths. It was often claimed, and sometimes shown, that money was misappropriated by project staff and partners, including NGOs. The projects were criticized for introducing commercial activities such as coffee plantations and sericulture, eucalyptus plantations that benefited paper mills more than the local population, and infrastructure that benefited large companies. These activities were perceived as posing threats to traditional livelihoods of *adivasis* while benefiting traders and money lenders and introducing dependency on government handouts.

Sources: IFAD (1999); Odisha Tribal Empowerment & Livelihoods Programme Plus, http://otelp.org/; Das (2003); ICAI (2013).

The livelihoods approach, like IRD, focuses on multisectoral and integrated development. It emphasizes that the poor derive their livelihoods from many sectors, jobs, and sources of income and that standard approaches that focus on specific sectors are inadequate, particularly in the most marginalized areas. It emphasizes the diversity of rural households' strategies, including not only agricultural production but also diversification and migration. It focuses not just on poverty and deprivation but also specifically on poor people's resources and assets. This is presented as an "asset pentagon" (Figure 5.2) that shows

Figure 5.2   The Livelihoods Framework

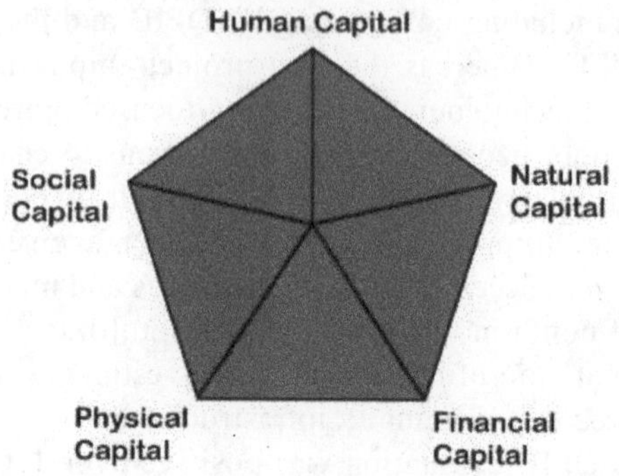

Source: Scoones (1998), reproduced by Arjan Rai Randhawa.

the multidimensionality of people's livelihoods and the relationships among their assets.

The livelihoods framework built on lessons from poverty analysis that over time had come to emphasize the multidimensionality of poverty, issues of vulnerability, and the idea that slightly better-off people are at risk of losing their income. Moreover, in a new wave of emphasis on participation and following work in particular by Robert Chambers and Gordon Conway (1992) that reflected on past problems caused by paternalism of development professionals, the sustainable livelihoods approach put participation and empowerment at the center. The livelihoods framework works across a range of sectors, whereas governments and donor agencies tend to work along sectoral lines. In the case of the project in China described in Box 5.4, project priorities defined through a participatory approach included a wide range of services and required the cooperation of (and often also counterpart funding by) different line agencies.

In addition to the focus on participation, but in practice much less developed, the sustainable livelihoods approach also highlighted policy dimensions. This was partly a response to the critique that technical project approaches paid little attention to the policy environment in which they functioned. The framework stressed the importance of strengthening policies and institutions—at a local level through direct participatory processes but also at higher levels of policy formulation and implementation—to enhance livelihood options.

Box 5.4   Poor Rural Communities Development Project in China

Starting in 2005, the World Bank and DFID jointly provided support to the Chinese government for a rural development project in eighteen counties of three of its poorest provinces (Sichuan, Guanxi, Yunnan). It was the fourth in a series of World Bank poverty projects in China that were generally considered successful. The objective of the Poor Rural Communities Development Project (PRCDP) was to improve livelihoods and security of the poorest people and to solicit their participation in project design, implementation, and monitoring and evaluation. Funding was provided through a World Bank loan (US$100 million), a DFID grant (US$32 million, which reduced the interest rate of the loan), and counterpart funding from the Chinese government and project beneficiaries (US$42 million).

In 2005, China was no longer among the poorest countries. But, it was argued in the project document, the numbers of poor in resource-poor areas were still very high, forming a large proportion of the world's poor, and addressing this required innovative development approaches. The project was targeted to China's poorest population, those living in remote and mountainous areas, often ethnic minorities. The project adopted a participatory approach, involving poor people in all stages of the project and increased involvement of NGOs. It was a multisectoral project that aimed to provide access to education and health in the poorest areas, as well as improve infrastructure and introduce diverse forms of agriculture. The project included a substantial financial allocation and technical inputs for capacity building to improve management capabilities of government staff and promote the use of a participatory approach.

While directly benefiting large numbers of poor households in the eighteen poor counties, the project also aimed to influence the Chinese government's broader poverty strategy. The government has been proactive in using such projects as part of its economic development programs and reforms, including strengthening management capacities to international standards.

The livelihoods approach, too, has come under criticism. In agencies such as DFID, where for some time it was seen as a major priority, attention shifted to other issues. In *World Development Report 2008: Agriculture for Development*, the livelihoods approach and the work by Chambers and Conway no longer were mentioned (though the report did describe the diversity in household income strategies). The livelihoods approach has been criticized for its ambition in aiming to work across a range of sectors. Indeed, in the project in China, ensuring that the many different line agencies cooperated and the aid provided matched the participatory plans developed continued to be challenging.

A version of a livelihoods approach has come back into the development debate with investment in and research on a "graduation approach." This approach evolved out of microfinance approaches (discussed next), and it was also promoted by researchers who focused on testing development interventions through randomized controlled trials. The Ultra Poor Graduation Approach promoted by Innovations for Poverty Action (IPA) focuses on providing households with assets to enhance self-employment. The evidence collected in six countries demonstrates the value of "big push" interventions that provide multiple types of support, including assets, cash, training, and health access.[7]

Microfinance

Microfinance became a popular instrument of the aid industry in the 1980s. Its development was based on the understanding that regular financial systems in many countries failed to provide financial services to the poor. In the 1960s, many countries experimented with massive subsidies and credit, but in the 1980s this approach was heavily criticized. In the early 1980s, the Grameen Bank in Bangladesh started with a group-based lending approach. The Grameen Bank was awarded the Nobel Peace Prize in 2006 for its work—at the time, some seven million borrowers had been granted a loan. The model was adopted by many microfinance institutions around the world, as have models developed by BRAC (the development organization based in Bangladesh), and the number of studies assessing the effectiveness of microfinance projects and institutions grew.

Microfinance targets finance to poor people. Small and accessible loans are very important for poorer people to fund new economic activities or provide support during crises. Grameen provides credit to groups of women with little or no land. Staff who have gone through extensive training assess households' wealth using visual indicators such as housing quality and assets. This is a quick and reliable mechanism that allows a rapid increase in coverage in contexts where little information about income exists. In many projects, loans are provided to groups instead of individuals. In the absence of collateral, the group members are jointly liable for the loan, which is thought to be a key to keeping up repayment.[8]

These schemes have had success and are regarded as a very effective and sustainable way to provide poorer households with loans. The approach is thought to be sustainable because repaid loans can be used to expand services and increase coverage of larger populations. Successful programs like Grameen's have shown very high rates of repayment, unlike earlier state-led approaches, which placed little emphasis on and had little success with repayment.

Because the loans are small, it is unlikely that the rich will capture project benefits. In the case of Bangladesh, lack of land has been regarded as a proxy for poverty, and the quick assessment done by Grameen Bank staff is a good indicator of the overall wealth of a household. In other cases, such as the small farm loan project in Thailand in the mid-1980s, finance was targeted to villages that had been identified as poor. In Indian states, village councils identified poor households eligible for loans.

But such approaches have encountered criticism too. Even in the celebrated Grameen case, "targeting errors" occur. The literature distinguishes two kinds of errors. First, "inclusion errors" allow people who are not poor to get the benefits; in the case of Grameen, for example, this would be people without land who are not poor. Second, "exclusion errors" prevent people who are poor from getting the benefits. People with a little land may still be poor. The poorest may also be excluded by project staff or by the borrowing groups themselves, particularly if there is high pressure for repayment.

Some studies have pointed at possible negative social consequences of microfinance. For example, Grameen borrowers have to sit on the floor and chant slogans, among other activities, which can be stigmatizing. Whereas group formation may enhance the "social capital" of group members, failing to repay loans may damage social connections. Providing loans to women can enhance their empowerment but also create tensions within households. Perhaps most important has been the question of whether the loans have a sustainable impact on improvement of income or well-being, particularly whether the poorest people can actually use loans for economic investment. Many loans are used for consumptive purposes, new small enterprises often fail, and expectations that microfinance lifts large numbers of people out of poverty may be too optimistic.

Over time, the microfinance approach has been replicated and has evolved. Grameen America was built on the Grameen model to provide microloans for women with income below the poverty line who could work in groups of five to start a business. The focus on microcredit for small groups expanded to a focus on access to financial services for poor families and addressing barriers to "financial inclusion," as highlighted, for example, by CGAP, the Consultative Group to Assist the Poor, which was created in 1995 by a group of major aid organizations, and by the creation of the Global Findex Database.[9] New technologies have been employed to enhance poorer people's access to financial services: Kenya's M-PESA, launched in 2007 by mobile network operators, became a model for addressing traditional barriers to banking services.

Social Investments:
From Social Funds to Social Protection

As described in Chapter 2, the largest share of traditional donors' aid goes to social sectors. Low-income countries, in particular, rely on donor funding for health and education investments, with grants rather than loans as the dominant modality. Donors, including philanthropic investors, have played a key role in the development of medicines to address diseases. Social sectors investments can be in the form of both projects and programs (as described in Chapter 3). Here, I focus on one specific social sector project, social funds, and how this has evolved to garner significant donor attention for social protection.

During the 1980s, when economic stabilization and adjustment were core concerns, the World Bank started to look for ways to ameliorate the impact of economic crises, including by focusing on people directly affected by crises. This approach obtained the name "social fund" and was adopted by regional development banks and often cofinanced by other donors. In 2000, social funds existed in over fifty countries, with the World Bank and the Inter-American Development Bank (IADB) as the largest funders. World Bank financing was estimated at about US$3.5 billion during 2001–2005, and government and other donor cofinancing total expenditure amounting to almost US$9 billion. Though social funds remained a small part of countries' social security activities, they formed a significant part of the government budget in a number of countries.

The first funds emerged in the late 1980s as emergency measures to alleviate the direct impacts of structural adjustment and economic shocks. Bolivia's Emergency Social Fund (ESF) aimed to address the social costs of adjustment, particularly unemployment of miners laid off after the collapse of tin prices and closing of state-run mines. The Program of Action to Mitigate the Social Cost of Adjustment in Ghana and the Program to Alleviate Poverty and Social Costs of Adjustment in Uganda were set up in a similar vein. Social funds were less important in Asia, but social fund support was given to the District Poverty Initiative Project in India. In Thailand, a social fund was created with a focus on establishing a new economy after the 1997 crisis. Funds were set up in the poorest countries, in former communist countries marked by crises of social security systems, and in fragile contexts, such as Yemen (Al-Iryani, De Janvry, and Sadoulet 2013).

Social funds were regular loans to countries, usually cofinanced with contributions from recipients and sometimes combined with additional grant funding. They acted as an intermediary for sending resources to small-scale projects for poor and vulnerable groups: a central administrative entity disbursing funds to local governments, private firms, and NGOs. The funds appraised, financed, and supervised implementation of small projects—but did not implement them. They operated as institutionally and organizationally distinct from government sectoral policies and services. Some funds were autonomous agencies outside regular government bureaucracies; others operated within ministries but with a substantial degree of independence. Many funds set up procedures that would overcome the time-consuming and bureaucratic procedures associated with the public sector and that avoided complex disbursement and procurement procedures. They recruited staff at higher rates than civil service standards to attract the best professionals, and sometimes offered performance contracts.

Social funds were set up to respond to demands from local groups, usually with a set menu of eligible and ineligible projects. They were intended to enable quick and targeted actions to reach poor and vulnerable groups. They aimed to stimulate participatory development initiatives by providing small-scale financing to local NGOs, community groups, small firms, and entrepreneurs and to provide pre-investments to promote participation. Beneficiary cofinancing was deemed central to ensuring that projects responded to demand and were more likely to be sustained after the end of project funding. They experimented with a range of community contracting models.

Social funds were praised for their rapid disbursement, flexibility, and ability to respond to demand from poor communities.[10] Of course, impact and project quality varied. For example, beneficiary-executed projects were found to benefit from broad participation in project definition and met the felt needs of the community, whereas private organizations and NGOs scored less high, usually because of project complexity and lack of continuity. Interventions provided through line ministries tended to lack participatory practices and resources to supervise interventions or work closely with beneficiaries.

A key concern with social funds was the potential for conflicts between efficiency goals and the time-consuming and costly processes of community ownership and decisionmaking. Reviews found that only a small proportion of the funds could be categorized as really demand-oriented. Adequacy of the methodology used to formulate community needs was questioned, and it was found that the resources supplied could increase corruption. Potential trade-offs between reaching the poor and demand-led approaches were also noted, as was the need to enhance the capacities of communities to participate.

As a reaction, often driven by donors, to the slowness of public sector reform, social funds tended to create new structures rather than work to reform existing government institutions. Evidence exists of negative effects of social funds on other national and local policy and public sector institutions. With parallel systems, when conditions for social fund staff were much better than conditions in mainstream public institutions, the morale and efficiency of government staff elsewhere were sometimes harmed. Integrating social funds into existing structures often was not envisaged at the planning stages. Finally, establishing funds could displace other sources of funding. As with other projects, social funds suffered from so-called fungibility, the risk that ministries would reduce their allocations to areas or activities that were targeted by social funds.

Over time, the emphasis shifted from short-term emergency relief to more general developmental programs. In line with an evolving World Bank social protection strategy, social funds moved away from a focus on risk coping toward a more proactive strategy dealing with risk mitigation and risk reduction with longer-term objectives. Social funds continued to pay attention to popular participation and facilitated community-driven development (CDD, discussed further in Chapter 7).

Since the late 2010s, the World Bank has reduced its investment in social funds. It moved its focus to supporting more permanent social protection and employment policies, working in collaboration with many other donors, particularly the ILO. Social protection also obtained a prominent place in the Sustainable Development Goals (SDGs) framework, for example, Goal 1.3, which includes "nationally appropriate social protection systems and measures for all, including floors, and by 2030 achieve substantial coverage of the poor and vulnerable."[11]

The World Bank social protection portfolio grew significantly to over $18 billion in lending by 2019, out of which more than $11 billion goes to International Development Association (IDA) countries. These funds include targeted resources for cash transfers, public works, school feeding, and safety nets but also aim to enhance economic opportunities and skills development. For example, World Bank social protection support in the Philippines focused on technical assistance to and project activities for the Department of Social Welfare and Development to improve the design of and scale up the national program of conditional cash transfers, building on experience in Brazil and Mexico.[12] This switch from social funds as distinct projects to support of (sub)national policies is an example of a move from a project to a program approach (discussed in Chapter 3).

Critique of Project Approaches

Projects thus have come a long way from their origins in the schemes of the late-colonial period and the early infrastructure projects of the period, where the emphasis was on kick-starting economies of former colonial countries and overcoming the savings gap through straightforward and visible projects. During the 1980s, countries' financial crises made many of the projects financially unsustainable, but even before that, criticism of project approaches had emerged (Mosley and Eeckhout 2000).

Experience showed that development projects can undermine local ownership. The aid industry discovered that demands for projects were not easily or quickly forthcoming. Industry staff had incentives to go out and design projects, and donor countries often had economic interest to supply certain goods. There are many stories of inappropriate projects, but even in the better cases, local ownership was limited. And if grants rather than loans were involved, recipients did not have strong reasons to say no to offers of aid.

Sustainability is a second concern, directly related to the question of ownership. Many infrastructure projects have had a poor track record of maintenance. Technical cooperation does not have a strong record of success in many places, often because the broader environment needed to sustain improvements does not exist. Aid projects have imposed large burdens on recipient governments, particularly in aid-dependent countries. Even the Indian government, for whom aid was only a small proportion of government budgets and administrative capacity, limited the total number of donors because of concerns over transaction costs. Each project comes with its own reporting requirements. Aid projects, which usually offer better conditions, often absorb the better-skilled workers from government services.

Third, projects and technical assistance have often become isolated "islands of excellence." With a strong focus on project outputs, donor projects have contributed little to broader government strategies. Project managers cannot be held accountable for changes at the policy level, and evaluations usually do not address the wider environment (even though project documents often state aims to that extent). As we saw in the description of social funds, aid projects tend to create parallel structures and increase administrative burdens.

Fourth, projects suffer from "fungibility" of funding. Aid to particular projects, or sectors, may lead governments to reduce their own contribution to these purposes. Unless aid agencies have insight into government planning and budgeting procedures, which is key to program aid and budget support (as discussed in the next chapter), this aspect is difficult to be certain about.

Fifth, projects not only are a heavy burden on governments but also may fail to contribute to wider development planning and can undermine government policy. In countries heavily dependent on foreign aid, projects can undermine resource planning. Budgets of many countries receiving aid show, for example, large year-to-year fluctuations in spending on sectors that receive substantial aid. Projects can undermine local accountability, for example, when elected leaders can attract voters because of impressive new bridges or schools.

Not all projects, of course, suffer from all these problems. Many of the issues have been addressed in newer-generation projects. In the case of larger countries, where aid flows are small relative to total country or government resources, projects, especially those focused on innovation, may continue to prevail and be successful (World Bank 2007). And many of the problems with projects also pertain to the newer instrument of the aid industry, the program approach, which was described earlier. Project success depends at least as much on the broader policy environment as it does on the project design itself. In terms of results, it is probably the ways in which projects are supported, both quality of implementation and recipient ownership, rather than the project approach, per se, that determines success.

Despite these critiques and concerns, and despite intentions to move toward a program approach, development projects continue to be the bread and butter of the aid industry. The World Bank funds projects, including major ones in the infrastructure sector. The bilateral agencies that have forcefully argued for changes away from the project approach also continue to fund projects. The new actors in the aid industry have expanded the numbers of projects. Projects, with their flexible and demand-driven nature and potential for innovation, suit the aid industry well, with its disbursement pressures and need to show results. And they can fulfill important needs of recipient countries.

Notes

1. Grove and Zwi (2008) proposed an additional tool to address these concerns: a "Health and Peace Building Filter" for health programs in conflict settings.

2. GIZ, www.giz.de.

3. OECD DAC, Network on Governance (2006, 9); Nastase et al. (2021) described how the concept of technical assistance has evolved.

4. Levy (2004); World Bank IEG (2021). The success of rural roads in contributing to poverty reduction is described in the World Bank (2004a) document *Reducing Poverty, Sustaining Growth: Scaling Up Poverty Reduction.*

5. During the 1990s, the World Bank's infrastructure investment lending declined by 50 percent. The decline in international lending was matched by a decline in government spending (Kessler 2005).

6. The Green Revolution had less impact in Africa than elsewhere. The Gates/Rockefeller initiative Alliance for Green Revolution in Africa aims to address this, showing the private sector taking a lead rather than the public sector, which led the 1960s Green Revolution.

7. "The Ultra Poor Graduation Approach: Case Studies," Innovations for Poverty Action, https://www.poverty-action.org/impact/ultra-poor-graduation-model.

8. A large amount of literature is available on the Grameen Bank. The documentary on Bangladesh in the series *The Quiet Revolution* provides a good introduction (World Neighbors 1995).

9. "Can Financial Services Support Platform Work?" Consultative Group to Assist the Poor, https://www.cgap.org/; "The Global Findex Database 2021: Financial Inclusion, Digital Payments, and Resilience in the Age of Covid-19," World Bank, https://globalfindex.worldbank.org/.

10. For example, in de Silva and Sum (2008), and the extensive study by Rawlings, Sherburne-Benz, and Van Domelen (2004). External and critical studies include Cornia (1999) and Tendler (2000).

11. Developing countries spend on average 1.5 percent of their GDP on social protection (World Bank 2018).

12. Elena Bardasi, "Not Just What, but How: A Strong Delivery System Was Key to the Success of the Philippines' Nationwide Social Protection Program," Independent Evaluation Group, March 2, 2020, https://ieg.worldbankgroup.org/blog/not-just-what-how-strong-delivery-system-was-key-success-philippines-nationwide-social.

Notes

1. (mostly illegible)

6

The Importance
of Governance

DURING THE 1970s, AS THE AID INDUSTRY MADE POVERTY REDUCTION
increasingly part of its core business, financial sustainability became a
growing concern, first gradually, but then dramatically so after the second oil crisis. This led to an emphasis on economic reforms, a "Washington Consensus," and structural adjustment, which gave at least part
of the aid industry a poor reputation and the 1980s the title "lost development decade." This, in turn, led to new development approaches, a
move toward a "post–Washington Consensus" (which is complemented
later with a discussion of a "Beijing Consensus"), and a growing
emphasis on governance within the aid industry.

In this chapter, I aim to explain this shift and the continued debates
around adjustment and its importance in the aid industry. The first section is an overview of what structural adjustment means, where it originated, and the main elements of the critique of this approach that came
to dominate the 1980s, including whether it has caused poverty.
Although the differences in views are likely to continue, criticisms of
adjustment exerted considerable influence on the development of newer
approaches, including the attempts to move toward program and sector
approaches, as described earlier.

In the next section, I focus on conditionalities, a practice that was
particularly important under adjustment and that continues to be central
to the functioning of the aid industry. Under adjustment, aid agencies—
particularly but not only the International Monetary Fund (IMF) and the
World Bank—imposed conditions of policy or administrative changes,

such as establishing financial stability, that were required to be implemented before loans or grants were given.

The next sections discuss governance and politics. The focus on restoring economic growth brought relatively little success in aid-dependent countries, and for the aid agencies, it became increasingly clear that this required good governance, an array of government functions and capacities, including tax policies, civil service, and public enterprise reform. These are complex processes and aid agencies came up with long lists of prescriptions, the implementation of which posed large challenges. The focus on governance made it increasingly clear that development, and hence aid provision, is a political process, and aid agencies started to incorporate this understanding.

Structural Adjustment Lending

The term *structural adjustment* raises more heated debate than perhaps any other term in the international development language. Structural adjustment was a response to debt crises that emerged after the oil crises of the 1970s. Brazil, Mexico, and Poland were among the countries unable to service their debts. The IMF—because of its mandate to ensure global financial stability—followed by the World Bank became the key agents in addressing the so-called debt crisis, and their response received widespread attention because of its focus on reducing government expenditure, reducing state intervention, and promoting liberalization.

"Structural adjustment" has been used as a simple term in critiques of the aid industry, but it consists of multiple objectives and instruments. It has involved not only the IMF and World Bank but also bilateral agencies. The subjects of adjustment are usually countries' governments, though in the case of India, the World Bank worked directly with state governments, as described in the example later in this chapter. Structural adjustment has characterized policy changes in the North as much as in the South—the discussion here focuses on how the aid industry approached adjustment and the impact it had on the recipients of aid.

Structural adjustment programs, or SAPs, have included two main sets of measures. The first is *stabilization*, immediate and short-term steps to address a country's internal fiscal and external balance of payments crises. This typically includes currency devaluation to make exports more competitive and addressing inflation. To achieve that, policies often freeze civil service and public sector wages and reduce government expenditure by cutting subsidies for public services and products, such as food and other basic commodities, health and education, and pensions. Increasing government revenue is also an important element of addressing fiscal imbalances.

The second main set of measures is called *adjustment*. These are meant to follow a phase of stabilization and are designed to enhance government efficiency, economic growth, and competitiveness in the longer run. SAPs often included the following measures:

- Following immediate stabilization attempts to reduce the government's salary bills, SAPs often recommended the number of civil servants be reduced usually in combination with attempts to reform the civil service and public sector to increase efficiency and, for example, improve recruitment and promotion procedures.
- Economic liberalization was recommended to enhance economic efficiency, for example, through reducing and streamlining regulation, liberalizing prices, reducing explicit and implicit subsidies, reducing taxes on productive activities, promoting privatization, and reducing the importance of state monopolies.
- Export promotion was considered key to addressing debt crises as well as promoting economic competitiveness. Recommended measures included reducing constraints in obtaining foreign exchange and promoting diversification, usually away from a focus on agricultural goods for which prices had been declining.

Over time, SAPs have been adapted. The distinction between stabilization and longer-term economic development was made clearer, which resulted in a separate mechanism to fund activities for economic recovery, such as the Enhanced Structural Adjustment Facility (ESAF). Although initially a blueprint approach, over time local circumstances came to feature more predominantly. Aid agencies increased their country presence and technical capacity commensurate with the wide range of areas highlighted in SAPs. The initial list of measures did not feature the reduction of poverty, and it has been argued that the agencies involved did not prioritize poverty reduction.

Uganda in the 1990s was seen as an African showcase of the beneficial effects of structural adjustment. Jim Wolfensohn and other donors worked very closely with its government, led by President Yoweri Museveni. Many of the new aid modalities were piloted and seen to be successful in Uganda. Indeed, Uganda, after it emerged from dictatorship and civil war, over the 1990s did achieve significant economic growth (including in agriculture) and poverty reduction. Aid dependency was reduced, and reforms seemed to have local ownership. There was a clear intention to communicate that the relationship was working. Peter Chappell documented the close relationship between the Ugandan government and the World Bank, despite difficult discussions about military spending to fight an insurgent movement, in his film *Our Friends at the Bank* (First Run/Icarus Films). Over time, Uganda lost its status of "donor darling."

Alongside financial assistance, aid agencies provided technical support, assisting recipients in building the capacity for economic and financial management, for example, through long-term assistance to financial systems reforms or secondments to finance ministries. Box 6.1 provides an example of such a loan, the Orissa Socio-Economic Development Program, provided by the World Bank in 2004, in collaboration with the Department for International Development (DFID). This is not a typical example—India's conditions are of course very different from those in African countries, and aid was provided to a state rather than to a country and relied on agreements between Orissa and the Central Government—but it does illustrate the main aspects of the structural adjustment aid approach at the time.

Box 6.1   Orissa Socio-Economic Development Program

The Orissa Socio-Economic Development Program was the first in a series to support the medium-term program for socioeconomic development in Orissa, India's poorest state, under severe fiscal stress. The loan was provided by the World Bank, and the UK's DFID contributed with a separate grant.

The project aimed to stabilize the fiscal situation and introduce growth-enabling reforms, reinforce government initiatives to accelerate economic growth, and improve public service delivery to reduce poverty. Expected benefits included more rapid economic growth, improved fiscal performance and reduction of public sector borrowing, and enhanced quality of governance and service delivery. The newly established Poverty Task Force produced overarching policy documents, such as *Vision 2020*, and documents on poverty reduction.

The donors thought the program had significant risks: implementation of the reform program could be slowed by institutional capacity constraints and by opposition from powerful interests, and

continues

Box 6.1   Continued

---

nonadherence to the targets set in the fiscal reform framework could derail Orissa's adjustment path. Several factors were thought to mitigate the risks: the government had already implemented up-front actions that laid the foundation for subsequent reforms, and donors ensured that significant technical assistance was available to follow through on the reform measures.

The program had a large number of policy actions and reforms required for disbursement of funds, including the creation or strengthening of systems to monitor outcomes and a communication mechanism to inform the public about the reforms. This list of requirements was the outcome of long discussions, and preparation of the project took several years. Some policy areas, for example, in education, were subject to separate collaboration with donors. It was argued the list of policy actions was too long and the project should focus on core areas of fiscal adjustment and governance reforms.

The support entailed a gradual approach to reforms. Some reforms had been supported previously and continued forward, such as power sector reform. Many of the actions consisted of drafting plans, policies, or legislation, and proposals for research and tracking of government expenditure. Some were more concrete actions (such as increased prosecution of cases of corruption), and a few highlighted specific outcomes of these policy actions (for example, price realization).

It is important to highlight here how radical a departure SAPs were from previous aid approaches. They implied a sharp change of direction from project approaches. Donor support under SAPs typically came in the form of budget funding to support a plan or policy program developed by the recipient government. This modality enhanced the role of the IMF—which was set up as and continues to be a global financial rather than an aid institution—and impacted the autonomy of aid-dependent countries in managing their public policies and financial planning. Aid in this form and particularly from IMF and World Bank comes with specific strings attached, or "conditionalities," as described later.

Questions about the role and impact of adjustment, and alternatives to adjustment, are complicated. Implementation of programs has often been very partial and slow, which also means that impact on economic recovery and poverty reduction remains limited. As mentioned earlier, there has been much debate around the impact of structural adjustment on poverty. Global debt relief campaigns and the Poverty Reduction Strategy Paper approach made poverty much more central to such forms of donor action.[1] A main argument was that poverty could not be addressed until some of the "basic" economic problems and government failures were addressed. In the case of adjustment in Orissa, experts argued that it would be undesirable to discuss increased spending in, for example, the health sector or poverty reduction programs as long as all government financial resources went to salaries of civil servants, public sector employees, and financial losses, particularly in the power sector; public finances and government functions had to be rationalized first to "create fiscal space."[2]

Structural adjustment has had a direct impact on particular groups, and hence created new forms of inequalities. Civil servants and public sector enterprise workers lost their jobs as a result of reforms; training and retirement schemes and social funds were created to ameliorate direct impacts. Changes in prices and subsidies as a result of reforms also have had varied impacts on groups of producers and consumers. The introduction of user fees and the reduction of subsidies in health and education have been much criticized; however, overall, and partly as a result of criticism, spending in these sectors has been protected. Also, much of the social spending does not benefit the poor, and donors have made efforts to shift spending toward primary education and social protection that benefits poorer groups. Many of the elements of adjustment do not have a direct or immediate link to the main causes of poverty. However, in the case of Orissa, issues of land and forest use by marginalized groups are central to poverty reduction but received very little attention in the policy discussions.

The impact of reforms and adjustments of course depends on political and other forms of power. Many country leaders and their constituencies paid little attention to poverty reduction. In the case of Orissa's state leaders, political analysis clearly showed that power was held by a very small elite, hardly accountable to large groups of deprived people and with little incentive to make existing government programs work properly (de Haan 2008). Many of the policy measures that were part of adjustment programs do not affect these power relations, which do not change easily and can hinder reforms.

As the debt situation in recipient countries eased, adjustment lending became less important. But it continues to remain an important topic. The IMF's role in the financial crisis in Greece was debated. In the second half of the 2010s, debt levels in Africa started to increase again and became increasingly unsustainable for a growing number of countries. This trend was amplified by the Covid-19 pandemic, even though many low-income countries' fiscal and monetary responses to the pandemic were very limited because of lack of fiscal space. Importantly, in the late 2010s the composition of debt changed considerably. Although the institutional creditors of the "Paris Club"[3] were central in the heavily indebted poor countries (HIPC) initiative, private sector and Chinese creditors play a key role in the 2020s, making debt relief much more complicated. The international community delivered a series of debt relief initiatives, and loans during the pandemic have been relatively free of conditionalities.[4] Concerns emerged, though, about IMF insistence on reducing expenditure and "demands for austerity" (Oxfam 2021; Kentikelenis and Stubbs 2021).

Debate about adjustment and the impact it has had on aid recipients is likely to continue. The debate represents different ideological positions, which technical assessments are unlikely to overcome. Over time the industry has come to recognize that there are different ways these problems can and need to be addressed. Critiques of adjustment did contribute to changes in approaches and increased attention on governance and politics, which I discuss in the rest of this chapter after a description of conditionalities.

Conditionalities

Donor support, and adjustment lending from the World Bank and IMF in particular, comes with specific strings attached, or conditionalities. Here is a definition provided by Tony Killick (2002, 481): a "conditionality consists of actions, or promises of actions, made by recipient governments only at the insistence of aid providers; measures that would not otherwise be undertaken, or not within the time frame desired by the providers." The World Bank and IMF have justified conditionalities on grounds that they would improve economic policy, economic growth, and ability to repay debts.

Conditionality in policy-based lending varies by context. In "better performing" countries, it focuses on financial stability, financial sector depth, or competitive environment for the private sector, for example. In "poor performing" countries, the focus is on public sector management and institution building, property rights, budgetary and financial management, efficiency of revenue mobilization, public administration, and corruption.

Conditionalities imposed through SAP and related approaches have been criticized. Uvin (2004, 59) argued that imposing conditionalities is unethical. Specific policy recommendations or conditionalities have been criticized as well: retrenchments of civil servants and public sector workers; privatization and reduction of spending in health and education have been heavily contested. Many argue that principles of conditionalities undermine governments' space and duty to formulate policies.

Over time, it has become clear that conditionalities often do not produce the intended results: "Generally, conditionality has not been effective in improving economic policies . . . it has failed to achieve its objectives and therefore lacks practical justification. . . . over-reliance on conditionality wasted much public money [and] the obstacles to adequate improvement are probably intractable" (Killick 2002, 483). Many have argued that aid allocation should follow governance indicators. Conditionalities may work better for certain aspects of governance than for others (Smets and Knack 2018), but they can be counterproductive: analysis has shown that they may have contributed to weakening bureaucratic quality (Reinsberg et al. 2019). The IMF's own evaluation highlighted the challenges of conditionalities.[5]

The agreement that conditionalities are difficult to implement and undesirable does not mean that they have disappeared. All donors have their priorities and requirements, and these continue to impact aid relationships and the effectiveness of aid. Discussion of conditionalities has focused deeper attention on governance, as discussed next.

Good Governance

Increased attention to governance was among the more important changes in development thinking and practice in the 1990s. It followed and was part of new developments in economics and signaled the move from the Washington Consensus to the post–Washington Consensus time (Stern 2002). Whereas the crises of the 1970s led to an emphasis on reducing state intervention, the 1990s pushed experts to look more closely at the institutions that govern market and financial processes. The 1989 *From Crisis to Sustainable Growth* was the first World Bank document to mention "governance."[6] As mentioned earlier, the aid industry's growing consideration of conflicts further increased attention on questions of governance. The governance agenda was always broad and has included economic liberalism, civil service reform, accountability and transparency, elimination of rent-seeking, managerial efficiency, democracy, participation, decentralization, respect for human rights, freedom of expression and association, and the rule of law.

Increased attention paid to "good governance" coincided with the collapse of the Cold War and more engagement with the former Soviet Union and other transitional countries. Globalization contributed to harmonization of institutions and norms of governance, which reinforced the focus on the role of institutions in development. The interest in governance also followed recognition that many of the reforms implemented during the 1980s had failed in part because they had been technocratic in nature, with quick-fix technical solutions and blueprint approaches, that paid little attention to local conditions, institutional capacity, and questions of incentives and motivation of political and administrative leaders. Moreover, the policy prescriptions under structural adjustment often had not worked because recipient governments did not have the capacity or the political will to implement them.

The emphasis on good governance coincided with increased focus on aid allocation and ensuring that grants or loans were provided to partners that were likely to use aid effectively.[7] Governance indicators became a component of aid delivery. World Bank resource allocation started to use policy and institutional assessments that rated countries against a set of criteria, such as economic management, structural policies, policies for social inclusion and equity, and public sector management and institutions, and relied on data tools such as the IDA Resource Allocation Index. Despite the large number of indicators, such assessments remained narrow against the wide array of existing governance and political dimensions, such as informal political voice or influence and inequality. Questions have been raised about how the indicators are constructed, what they really measure, and their hidden assumptions (for example, rules associated with liberal democratic societies).

The emphasis on governance led aid agencies to develop a range of instruments to analyze and support better governance and increasingly also to address conflict. Table 6.1 illustrates this diversity.

As mentioned in Chapter 2, the Millennium Challenge Corporation (MCC) set out to provide an additional $5 billion for international development and support countries living by three standards: "ruling justly, investing in their people, and encouraging economic freedom." It uses measures of policy performance as a basis for aid investments, rewarding countries that demonstrate "real policy change" and challenging those that have not implemented reforms. It was created both to depoliticize US aid allocations and to support local ownership and

Table 6.1 Agencies' Instruments to Analyze Governance

Area or Instrument	Description	Examples/Studies
Civil Service Reform	Interventions that affect the organization, performance, and working conditions of employees paid from state government budgets	"Comparative Experience with Public Service Reform in Ghana, Tanzania and Zambia" (Stevens and Teggemann 2004)
Drivers of Change	Approach to apply political economy analysis to the development of donor strategy	"Uganda's Political Economy" (Moncrieffe 2004)
Fragile States	Fragile states are countries where the government does not deliver core functions to the majority of its people	The OECD in 2005 produced draft principles for good international engagement in fragile states
Human Rights	Donor approaches to promoting human rights, with a diverse range of tools, varying between donors and NGOs, including the extent to which rights-based approaches are integrated	"Country Strategy Development: Guide for Country Analysis from a Democratic Governance and Human Rights Perspective" (Sida 2003)
Institutional Development	Concerned with helping organizations to improve performance, focusing on formal and informal aspects of organizations	
Justice	An accessible and effective justice sector is essential for development: security of property and protection of assets; access to legal protection; effective justice institutions for economic growth	DFID program, Justice and Poverty Reduction: Safety, Security and Access to Justice for All
Measuring Governance	Indicators to measure governance to assess governance capacity and performance, understand determinants and impacts of good governance, identify priority areas for aid allocations	"Sources for Democratic Governance Indicators" (UNDP 2004); World Bank, Country Policy and Institutional Assessment

continues

Table 6.1   Continued

Area or Instrument	Description	Examples/Studies
Public Financial Management and Accountability	Encompasses government capacity to raise revenues, set spending priorities, allocate resources, and effectively manage the delivery of those resources	IMF training focusing on accountability and corruption: Antoinette M. Sayeh, "Governance and Accountability in Africa: Progress and Road Ahead," International Monetary Fund, June 13, 2022
Voice and Accountability	Emphasis on creating inclusive spaces for dialogue between citizens and the state; support to citizen-driven initiatives, participatory budgeting, community scorecards, watchdogs	R. Eyben and S. Ladbury, *Building Effective States: Taking a Citizen's Perspective* (Development Research Centre, 2006)

sustainability. It was expected that this would contribute to attracting foreign investment and trade revenues and making these sources of capital more effective while creating more jobs.[8] After a slow start, it has received favorable review. MCC has managed to depoliticize the aid allocation process by using third-party and transparent indicators of policy performance. It has promoted local ownership and sustainability,[9] and research indicates it has been successful in supporting reforms (Parks 2019).

The good governance paradigm came under criticism from different sides. For critical observers, the emphasis on governance meant a less radical departure from the Washington Consensus than suggested by some. Mosse's (2005) anthropological study of social processes and aid relationships argued that emphasis on policy reform was part of a new "managerialism" in international development and a more intrusive form of aid: "The *means* of international aid have expanded from the management of economic growth and technology transfer to the reorganisation of state and society needed to deliver on targets" (Mosse 2005, 5).

A predominant critique internal to the aid community came from Merilee Grindle. She developed the idea of "good enough governance" in a paper for the World Bank (2002) at a time when the Poverty Reduction

Strategy Paper (PRSP) approach had become popular. She highlighted that the expectations for poor countries regarding governance perform-ance and policy reform were unrealistically high. The "must be done" lists presented by donors to partners were too large and often did not spot-light priority areas or advise on sequencing of actions. As mentioned in a paper by the Organisation for Economic Co-operation and Development (OECD) Development Assistance Committee (DAC) Network on Gover-nance (2006, 3), capacity development had an "overemphasis on what were seen as 'right answers' as opposed to approaches that best fit the country circumstances and the needs of the particular situation."

The development success of China and discussion about a "Bei-jing Consensus," a term coined by Joshua Cooper Ramo as an alterna-tive to the "Washington Consensus," have reinforced attention on gov-ernance. Much literature and debate have emerged around the distinct approaches behind China's rapid growth and poverty reduction. Although the terms and narratives of China's success are often used as a rhetorical device, one of the key lessons has been that governance is critically important—under China's distinct political system—but that there are no simple recipes. If anything, the distinctiveness of the experience appears to have been pragmatism, thus reinforcing an emerging consensus within the aid industry.

Although Grindle argued for donors to focus on a minimally accept-able level of government performance and civil society engagement, this did not provide a clear guide to making decisions, as Grindle (2007) acknowledged in an article five years later. She highlighted, again, the need to prioritize and to choose interventions depending on local contexts. Interventions should be informed by an understanding of possibilities for and dilemmas in promoting change and the potential impact of specific interventions or reforms. As with the question of con-ditionalities, the realization that the goals of governance agendas were overambitious has not meant that the questions and dilemmas with aid relationships have disappeared. In the context of conflict and instability, they have emerged even more. Alongside the debates on governance, there has been a growing interest in the role of politics in these aid rela-tionships, as discussed next.

The Role of Politics in Aid Modalities

Aid modalities were also influenced by a renewed focus on politics, including questions of democracy. Most development professionals share a commitment to democracy, and the end of the Cold War provided a good deal of optimism about transitions to democracy. In comparison, some development success stories have happened under nondemocratic regimes, and China's experience has changed the contours of the debate. The project approach enabled ways of working that allowed aid agencies to avoid politics, and even the early approaches to governance in the 1990s often had a technocratic character. But increasingly, and with the increased attention on local context, questions of legitimacy of reforms and participation in politics have moved to center stage (de Haan and Everest-Phillips 2006).

Questions about corruption and increased accountability to taxpayers, including the question of how aid could promote revenue generation, led to the realization that donors were part of recipient country politics. In governance analysis, it became increasingly apparent that reform feasibility required a better understanding of local politics. This also showed that "political will" and "political context" needed to be understood much better: for example, legal reforms, though actively encouraged by teams of highly paid lawyers and consultants, should not be seen as solutions without an understanding of whether new laws were really needed or would be implemented. Over time, there has been growing interest in the role of elites in promoting development, as shown in Naomi Hossain's (2017) research on Bangladesh.

The Monterrey Consensus in 2002 helped strengthen politics as part of development, domestically and internationally. While acknowledging that geopolitical considerations continue to play a key role in aid allocation, according to the Monterrey final report (UN 2002):

> Governments must build within their countries—both developed and developing—the public support necessary to translate their collective vision into action. That would require political leadership—in the developing countries to overcome the many difficulties in undertaking institutional and policy reform, and in the developed countries to develop engagement and solidarity with the developing countries in their efforts to reduce poverty. . . . To translate the draft Consensus into action will involve a process of arriving at politically acceptable decisions at the national and international levels. There is a need for strong political will.[10]

A growing number of instruments started to integrate politics into aid delivery. Forms of political analysis were introduced through DFID's Drivers of Change and the World Bank's Institutional Governance Reviews with a strong focus on sources of corruption, and various agencies began to use the term *political economy*. Sida's (2006) "power analysis" focused on understanding the "underlying structural factors" that create incentives and disincentives for pro-poor development, a form of political analysis that tries to highlight potentials for "transformative" processes. Analysis of actors, interest groups, and structures intends to show where "real power" in a society lies and how power is distributed and exercised. It highlights both formal and informal power relations, whether resources and authority are transferred in support of decentralization, why women are not allowed to inherit land, or why human rights tend to be neglected. It also analyzes the impact that development cooperation has on power relations and agents and incentives for change.

For the aid industry, this raised more questions than answers. Political analysis almost inevitably is disputed, and the credibility of donor-commissioned studies remains an issue. As an Overseas Development Institute (ODI) paper on public financial management put it, "the apparent consensus that politics matters begs the question of what reformers should do when the necessary political impetus is weak or missing" (Hedger and Kizilbash 2007).[11] The OECD DAC Network on Governance (2006) paper noted the tensions "emerging between corporate objectives and the implications of Power and [Drivers of Change] analysis, which emphasize the prime importance of local political process and incremental change, in the face of pressures on donors to meet short term spending targets, and to be accountable to their own taxpayers."

Programming in "fragile" and "postconflict" contexts further highlighted the importance of politics. Programming in these contexts perhaps has not presented unique challenges to donors but has amplified many of the challenges around governance and the political nature of aid. Donors' own political role is deepened when aid programs are linked to economic and political interests. The possibility of creating ownership is made more difficult in such contexts, and the likelihood that donors try to impose one governance system is larger. A "rentier effect"—as with natural resources, the source of income is concentrated and not linked to productive resources—tends to predominate. In a context of military roles and human losses, it is likely that reporting inflates development gains, and accounting for results and corruption usually is more difficult.

Many authors who stress the problems of donor intervention in such contexts still conclude that development gains, such as improving education, can be successfully supported by aid programs. Mary Anderson (1999) discussed whether aid can support peace or war; she describes a number of case studies of aid projects in conflict situations. Browne (2007), who has discussed many challenges of donors working in fragile contexts, concluded that political engagement can promote positive change because it helps build connection with global values and because it can, and should, help build solidarity and support humanitarian needs. Booth and Unsworth (2014) documented case studies where donors found ways to work politically and achieve positive change: "Keys to success included iterative problem-solving, stepwise learning and brokering relationships to discover common interests."

As described in Chapter 2, after 9/11 aid programs increasingly supported efforts in situations of overt conflict, including in Afghanistan and Iraq with the US-led military engagements, and coordinated defense, diplomacy, and development objectives and agencies of donor countries. With the chaotic 2021 withdrawal from Afghanistan, there is a general sense of failure of such ambitious efforts and an urge to focus on continuing support for humanitarian objectives and NGOs.

Continued Dilemmas in the Provision of Aid

Even if traditional structural adjustment has disappeared—and some argue it has not—many of the old questions remain. In the early 1980s, the state had been charged with responsibility for whatever went wrong, but ten or twenty years later it was recognized that rolling back the state did not provide the solution. China's development success, and East Asia's more broadly, has challenged much conventional thinking. In fragile states, for aid to contribute to sustainable development and poverty reduction clearly is very challenging. It has become increasingly clear that state capacity—or governance—remains critical, and that strengthening that capacity ought to remain a significant element of providing aid.

Imposing conditionalities through donor grants or loans is now generally thought to be undesirable and ineffective. However, the debates on conditionalities still point to enduring dilemmas in the aid industry that merely avoiding the term will not resolve: sustainable poverty reduction requires the right conditions, with a governance agenda that remains challenging, while aid agencies continue to have to show the result of their efforts.

The questions on governance and politics are not easy ones to answer. In many of the new aid modalities, including cash transfers and sector approaches, or, for example, in attempts to raise taxation, political analysis remains absent and application largely dependent on individuals within donor organizations. Predominantly, aid modalities have tended to remain technocratic: monitoring of progress is outcome focused, with little analysis of the why or the causes and political economy of change.

Strengthening governance capacity remains essential, but it is also a very slow process and uncertain. The aid industry does not have a strong track record in capacity support. Donors need to show results. For most taxpayers, this needs to be in hospitals built, children brought into schools, or lives saved—long-term support to financial management within ministries does not provide the "photo opportunity" that ministers of donor countries require.

Notes

1. For example, Mkandawire and Soludo (2002) presented "African voices" on adjustment. Killick (1999) concluded that "the strongest criticisms that SAPs cause poverty are not borne out, and concern about poverty effects is not a sufficient reason for deferring adjustment. But SAPs have done avoidable harm and could be made more pro-poor."

2. An exception to this was funding for education: increased funding for primary education was seen as desirable, partly because increased funding for education would leverage additional central government funding.

3. The Paris Club (https://clubdeparis.org/) is an informal group of official creditors that aims to help resolve solutions to the payment difficulties of debtor countries. Since its inception in 1956 it has concluded 477 agreements worth US$612 billion.

4. See this IMF description: "Covid-19 Financial Assistance and Debt Service Relief," International Monetary Fund, March 9, 2022, https://www.imf.org/en /Topics/imf-and-covid19/COVID-Lending-Tracker.

5. A 2007 report by the IMF's Independent Evaluation Office concluded that, despite efforts to reduce and streamline conditionalities, many of the problems continued to exist (IMF Independent Evaluation Office 2007). According to Tom Bernes, director of Independent Evaluation Office, progress was made in aligning IMF conditionality to areas of IMF responsibility and expertise, but one-third of conditions continued to reach outside these areas (quoted in: Aslam 2008).

6. This argued that a crisis of governance, the exercise of political power, was behind many of Africa's development problems. "African governments . . . need to go beyond the issues of public finance, monetary policy, prices, and markets to address fundamental questions relating to human capacities, institutions, governance, the environment, population growth and distribution, and technology" (World Bank 1989, 1). Key subsequent World Bank documents include *Governance: The World Bank's Experience* (1994); Kaufman, Kraay, and Zoida-Lobaton (1999); and *World Development Report 2004*. In the UK, its status was elevated by DFID's (2006) white paper *Eliminating World Poverty: Making Governance Work for the Poor*.

7. In providing grants or loans, donors are also concerned about "fiduciary risk": the question of whether donor funds are properly accounted for, are used for the intended purposes, and represent value for money.

8. President George Bush's speech at the Inter-American Development Bank, March 14, 2002; see the Millennium Challenge Corporation (http://www.mcc.gov).

9. Parks (2019); Lancaster (2008); and Radelet (2007) described the early experience of MCC.

10. This report stressed that technical efforts needed to be accompanied by a strong and persistent political will, in both the developed and the developing countries. The head of the IMF added a note of caution, observing that slow progress in reforms often reflected lack of institutional capacity rather than lack of political will.

11. Based on experience as a researcher and DFID chief economist, Dercon (2022) concluded that successful growth and development requires a "development bargain" among those who can make development happen.

7

Cross-Cutting
Themes

THE THEMATIC FOCUS OF THE AID INDUSTRY HAS CONTINUED TO EXPAND.
More donors are entering the field, and many are expanding their focus
and thematic interests, integrating different approaches into existing
programming. In this chapter, I focus on how the industry has integrated, or "mainstreamed," gender, participation, rights, and environment into programming. Each of these themes has substantial and growing literature. Climate change, in particular, has grown into a field of its
own over the last decade. This chapter places these cross-cutting themes
in the context of wider development debates and looks at how
approaches have or have not influenced aid practices and where the
areas of contestation and institutional constraints are.[1]

The term *mainstreaming* has been most explicitly defined with
respect to gender and is often associated with the call of the Beijing
Platform for Action that "governments and other actors should promote
an active and visible policy of mainstreaming a gender perspective in all
policies and programmes." Mainstreaming a gender perspective means
assessing the implications for women and men of any planned action,
including legislation, policies, and programs, at all levels and in all
areas. It has been associated with an organizational strategy to bring a
gender perspective into all aspects of an institution's workings, including strengthening capacity and accountability.

The question of mainstreaming is relevant for the four issues
described in this chapter. They can be described as separate themes or
as relevant to all aspects of the aid industry. Often, consideration of

these objectives leads the industry to look outside its own bilateral agencies and to work with other government departments, for example, on climate change and human rights. The themes are the subject of strong advocacy by people within and outside the aid industry. Some advocates have expressed doubt whether mainstreaming is the right way to promote goals because they feel that integration of radical objectives in the practices of the industry leads to a loss of their transformative potential.

Gender and Development: Advocacy and Mainstreaming

Observers have noted that gender and development have never had an easy relationship,[2] and differences continue to prevail over issues of women's rights. Much progress has been made in bringing gender to the development agenda, as shown now in the articulation of SDGs 5, and global conferences and alliances as a result of sustained advocacy. Although the aid industry's investment in gender programming has remained limited, a growing number of programs have emerged that are focused on women's entrepreneurship, financial inclusion, and most recently women's care burden. In this section, I discuss this relationship in terms of development goals, analysis, and mainstreaming in aid practices, and present critiques of the mainstreaming approach.

It is common to make a distinction between two approaches to gender. A Women in Development (WID) approach "calls for greater attention to women in development policy and practice and emphasizes the need to integrate them into the development process." The alternative approach, Gender and Development (GAD), "focuses on the socially constructed basis of differences between men and women and emphasizes the need to challenge existing gender roles and relations."[3] Over time, approaches have shifted from WID to GAD, fueled by earlier dissatisfaction of the impact of a WID approach, though in practice the differences between the two approaches are often not clear-cut.

MDGs 3 focused on the promotion of gender equality and the empowerment of women, with targets to eliminate gender disparity in primary and secondary education. With SDGs 5, "Achieve gender equality and empower all women and girls," gender equality has become more important in the international development debate, with a growing number of targets and indicators. It is commonly pointed out that gender equality is important for achieving the other MDGs, too, a so-called instrumental case for reducing gender inequalities.

Over the last two decades, various measurement instruments have been introduced, reflecting the growing acknowledgment of gender as central to all development efforts. These tools allow for comparisons over time and between countries, and they show slow progress as well as large differences across the globe. Many spheres and places lack gender-disaggregated data, and there are now international efforts to address this. It is worth noting that few measures cover people's attitudes to women or gender equality, though data for this are available through the World Value Survey.[4]

The Human Development Report incorporated two measures of gender equality. The Gender Development Index (GDI) is an indicator of gender inequality in basic capabilities and it is based on the Human Development Index, which focuses on gender disparities in life expectancy, educational attainment, and income. The Gender Empowerment Measure (GEM) measures gender inequality in key areas of economic and political participation and decisionmaking, such as seats held in parliament and percentage of managerial positions held by women.

The World Economic Forum (WEF) launched its Global Gender Gap Report in 2006, with regular editions since (WEF 2021). Similar to GDI and GEM, this report assesses countries on how well they divide resources and opportunities among their male and female populations, regardless of the overall levels of these resources and opportunities. It focuses on four critical areas of inequality between men and women: economic participation and opportunity, educational attainment, political empowerment, and health and survival.

In the aid industry, and for advocates within, the Convention on the Elimination of All Forms of Discrimination Against Women, or CEDAW, adopted in 1979 by the UN General Assembly, has been the most important international framework.[5] The Platform for Action promoted the idea of mainstreaming gender—ensuring that gender equality is a primary goal in all areas of development—as an international strategy for promoting gender equality and was adopted at the UN Fourth World Conference on Women held in Beijing in 1995. In 1997, the UN defined the concept of gender mainstreaming as follows:

> Mainstreaming a gender perspective is the process of assessing the implications for women and men of any planned action, including legislation, policies or programmes, in any area and at all levels. It is a strategy for making the concerns and experiences of women as well as of men an integral part of the design, implementation, monitoring and evaluation of policies and programmes in all political, economic and societal spheres, so that women and men benefit equally, and

inequality is not perpetuated. The ultimate goal of mainstreaming is to achieve gender equality. (ILO 2002)

Mainstreaming is not about adding a "woman's component"; that is insufficient—notwithstanding the need for activities that target women specifically and affirmative action. Mainstreaming includes but goes beyond increasing women's participation, for example, through quotas for women and girls in school and on watershed management committees, and ensuring women have equal access to training in development projects. Mainstreaming gender means bringing the experience, knowledge, and interests of women and men to bear on all aspects of development agendas. The goal of mainstreaming gender is to transform unequal social structures into equal and just structures for both men and women (this is also a common emphasis in "transformative" approaches, discussed below). To ensure mainstreaming, development agencies should have institution-wide mechanisms for ensuring gender equality, with high-level support, monitoring of progress, and recognition that all actions and programs *can* have a gender aspect and that gender analysis should always be carried out.[6] A gender mainstreaming approach focuses on the "intrinsic value" of gender equality: whereas a women's empowerment approach contributes to other goals, such as child health, repayment of microcredit, and economic growth, a gender mainstreaming approach highlights that gender equality is a value in itself.

What does a gender approach in development projects look like? In the example of the Poor Rural Communities Development Project (PRCDP) mentioned in Chapter 5, mainstreaming gender had the following components. The pre-project analysis highlighted the strong gender differences in project areas, noting their direct linkage to level of poverty. Despite official commitments to gender equality, significant disparities existed in literacy rates, the ratio of newborn boys to girls, maternal mortality in poorer regions, ratios of women infected by HIV, and levels of medical care or school attendance of girls compared to boys. The project chose to use a participatory approach as the main vehicle to support women's participation throughout the project cycle. It was proposed that each of the three provinces (Sichuan, Guanxi, Yunnan) would produce its own gender mainstreaming strategy, including gender training for building management capacity, disaggregating data and monitoring project benefits for and impacts on men and women, and supporting specific initiatives to meet women's needs.

Whereas mainstreaming gender in projects is demanding, the challenges are even bigger in sector approaches, program and adjustment lending, and the Poverty Reduction Strategy Papers (PRSP) approach. In sector approaches, a first step to mainstreaming gender is analysis of gender disparities in the relevant sector, including legal and regulatory framework, budgets, service delivery aspects, wage differentials, and women's time availability (OECD DAC 2002). Another example is donors supporting gender mainstreaming in climate policies through the NDC Partnership.[7] As Box 7.1 describes, gender budgets are a way to maintain a gender focus and improve participation in budget-making processes. Second, as noted above, preparation of sector approaches is time-consuming and requires the involvement of large numbers of stakeholders; a gender approach highlights this need and ensures that women and representative groups are adequately consulted. Third, sustaining gender mainstreaming often requires attention be paid to the gender balance in institutions and any existing gender stereotypes are dispelled. An example is the introduction of "gender champions": relatively senior managers who ensure gender is addressed in all parts of the organization, through regular reporting and inclusion of discussion in meetings. Finally, gender mainstreaming needs to be reflected in monitoring.

Reviews have highlighted the challenges of gender mainstreaming in sector approaches (OECD DAC 2002). The Organisation for Economic Co-operation and Development (OECD) Development Assistance Committee (DAC) found that the approach to gender focused on narrowly defined investments in women or girls and did not address the underlying conditions that produce unequal opportunities. It found that organizing the consultations in a gender-sensitive way was challenging in many cases, that limited progress was made in addressing gender imbalances within the institutions responsible for implementation of sector approaches, and that gender-sensitive monitoring was weakly developed.

Similarly, gender mainstreaming was found to be challenging in PRSP approaches, despite explicit guidance given in a "PRSP Sourcebook" (Kabeer 2003). Reviews showed that only in half of the PRSPs was there a detailed discussion of gender issues. Poverty analyses often did not highlight the different ways in which women and men experience poverty, and gender priorities were not fully or systematically reflected in discussions of policy priorities, budgets, and monitoring. It was noted that people responsible for drafting PRSPs often lacked knowledge of gender issues, and gender advocates often lacked the technical expertise to engage effectively in discussions on budgets.

A more radical critique emerged from feminists and activists. According to Ines Smyth, former Oxfam GB gender adviser, "Terms

156

Box 7.1   Gender Budget Initiatives

Gender budgets are a mechanism used to strengthen a gender focus and participation within budget-making processes. The idea emerged in Australia in 1984, and it has inspired initiatives in South Africa and the Commonwealth Gender Budget Initiative. The approach arose outside the aid industry, but many aid agencies have come to support it as a civil society initiative and a way to inform, for example, the budget support process. The International Budget Partnership has recorded over 100 exercises for improving budget systems across the world.

A gender budget initiative analyzes public expenditure or taxation from a gender perspective, identifying the implications and impacts on women and girls. The initiative may be located inside government departments and be organized by officials and ministers or by researchers and civil society. It can cover the whole budget or selected departments or programs and can focus on different stages of the budget cycle.

The South African initiative was a collaboration of nongovernmental organizations (NGOs), research and policy institutions, and parliamentarians. In 1997, the South African government initiated a gender budget initiative, coordinated by the Ministry of Finance, that involved citizens in the policy area of budgets. They analyzed various years of national ministries and provincial budgets, the position of women and men and girls and boys within each sector, whether government policies adequately addressed problems, resources allocated to implement gender-sensitive policies, and how well resources reach intended goals.

The Ugandan gender budget initiative was started by the Forum for Women in Democracy, a women's rights group of female members of Parliament (MPs). They commissioned national-level and district-level research on gender and budget issues and provided support to local initiatives. Research was carried out by university researchers, with parliamentarians and civil servants, journalists, and civil society activists, and some of the findings appeared in parliamentary budget reports.

Sources: International Budget Partnership, www.internationalbudget.org; Commonwealth Secretariat (1999); Judd (2002); Budlender (2003).

such as 'empowerment,' 'gender,' and 'gender mainstreaming,' which originated in feminist thinking and activism, have lost their moorings and become depoliticized" (Smyth 2007, 582). As gender is mainstreamed, fewer resources may be made available to addressing women's needs explicitly. The way gender is mainstreamed often relies on "instrumental" arguments about the beneficial impact of gender equality on other goals. It also may lack attention to the need to transform institutional rules and structures.

Central to some of the thinking on transformative approaches to gender are questions of intersectionality, as defined by Kimberlé Crenshaw: "a prism for seeing the way in which various forms of inequality often operate together and exacerbate each other" (Steinmetz 2020). Although much of the gender focus is closely linked to a poverty focus, much less attention has been paid to other forms of exclusion, such as ethnicity and race. Observers in Latin America concluded that the record of gender advances in the region had been impressive, but attention on social exclusion and race discrimination had been more limited (Buvinić and Mazza 2008); this seems to still hold true and is relevant to other regions too.

Some advocates emphasize the need for "gender-transformative approaches" (Moser 2020). A growing number of countries now underpin their aid programs—and foreign policies, more broadly—with a feminist focus. In recent years, the commitment to funding gender equality has increased significantly, as shown by global-coalition-forming events such as Women Deliver and Generation Equality—US$40 billion was committed in the latter (Focus 2030 2021). Investing in women's (rights) groups, according to analysis largely neglected in development funding, is an important component of the recent advocacy and commitments.

Thus, gender has become much more central to the practices of the aid industry, and discussions about approaches continue. Alongside continued advocacy, analytical work and tools such as gender budgets have made gender concerns much more central to development thinking and national policies. The advocacy for and debate around gender mainstreaming and investment in women's groups indicate that the development agenda remains complex with trade-offs. There are different ways of measuring progress and differing objectives and expectations among the advocates of gender equality. Capacity to implement these is uneven, and recent international financial commitments will be critical for this agenda. Finally, the emphasis on mainstreaming is contested. Feminist advocates argue that the gains in terms of integrating women's issues into existing policy have been modest, not transformative, and that political commitment and civil society mobilization remain essential to ensure such progress.

Participation

The aid industry's emphasis on participation and community organization has moved in waves. Though the basic idea that participation by beneficiaries is important is not disputed, there is much debate over how participation should be integrated into design, how many resources should be devoted to the process, whether it is a value in itself or merely of instrumental importance, and what can be expected from processes of participation.

Participation can be defined as the process through which primary stakeholders influence and share control of development initiatives, decisions, and resources. It is believed that individuals, poor or rich, man or woman, have the capacity to analyze their own reality and act based on this analysis. Mainstreaming participation is about the full and systematic incorporation of participatory methodologies into the work of institutions. According to advocates such as Robert Chambers, mainstreaming participation will require drastic changes in the attitudes of aid officials.[8]

Korten (1980) described the early waves in participatory approaches. The community development movement started in the 1920s, and the Ford Foundation funded a pilot project in Uttar Pradesh, India, in 1948—in a context where Gandhian principles favored community-based approaches even though Nehruvian-style modernization was proceeding simultaneously.[9] Indian community development efforts inspired programs in over sixty nations during the 1950s, which were described as "community development's decade of prominence."

Within a decade or so, the optimism seemed to wane, partly because of the growing popularity of central planning, partly because the experiments showed a series of weaknesses. It was noted that community development experiments did not change existing power structures, which contributed to capture of project benefits by local elites. Limited attention was paid to building up local organizations and capacity to solve problems and deal with broader administrative systems. Social funds set up agencies separate from regular line departments, which caused coordination problems and bureaucratic conflicts. Finally, when conventional bureaucracy was involved, project implementation was not very responsive to people's willingness and capability to participate (Korten 1980, 482).

Advocacy for strengthening the participatory processes in development practices continued, as it did in other parts of public policy. Michael Cernea joined the World Bank as its first sociologist, in a new Rural Development Division. From the late 1970s, he worked on guidelines for resettlement that became World Bank policy in 1980, and in the mid-1980s he organized an influential seminar series that resulted in the publication *Putting People First*. Robert Chambers became influential through his idea of "reversals" of development reality and the need for "putting the last first" and "farmer first." In Latin America, ideas around "participatory democracy" flourished in the second half of the 1980s, such as in Porto Alegre in Brazil, as described Box 7.2.

Under adjustment—when enhanced participation was often seen as alternative while the state was rolled back, and instruments such as social funds became popular to ameliorate the effects of crisis and adjustment—a series of initiatives emphasized the need for participation.

Box 7.2   Pro-Poor Participatory Budgeting: Porto Alegre, Brazil

Decentralization in Brazil resulted in a three-tiered structure of the public budget: federal, state, and municipal. The 1988 Constitution gave some autonomy at the municipal level in determining revenues and expenditures around investment decisions. In 1989 in Porto Alegre, the decentralization of budgetary decisions and the long history of democratic civil society action contributed to the establishment of participatory budget making.

The creation of this new democratic institution enabled citizens to participate in budget discussions through regional and thematic plenary assemblies. All citizens are entitled and encouraged to participate in discussions about transportation, education, health, and economic development. The assemblies and preparatory meetings define and rank regional or thematic demands and priorities. They elect delegates and councilors and evaluate the executive's performance. The councilors then use general criteria to rank the demands of the assemblies to determine the allocation of funds and vote on the investment plan proposals of the executive. Although conflicts have arisen, most citizens believe that the participatory budget has resulted in improved services, for example, in water services and school enrollment.

A wide range of instruments and resources have been developed that often draw on initiatives like the one in Porto Alegre.

During the 2010s, the World Bank spent about US$8 billion a year on local participatory development; an in-depth study by Mansuri and Rao (2013) describes the experiences. It has also put measures in place to support citizen engagement, such as two "Global Practices," a secretariat and focal points. The impact has been varied: research by the Accountability Research Centre among World Bank staff shows that there are differences in terms of commitment to the principles, and implementation across the diverse World Bank operations is further hampered by financial and human resources (Nadelman 2021).

Within the World Bank, community-driven development (CDD) emerged and draws on participatory approaches, considerations of social capital, and social fund approaches. CDD was seen as an approach that would give control over planning decisions and investments to community groups and local governments. The CDD portfolio formed approximately $2 billion a year and focused on building the capacity of communities and enhancing their access to information. CDD is based on the assumption that, with support, communities can become their "own agent of development" by promoting reforms in the institutions that affect their well-being and strengthening relations between the community and local government (Oshima 2013). CDD programs have been extensively studied (Casey et al. 2021).

Participatory approaches also came to influence the analyses that inform aid industry practice. Participatory rural appraisal (commonly known as PRA) evolved from rapid rural appraisals, which were a set of informal techniques to quickly collect essential data. PRA is a set of methods that emphasizes local knowledge and enables local people to make their own appraisal, analysis, and plans for development projects. Methods often involve group discussions and semistructured interviews. Material and visual tools are used to help groups analyze development problems (through mapping and seasonal diagrams), prioritize solutions (through preference ranking), and facilitate joint action.

Similarly, participatory approaches have influenced poverty analysis, which had a predominantly quantitative focus. Participatory poverty analysis, or PPA, became a central feature of the development of many of the PRSPs. An example of this was in Vietnam. International NGOs started with small-scale PPAs at the local level to guide projects, and then *World Development Report 2000* and World Bank support helped to start PPAs with much broader scale. Later on, village consultations were used to get feedback from villagers on the draft of the PRSP, and in the end twelve provinces were covered. These consultations are thought to have influenced the PRSP, for example, by highlighting the high costs of basic services in health and education, recognizing the importance of exclusion of migrants, and enhancing community participation in infrastructure projects and communication about and transparency in government projects.[10]

Two other examples illustrate participatory approaches in aid projects. The Rural Integrated Project Support program in Tanzania, started in 1988, was a district-level project that included water, health care, education, agriculture, local government, savings and credit, transport and marketing, and natural resource management. After an evaluation of phase one in 1993 showed weaknesses in program delivery at the community level, a participatory planning process was introduced, with a commitment to long-term support for strengthening participation. The program supported local communities and government authorities in the identification of priorities and action. According to reviews, this led to improvements in all aspects of the program, despite fairly limited resources (Blackburn, Chambers, and Gaventa 2000, 9).

The PRCDP project in China emphasized inclusive and transparent project planning, implementation, and monitoring at the community level and building capacities for participation within the project management system. It also tried to link village-level planning to county-level planning and implementation. The project developed specific participatory methods of poverty analysis, planning, implementation, and monitoring; trained facilitators at county and township levels; and developed a pilot program to maximize community participation.[11]

In 2005, Robert Chambers concluded that participation had been mainstreamed, but it is probably fair to say this remained subject to debate. The importance of participation was recognized in most aid agencies and in most sectors. Data showed participation had an impact on improving project quality and sustainability, the extent of targeting and capture by elites, and possibilities for scaling up (Mansuri and Rao 2004). The industry recognized that participation was no panacea, that time and resources needed to be invested to make participation effective, and that participation at local levels needed to be accompanied by changes in mainstream policymaking and implementation.

Resistance to participation was common, too, partly because of doubts about what it could achieve and partly because of the resistance of traditional top-down planners and aid agency staff. The use of participatory approaches in development practice came under fierce criticism

(Cooke and Kothari 2001). It was argued that participatory methods by large aid agencies was used more to legitimize their actions than to give people the power to make their own decisions and that it was more about solving the delivery problems of aid agencies than empowering its beneficiaries. Evaluations found that only a few projects categorized as participatory had appropriate approaches in place. As in debates on gender equality, some advocates concluded that mainstreaming participation meant the process lost its critical and its political content. A question that emerged was whether participation is a human right, to which we come back in the next section.

Rights-Based Approaches to Development

Among the cross-cutting issues discussed in this chapter, approaches to rights probably have found the least traction. The aid industry has opportunities to integrate rights further, and this is, as Peter Uvin (2004) stressed, critical, because aid can do harm.[12]

International conferences have emphasized development as a human right. Human rights, central to the US and French Constitutions and prominent in discourse since the late eighteenth century, became part of global governance frameworks with the advent of the Universal Declaration of Human Rights and subsequent human rights treaties and bodies. Human rights was integrated into the development discourse during the early 1970s. The Declaration on the Right to Development was adopted by the UN General Assembly in 1986. The World Conference on Human Rights, held in Vienna in 1993, stressed that "development exists within a human rights framework . . . [and] should be seen as an integral part of human rights" (quoted in Johnsson 2005, 47). NGOs and bilateral and UN agencies have developed policy papers and courses on mainstreaming rights and advocating for rights-based approaches to development.

Kofi Annan tried to move human rights to the core of the UN agenda. The United Nations Development Programme (UNDP) stressed that human rights and development were two sides of the same coin and proposed four main human rights principles (UNDP 2003). First, universality and indivisibility, that every person is entitled to enjoy their human rights simply by virtue of being human, and enjoyment of one right is indivisibly interrelated to the enjoyment of other rights. Second, equality and nondiscrimination, that human rights are for everyone, as much for people living in poverty and social isolation as for people who are rich and educated. Third, that everyone is entitled to participate in, contribute to, and enjoy civil, economic, social, cultural, and political development. And fourth, that states have the responsibility to create the environment in which all people can enjoy their human rights and have the obligation to ensure that respect for human rights norms and principles is integrated into all levels of governance and policymaking.

Despite commitment to mainstreaming rights and making rights central to aid practices, the industry faces challenges with integration for a range of reasons. First, many rich countries, and the United States in particular, often refuse to ratify international conventions that define rights, partly because of ideological objections, partly because of the potential implications of justiciable rights. Second, debates about human rights often become debates between North and South, and there are concerns that the concepts of rights reflect Western norms and do not allow for different and culturally specific manifestations. The growing importance of donors such as China provides an additional layer of complexity. Third, economic thinking has an aversion to debates on rights, apart from basic property rights, and particularly to the idea that human rights are indivisible and universal. Further, advocates of rights-based approaches have been criticized for overreaching aid agencies' capacity, for politicizing development projects, and for creating false hope (Gready and Ensor 2005, 28–40).

There are different ways in which human rights and development can be brought together. First, there is what Uvin (2004) calls "rhetorical repackaging," which, he stressed, was popular among aid agencies that needed to maintain a moral high ground. Rhetorical repackaging can obscure a critical difference between a service-based and a rights-based approach to development. A focus on the distribution of goods and services to recipients is not incompatible with—but also is not identical to—those recipients having entitlements to these services.

Second, donors can use conditionality and shape donor behavior to be more in line with human rights approaches. This could, in principle, be done if the principles of the Paris Consensus, described in Chapter 3, were binding or through PRSP approaches (Nankani, Page, and Judge 2005). However, observers have stressed that conditionality about human rights is unlikely to be successful and never fully implemented, as with other forms of conditionality (Wei and Swiss 2022). More specifically, aid conditionality is situated in contracts between governments and aid agencies and does not directly impact the relationship between a government and its citizens.

Third, aid agencies can provide constructive support, such as for strengthening the institutions that promote human rights. Many agencies, including the World Bank, have supported projects related to legal and judiciary reform based in governance approaches, as described in Chapter 5.[13] Aid can support advocacy for rights, such as ActionAid Brazil's support for achieving the right to food and sustainable nutrition (Antunes and Romano 2005). A Department for International Development (DFID)–funded project helped poor communities in Bolivia gain identity cards that would allow them to vote for the first time and access social and health services. There is a growing field of and support for legal empowerment (UN Commission on the Legal Empowerment of the Poor 2008).

Finally, rights and development can be brought together through a "rights-based approach to development." This provides a normative framework for achieving development priorities. This approach redefines the nature of the aid relationship and moves aid from being a charitable activity to one that is based on claims and justiciability. It sees beneficiaries as rights holders and project staff and policymakers as duty bearers.

Examples of moves toward rights-based approaches can be found among organizations that support children. Child welfare agencies have usually treated children as passive and have hardly involved them in project or policy development. But, under the influence of the UN Convention on the Rights of the Child, agencies such as Save the Children started to see children as holders of rights, for example, to express their views, access information, and participate in policy development (Theis and O'Kane 2005).

A rights approach takes participation a step further. For example, for CARE International, a human rights approach to their work signifies that "we view the people we assist as rights holders, and not simply as beneficiaries or project participants," and the overarching aim would be to facilitate the ability of marginalized and vulnerable people to progressively achieve their rights.[14] In a project in Rwanda, CARE stressed that adopting a rights approach called for an internal transformation of the organization and construction of a culture of rights within the organization. It carried out a participatory analysis of the causes of poverty in Rwanda, highlighting the rights issues underlying poverty (such as discrimination, unaccountable governance), and based choices for programming on this analysis. It introduced rights-based monitoring, or "bottom-up accountability," into its programs as a way to ensure that the children it supports hold CARE to account.

UNDP (2003) uses the language of mainstreaming rights. This emphasizes that values, principles, and standards of human rights must guide and permeate the entire development programming process. Such an approach presupposes that human rights are reflected in a country's norms and institutions. Mainstreaming rights also implies investing in advocacy and sensitization of partners around human rights, support for a sustainable system of legal and nonlegal forms of enforcement, application of human rights in law and reality, and effective systems for societal monitoring of human rights enforcement; however, mainstreaming may also lead to weakening of the principles of a rights approach (Broberg and Sano 2018).

According to Peter Uvin (2007, 598), one of the main advocates of rights-based approaches, "The track record of the rights to development is catastrophic." The conclusion that human rights are poorly integrated into development approaches still seems to hold true, and as mentioned, this is critical because donors can do harm. Newer donors have not engaged actively in the promotion of rights in aid practices.

A rights-based approach to development poses significant challenges to the aid industry—even though expanding international frameworks provide the space for moving from a charitable approach to one where rights and duties drive the industry. Support for strengthening legal institutions and awareness of rights is given by only a few agencies. NGOs have developed various ways to strengthen advocacy for rights in many countries but are mostly not, and should not be, "duty bearers" themselves. Moving from current aid practices to a rights-based approach is a deeply political process. The transformation from the current way in which the aid industry works, where it is largely accountable to donors' taxpayers and stakeholders, to one where donors are accountable as duty bearers to rights holders is a long way off.

Development, Environment, and How Climate Change Impacts the Aid Industry

The aid industry traditionally has made significant investments in environmental conservation (Bass et al. 2005). This has included long-term engagement of NGOs such as the Aga Khan Rural Support Programme in Pakistan's Northern Areas, which started with social organization and leadership development and subsequently took up support in communities for livelihood development and environmental conservation through joint forestry projects. In China, the World Bank supported projects integrating reforestation and soil improvement into, for example, the Yangtze Basin project and projects with a central focus on sustainable land use, as in the Loess Plateau Project (Taylor 2005).

Environmental concerns have been integrated into projects through environmental appraisals or assessments. For the World Bank, the "environmental assessment" is one of the safeguard policies that exist for social and legal areas as well as environmental issues. The assessments focus on mitigating the potential negative environmental impacts associated with lending operations to ensure that project options are sound and sustainable and to ensure that the people who will potentially be affected have been properly consulted.[15] As the impacts of climate change grow, it is becoming more important to integrate vulnerabilities assessments into project design.

In the case of the PRCDP project in southern China, the World Bank environmental assessment concluded that the overall environmental impact of the project was likely to be positive, including improved soil and water management, increased permanent vegetation cover, improved agricultural and livestock raising practices, and training in environmental practices. The participatory approach was expected to contribute to reducing environmental degradation. The project put in place an Environmental Management Plan, with measures to mitigate negative impacts and ways to monitor them. It highlighted that potential negative environmental effects could occur, but that these would likely be modest and localized, that negative consequences would be outweighed by positive ones, and that more negative development could be expected if the project did not take place (World Bank 2004b).

The aid industry has often focused on the links between climate and poverty or development objectives.[16] Poor people tend to be disproportionally impacted by environmental degradation because they often live in the most vulnerable areas and have the least ability to protect themselves. Although poor people can contribute to environmental degradation because they often have no options or alternatives, their practices or livelihoods typically contribute to conservation of the environment. Degradation, such as deforestation, often follows poorer groups' loss of access to such resources. Environmental stress can also have an impact on conflict, for example, competition for land resources, and this affects poor people as well as the better-off.

Over the last two decades, global debates have made climate increasingly central to the aid industry. Environmental sustainability was part of the MDGs framework, in Goal 7, which committed the international community to integrating the principles of sustainable development into country policies and programs and to reversing the loss of environmental resources. It also had specific people-related goals: to reduce the proportion of people without sustainable access to safe drinking water and to improve the lives of slum dwellers. The

SDGs framework, with Goal 13, has more ambitious goals. It emphasizes building resilience to climate change, support to national policies, and plans to address climate change, provide education, and build capacity in the least developed countries and small island states.[17]

The UN has paid attention to environmental issues at least since the First Earth Summit in 1972 in Stockholm,[18] where Indian prime minister Indira Gandhi predicted that "the environmental crisis which is confronting the world will profoundly alter the future destiny of our planet" (in Biermann 2022). It set out principles for the preservation of the human environment, devised an action plan for international environmental action, and proposed the monitoring of long-term trends in climate changes. In 1987, the UN General Assembly adopted the Environmental Perspective to the Year 2000 and Beyond, a framework for national action and international cooperation to promote environmentally sound development.[19] The Intergovernmental Panel on Climate Change (IPCC), set up in 1988, has produced a series of assessment reports, issuing increasingly dire warnings for devastating climate change trends.

The 1992 Earth Summit in Rio de Janeiro stressed that "nothing less than a transformation of our attitudes and behaviour would bring about the necessary changes." Governments recognized the need to take into account the environmental impact of any policy decisions and mandated the UN to monitor environmentally damaging practices. It resulted in Agenda 21, according to the UN itself "the most comprehensive . . . programme of action ever sanctioned by the international community." Many countries developed Agenda 21 plans and Local Agenda 21. Reviews of Agenda 21 show mixed and often disappointing progress (SD21 2012). Yet the importance of these plans should not be underestimated, and Local Agenda 21 has led to significant changes in local action linked to the global goals.

During the Rio Conference, the United Nations Framework Convention on Climate Change (UNFCCC) was established and signed by 158 states in 1992. In 1997, UNFCCC adopted the Kyoto Protocol, considered the most significant international action to date. The protocol came into force in 2005 and is focused on reducing industrialized countries' emissions of carbon dioxide and other greenhouse gases. These global summits were followed by meetings and accords in Durban, Bali (2007), Copenhagen, Paris (2015), and Glasgow (2021) that reinforced and renewed commitments to climate action[20] and systems of reporting.[21] Under the Paris Agreement, countries have committed themselves to producing National Determined Contributions, or NDCs, national plans for the reduction of emissions and adaptation to climate change.

Because of the recent interest in and evidence on climate change, environmental concerns now are at the heart of the practices of the aid industry (OECD 2021b). The International Monetary Fund (IMF) now considers climate "macro-critical." During the 2010s, the share of official development assistance (ODA) for climate funding doubled. The Green Climate Fund (GCF), for example, was set up in 2010 to assist developing countries to counter climate change. There are growing demands from developing countries for support for managing the impact of climate change caused by industrialized countries. Development agencies are likely to continue to increase climate funding,[22] and many of the recent efforts also involve agencies and ministries outside the traditional aid industry.

However, rich countries' commitment in 2009 to provide $100 billion in climate funding has not been met. It is also insufficient to need, and increasingly so. The disbursement of the $100 billion is fragmented, as Figure 7.1 shows. The agreement did not include clear guidance on how the contributions should be measured.[23] NGOs such as Oxfam have criticized the support for not meeting the most important priorities of the poorest countries. There is a growing demand for funding for "loss and damage," which reflects the idea that countries in the Global South suffer the consequences of climate change caused by the North.[24]

The Challenges of Mainstreaming

The cross-cutting themes discussed in this chapter illustrate the complexity that the aid industry must address. The industry has moved a long way from postwar technical projects and savings-gap financing and has incorporated an increasing number of issues, often following sustained advocacy. Importance given to these issues moves in waves, to some extent, with the environment now at the center of attention as the impacts of climate change are becoming all too evident.

Different parts of the industry and different people within agencies continue to define main objectives in different ways and continue to differ about whether they can focus on issues of gender and rights. Mainstreaming remains an important strategy for advocates that see gender, rights, and other considerations as values in themselves, and as a strategy to connect these to address other development goals.

The questions that these cross-cutting issues pose are not unique to the aid industry. Most public and often also private institutions are challenged to address questions, for example, of gender and rights more forcefully, and instruments like Gender-based Analysis Plus (GBA+) are

Figure 7.1 How Is the $100 Billion Climate Finance Disbursed?

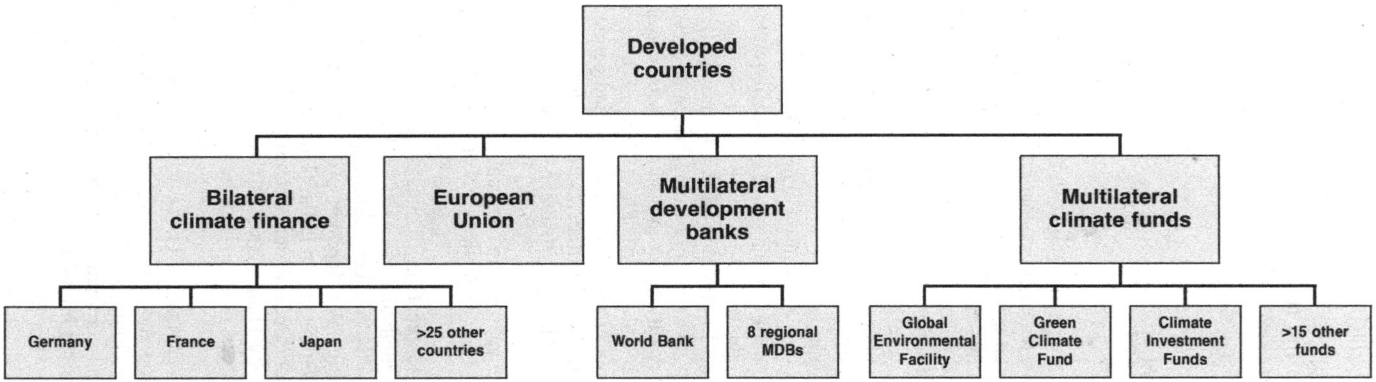

ODI Think Change

not restricted to aid departments. What makes the challenge for the aid industry distinct is that agencies need to translate pressures from their own constituencies to the realities in which they work. This highlights questions of or differences in both commitment and capacity. It also underlines the need for increased aid flows, particularly in the case of climate change.

Notes

1. The World Bank Social Development Department's (2003) *Social Analysis Sourcebook* focuses on how social dimensions can be incorporated into project design.

2. An article by scholar-practitioner-advocate Caroline Moser (2020) provides an insightful description of efforts to make gender central to different spheres of development thinking and practice. Diane Elson is one of the best-known scholars and feminist economists (Simon 2019).

3. Reeves and Baden (2002, 3); "sex" refers to the biological and physiological characteristics that define men and women, and "gender" to the socially constructed roles and behaviors, activities, and relationship between both sexes that a particular society considers appropriate.

4. Seguino (2007), on the basis of the World Values Survey, highlighted global progress toward valuation of gender equality and hypothesized that economic growth does contribute to this.

5. Convention on the Elimination of All Forms of Discrimination Against Women, UN Women, http://www.un.org/womenwatch/daw/cedaw/cedaw. The 1945 UN Charter recognized equality between men and women as a global goal.

6. Canada's Gender-based Analysis Plus (GBA+) is an example, "an analytical process used to assess how different women, men and gender diverse people may experience policies, programs and initiatives" ("Gender-based Analysis Plus [GBA Plus]," Government of Canada, https://women-gender-equality.canada.ca/en/gender -based-analysis-plus.html).

7. The mainstreaming approach in Nationally Determined Contributions (NDCs) is described in the article "Gender in NDCs," NDC Partnership, https://ndcpartnership .org/gender.

8. An important resource from IDS is available at Participatory Methods, https://www.participatorymethods.org/.

9. Albert Mayer was the pioneer behind the Etawah project, which became a model for other community development projects in India (Robert C. Emmett, "Guide to the Albert Mayer Papers on India," University of Chicago Library, http:// www.lib.uchicago.edu/e/su/southasia/mayer.html).

10. See the short note by Thanh (2005, 78), who led community consultations in two provinces; the experience in Vietnam is described in some detail by Shanks and Turk (2003).

11. The UK-based organization ITAD was responsible for working with the three provinces to develop and implement the participatory approach ("The Poor Rural Communities Development Project in China," ITAD, https://www.itad .com/project/the-poor-rural-communities-development-project-in-china/). The experiences from practitioners are brought together in Pennarz et al. (2011).

12. The book *Reinventing Development?* edited by Gready and Ensor (2005) gives a good overview of the history of rights approaches and a dozen case studies;

the volume by Alston and Robinson (2005) is a good source on rights approaches in different aspects of the aid industry.

13. Sage and Woolcock (2007) discussed approaches to strengthening justice systems for poverty reduction. Dawson and Swiss (2020) described results.

14. Quoted in Jones (2005, 79). The following is based on Jones's article; Jones worked for CARE in Rwanda and as the organization's rights programming adviser.

15. World Bank Environmental Assessment website (http://web.worldbank.org /archive/website01541/WEB/0__-2097.HTM). The policy and processes are described in Operational Policy (OP)/Bank Procedure (BP) 4.01: Environmental Assessment, an umbrella policy for the environmental "safeguard policies," which among others include natural habitats, forests, and dam safety.

16. The extent to which environmental objectives link to poverty and development goals depends on how *poverty* and *development* are defined; traditional measures of GDP and poverty are inadequate to capture environmental issues.

17. "Goal 13: Take urgent action to combat climate change and its impacts," Sustainable Development Goals, https://www.un.org/sustainabledevelopment/climate -change/.

18. Peter Jackson, "From Stockholm to Kyoto: A Brief History of Climate Change," *UN Chronicle* "Green Our World!" 54, no. 2 (June 2007), https://www.un .org/en/chronicle/article/stockholm-kyoto-brief-history-climate-change.

19. The World Commission on Environment and Development, better known as the Brundtland Commission, in 1987 provided a common definition of sustainable development: "meeting the needs of the present without compromising the ability of future generations to meet their own needs."

20. The global attention was reinforced at high levels through, for example, the work of Al Gore (2006) and Nicholas Stern (2006). Following the Stern Report, the UK announced £800 million of funding through the International Environmental Transformation Fund for reducing poverty through environmental management and helping developing countries respond to climate change, and £50 million of funding for tackling deforestation in the Congo Basin.

21. "Introduction to Transparency," United Nations Climate Change, https:// unfccc.int/process-and-meetings/transparency-and-reporting/the-big-picture/what-is -transparency-and-reporting.

22. Recent data on climate finance is available at Donor Tracker, https:// donortracker.org/.

23. Independent Expert Group on Climate Finance, *Delivering on the $100 Billion Climate Finance Commitment and Transforming Climate Finance* (Independent Expert Group on Climate Finance, December 2020), https://www.un.org/sites/un2.un .org/files/2020/12/100_billion_climate_finance_report.pdf; Jocelyn Timperley, "The Broken $100-Billion Promise of Climate Finance—and How to Fix It," *Nature*, October 20, 2021, https://www.nature.com/articles/d41586-021-02846-3.

24. George Monbiot wrote in 2021: "What poor nations are owed is reparations" (George Monbiot, "Never Mind Aid, Never Mind Loans: What Poor Nations Are Owed Is Reparations," *The Guardian*, November 5, 2021, https://www.theguardian .com/commentisfree/2021/nov/05/the-climate-crisis-is-just-another-form-of-global -oppression-by-the-rich-world).

8

What Works?
And How Do We Know?

THE AID INDUSTRY HAS WELL-DOCUMENTED SUCCESSES. AID HAS CONtributed to the Green Revolution and has combatted diseases such as smallpox and polio; case studies of successes in global health are documented in *Millions Saved* (Glassman and Temin 2016). UN agencies have provided significant support for refugees. Private companies have contributed to eradicating river blindness. Aid programs in China have helped improve poor people's lives, which happened probably faster than lives would have been improved without the presence of aid agencies.

At the same time, as highlighted in this book, the performance of aid, its successes and failures, remains contested. The critiques are diverse and different analysts see different problems with aid, and the scorecard for new donors also shows mixes of successes and failures. The Sustainable Development Goals (SDGs) have provided a uniform set of goals, but not agreed ways of how to get there. Donors are driven by political as well as humanitarian motives, making John Norris, author of a book on the sixty-year history of the US Agency for International Development (USAID) exclaim:

> How do you fairly evaluate U.S. foreign assistance overall when, on the one hand, it helped make South Korea and Taiwan economic powerhouses but, on the other, it squandered billions in Afghanistan, Iraq, and Vietnam? How do you properly value the worth of the assistance that directed tens of millions of dollars to Mobutu Sese Seko in Zaire, yet also introduced simple, lifesaving health

interventions that have saved the lives of millions of children around the globe?[1]

In an overview of evaluating the impact of development projects, Judy Baker (2000, vi) stressed that little was known about the impact of aid projects on the poor, and that aid organizations were reluctant to carry out impact evaluations, including because the findings could be politically sensitive. As a result of criticisms of aid—that it should focus on sending aid to poor countries and groups *and* do so effectively, that it should show results for taxpayers' money, and that it should focus on aid effectiveness and the Sustainable Development Goal frameworks[2]—the field of aid impact analysis is growing.

Aid agencies differ in the extent to which they measure results. Principles of evaluation are promoted by the Development Assistance Committee (DAC) and the Global Partnership for Effective Development Co-operation, including regarding the role of the private sector.[3] The World Bank has relatively strong systems of peer review at the design stage of projects and during monitoring or supervision; a relatively independent evaluation department provides post-project evaluations.[4] The UK also has a fairly well-developed system for assessing its aid program, including through the National Audit Office—which normally focuses on auditing government offices' accounts—and the Independent Commission for Aid Impact.[5] Agencies such as the Gates and Hewlett Foundations and the Millennium Challenge Corporation (Parks 2019) emphasize the need for better understanding whether investments, including blended and private finance, are well spent (Carter 2021).

This interest has led to a wide diversity of measures and methodologies. Studies have used cross-country statistical analysis that assesses the impact of aid on economic growth. Program and sector-wide approaches have developed their own forms of evaluation and monitoring. Many studies focus on the results of development projects, and the field of impact evaluation using controlled trials has formed its own niche over the last two decades. This chapter describes different approaches in different parts of the aid industry.[6] First I describe assessment principles and practices and the difficulty of assessing "impact." Then I discuss the ways in which programs can be evaluated and, perhaps most controversial, the impact of aid on economic growth.

The main terms used in this field are defined in Box 8.1, and Table 8.1 is an overview of principles and examples of evaluation across development approaches.

Box 8.1   Definition of Terms in the Field of Evaluation

In the assessment of the aid industry, and of public policy more generally, the following terms are important:

- Program *monitoring* assesses whether a program is implemented according to plan, which enables feedback and highlights implementation problems. For example, does a livelihoods program spend according to schedule on promoting food crops or investments in roads?
- *Cost-benefit analysis* assesses whether money is spent in the right way, compared to other possible uses, and related to benefits created. For example, what are the realized returns on investments in primary education?
- *Impact evaluation* determines whether the program has the desired effects on its beneficiaries. For example, have incomes increased as a result of a project or policy change promoted by an international agency? This is often also captured as *effectiveness*.
- Related, *proving causality*, or attribution, means showing that observed changes do not merely coincide with inputs from donor agencies but are the direct result of these actions. This is generally considered one of the most difficult technical questions. *Experimental and quasi-experimental* approaches address this and work for a small proportion of development project types (discussed below).
- Impact evaluation is normally *ex post*, after a project or program has been completed. It is also possible to make *ex ante* assessments to ensure that the best knowledge of likelihood of impact is made available; an example of the latter is presented later as well.

Evaluating Projects

Most if not all aid agencies have systems for monitoring programs as a form of regular supervision and feedback during the project cycle. Self-assessment of projects by program managers is the most common form of assessment, and a small number of projects are evaluated either externally or by a relatively independent evaluation department in an agency. Box 8.2 presents an example of the latter from an Asian Development Bank project in the Philippines.

Table 8.1 Principles and Examples of Evaluation in Types of Aid Approaches

	Input	Output	Outcome	Impact
Definition	Financial, human, and material resources used for aid investment	The products, capital goods, and services that result from aid; changes resulting from a project	The short-term and medium-term effects of an intervention's outputs Achieving outcomes is captured as "effectiveness"	Positive and negative, primary and secondary, long-term, direct or indirect, intended or unintended
Project examples	Total project investment and personnel working on the project	Number of loans disbursed Repayment rates	Poor households have access to loans Increased incomes Poverty reduction	Dependence on informal lenders Inequality between poor and less-poor
Examples of sector-wide approaches	External resources coordinated with national plans Measures to strengthen national policy	Strengthened government policies Improved measurement of policies	Implementation of policies Greater efficiency in use of resources	Better use of resources lead to better development outcomes

**Box 8.2   Project Evaluation Example:
Asian Development Bank's Microfinance in
the Philippines**

A special evaluation study assessed whether microfinance projects—including the Rural Microenterprise Finance Project in the
Philippines, which provides small loans—reduced the poverty of
rural poor households and improved the socioeconomic status of
women. The study used quantitative tools through a nationwide
survey that covered 2,274 households and twenty-eight microfinance institutions. Qualitative tools such as focus group discussions were used to gather information on intra-household dynamics
and the effects of microfinance on the status of women. Sample
surveys that covered 566 women were designed to validate the
focus group discussions.

The impact study used a "quasi-experimental" design (which I
discuss further in the next section) that required treatment and comparison areas for each of the twenty-eight microfinance institutions.
These areas were geographically different from each other. Two
types of household respondents were surveyed: households that
received microcredit loans, and households that did not receive loans
but qualified to join the program. Statistical techniques used to esti-
mate impact showed the following:

- Microcredit loans had positive ("mildly significant") impacts
  on beneficiaries' income and food expenditure. The income of
  beneficiaries increased by P5,222 per year compared with
  those that did not receive a loan (P8.6 billion for the total of
  1.6 million women clients reached with microcredit).
- But the impact on per capita income and expenditures was
  found to be regressive. The project reached poor households,
  but not in significant numbers, and the impact was negative
  for households with lower incomes. The study concluded that
  targeting microfinance to the poorest households may not be
  the most appropriate way to help them escape poverty. The
  household survey found that only 10 percent of the respondents were classified as poor (using the official Philippine
  poverty line).

continues

Box 8.2   Continued

- The evaluation showed that the project helped to reduce the dependence of participating households on informal money-lenders and more expensive loans from financial institutions. The proportion of participating households with savings accounts increased, as did the saved amounts. The program increased the number of microenterprises and number of persons employed.

Source: Asian Development Bank, Operations Evaluation Department (2007).

In such project-level evaluations, the following issues are important. First, the choice of indicator: even if measurement is limited to using an income poverty indicator, it is important whether one looks at only the number of people in poverty (headcount) or the extent of their poverty (poverty gap) too. Much research on microfinance—such as the evaluation in the Philippines—shows that poor households benefit, but the poorest benefit less so. Further, impact can be measured on wealth or assets, food security, child nutrition, quality of life, gender relations, or beneficiary satisfaction. But information for evaluation is often not easily available, and few projects decide to invest heavily up front in establishing baselines, thus restricting choice of indicators.

Many outcome or output indicators may provide only part of the picture. Repayment rates may be a sign of improved income but can also be the result of, for example, pressure to repay (common in group-based lending). Impact can vary for different groups, for example, the poorest people might not be able to use microcredit effectively, and impact can be measured at different levels (individual, household, village, etc.). Within households, men and women are likely to be impacted differently, and access to credit may change the relationship between household members. There may be impacts, positive as well as negative, on people not directly included in the project.

Projects that are targeted to poor people are usually assessed on errors of "inclusion" and "exclusion." Inclusion errors describe whether and how many people benefit from the project though they were not eligible, also called leakage. A measure of exclusion errors describes how many people who were eligible did not receive project benefits—which of course can be for a variety of reasons and not just because of the project, but this error rate does give an important indication of how well projects perform. For example, incentives to project staff for increasing lending may lead to exclusion of the poorest borrowers, a finding in some analysis of microfinance projects, including the example from the Philippines described above.[7]

Various methods of data collection are used in evaluations. Forms of impact assessment usually rely on data generated by the project itself combined with surveys on income, health, education, and so forth. For example, a World Bank evaluation of social funds used baseline data created in each social fund and compared different funds with similar design in different countries.[8] Qualitative techniques—case studies, focus groups, interviews—can be used, usually to better understand changes in processes or beneficiaries' perceptions of changes. Participatory methods typically include ways of reporting that are driven by communities and facilitated by outsiders of the aid industry.

Longer-term changes and impacts are difficult to assess and seldom addressed in aid projects because of the short-term and project-centered engagement of agencies. The Southwest Poverty Project in China, for which the World Bank lent $400 million in the second half of the 1990s, shows important insights from an evaluation that focused on the long term. The project worked with the National Bureau of Statistics to carry out surveys every year during the project, in project and nonproject villages, with a follow-up survey four years after the end of the project. The evaluation found that the project was well targeted in terms of having selected poorer villages, and that during the project, villages improved compared to nonproject villages. A follow-up survey showed that the positive impact could still be found after four years but that these impacts were much smaller.[9]

A Japan International Cooperation Agency (JICA) evaluation of infrastructure projects in Africa and East Asia showed how changes in institutions—critical for the sustainability of infrastructure—can be measured. It identified projects' intended and unintended institutional effects, impacts on government activities and funding outside the project, sector policies, regulation, and capacities. The evaluation ranked the projects from "unsustainable" to "best practice" and highlighted the idea that investment in infrastructure is about much more than "bricks and mortar" (Jerve and Nissanke 2008).

Evaluating the impact of projects is often harder in fragile contexts because of increased difficulty of data gathering and making valid comparisons. An analysis of "securitized" aid projects by the UK was able to identify that projects in fragile contexts had enhanced security, but they struggled to achieve intended outputs (called "effectiveness"). The study showed that the projects reviewed did not significantly strengthen the recipient countries' institutions, stability, or security and instead had some negative side effects.[10]

How to Understand Impact and the RCT Revolution

Project evaluations assess "impact" and "effectiveness"—two commonly used terms with distinct connotations and meanings. Put simply, the question is whether changes observed in project monitoring or evaluation are caused by the project or by other factors happening at the same time as the project.

To assess impact, an evaluation can compare the changes in the project area with the changes in an area that is comparable in all aspects except that it did not have the development project; this is the core question of the randomized controlled trial (RCT) methodologies discussed in Chapter 4. For example, if a project shows an increase in school enrollment in project areas, it is essential to know whether this increase also occurred in areas outside the project areas. This question is often called the "counterfactual": What would have happened if the project did not exist?

Project evaluation can also use comparisons of beneficiaries and nonbeneficiaries with a similar socioeconomic status (for example, villagers in a nearby, nonproject village, as in the example from China above). There are two main approaches for this type of evaluation. First, in experimental designs, similar to medicine trials, project benefits are distributed randomly among eligible beneficiaries, and a control group with similar characteristics does not receive them.

Although this type of experimental framework is often seen as technically the best way to track the effects of an intervention, it has a number of problems. Many purposes, projects, and certainly programs do not allow for the creation of randomized experiments. In some cases, the cost of random design can be prohibitive because the coverage and sample size need to be large enough to establish statistical validity. There is also an ethical question of denying benefits to eligible participants in the control group: although this may be justifiable if full coverage is not achievable or if the benefits from the experiment are so large as to outweigh ethical objections, it may not be justifiable if randomization into experimental and control groups is essentially for a donor purpose.

An example of a randomized trial approach is from an International Food Policy Research Institute (IFPRI) evaluation of the Red de Protección Social, a conditional cash transfer program in Nicaragua, that supplemented income to increase household well-being. The randomized experiment meant that half of the communities received the benefits, while the other half did not. The moral justification for this was twofold: it was thought that there was not enough evidence that this kind of intervention would be effective, and there was limited capacity to implement the project in all communities (Maluccio and Flores 2004).

"Quasi-experimental" and "randomized natural" methods are the second best and usually more practical alternative to randomized controlled trials, and a technical literature has accumulated on different ways of implementing these methods. The comparison uses statistical techniques rather than actual comparisons, and comparison groups are selected after project implementation. These methods use existing data from comparable groups rather than randomly selected eligible groups.

A World Bank evaluation of a Japan-supported secondary school scholarship program in Cambodia—that found improvements in student retention and completion—is an example of a randomized natural experiment. It was based on comparisons between recipients and nonrecipients and used samples of application forms and unannounced visits to the schools where enrollment and attendance was recorded (Filmer and Schady 2006).

The number of impact evaluations has grown tremendously, driven by pressure on donors and even NGOs to understand and show impact. The movement has also been driven by an academic community mostly located in the Global North, and that drive has received significant criticism. From the aid agencies' viewpoint, whereas these evaluations can be technically superior, they are also time-consuming and expensive, may be particularly difficult for smaller organizations to complete, and are not suited for many types of interventions.[11] They are not suited for evaluating programs, to which we turn next.

Evaluating Programs

The previously mentioned forms of evaluation focus on projects with clearly identifiable inputs and measurable outcomes. It is more complicated to assess results and effectiveness of the program approaches, described in Chapter 3, and evaluations rely more on descriptions and qualitative assessments than quantitative techniques.

Sector-wide programs and other programs focus on changing the way that aid is delivered, particularly on changing the way donors work with governments. They are not just sets of projects and activities but also a way to coordinate and support sector activities and improve policies and resource allocation. The evaluation methods described above do not allow for identifying the effect on policy quality or whether policies have contributed to increased resource allocation to priority sectors. For example, improvements in health service delivery may be as much the result of policymaker or administrator leadership as they are the result of existing donor programs, or both. Making comparisons with other countries is virtually impossible because contexts are too different to allow such comparisons to be meaningful.

Instead, different kinds of indicators are proposed for programs—but there are fewer examples of this. Because the purpose of a sector approach is usually to better use resources, both private and public, indicators ought to reflect broader development outcomes, not just those of projects. To measure improved resource allocation, aid agencies have used indicators, for example, related to mechanisms to reduce inappropriate investments in hardware and training, drug quality control, and public knowledge about appropriate treatments. Indicators around policy implementation can include measures of whether implementation reflects the agreed-on expenditure patterns, expenditures focus on key objectives such as increased spending in rural areas and for primary care, or whether difficult policies have been implemented, for example, hospital rationalization, contracting, and regulation; and improvement in administrative capacity and technical efficiency (Walford 2003).

Many of these intended program outcomes are difficult to measure. For example, it is difficult to assess the extent to which government feels ownership and accepts agreed-on priorities for allocation, the extent to which other stakeholders—the medical sector, a patient representative organization—feel they have an influence on sector policy and plans, and the extent of participation in policy development. Indications of strengthened national systems and planning equally are not easy to capture, for example, relating to procurement, the role of the private sector (e.g., using health accounts), the extent to which budgets reflect available domestic and aid resources, and improvements in capacity to monitor quality and uptake of services.

Similarly, the monitoring of Poverty Reduction Strategy Papers (PRSPs) focused on processes combined with a wide range of monitoring systems for various elements of public policy. In a chapter in the World Bank (2002) PRSP "sourcebook," the components of a monitoring system are described, indicating that capacities for monitoring and dissemination of evaluation may need strengthening. A poverty-monitoring system tracks key indicators over time, including public expenditure and outputs, and quick measures of household well-being. The World Bank document highlighted the need for rigorous assessment of intervention impact on poverty, which is a key component of the strategy—Box 8.3 describes an instrument that donors proposed to assess impact ex ante, before decisions on policy directions were taken, and to assess the most likely outcomes of different scenarios. Because a PRSP is a strategy involving multiple sectors and ministries, the evaluation of impact—as opposed to evaluation of the impact of a specific component of a strategy—is especially challenging.

Box 8.3   Poverty and Social Impact Analysis

Poverty and Social Impact Analysis (PSIA) was developed in the context of PRSPs as a way to consider the poverty and social impact of major reforms in lending programs to poor countries. PSIA is an ex ante analysis of intended and unintended consequences of policy interventions on the well-being of different groups, particularly the poor and those at risk of falling into poverty. It intended to promote understanding of the impacts of policy reforms and evidence-based policy and to evaluate the trade-offs between policies.

In Mozambique a PSIA was organized during the process of developing its PRSP covering 2000–2005. The PSIA focused on the impact of a possible rise in fuel tax, which was then under debate, because the price of fuel had not changed in five years despite inflation. The revenue raised from an increased tax would be used to support development priorities, such as road maintenance, but many argued that increasing fuel tax would cause increases in poverty. To analyze the potential impacts, researchers used a range of approaches, including interviews with key decisionmakers in government and the private sector, household surveys to prepare a poverty profile, qualitative research about the use of fuel and transport among vulnerable groups, and quantitative analysis of how fuel prices would be transmitted through the economy using a social accounting matrix.

The PSIA concluded that the aggregate short-term impact on poverty of a rise in fuel tax would be modest. And though the analysis did not look at the potential use of the additional government revenue, it did highlight that possibly more people could be lifted out of poverty through more pro-poor spending than the number of people who would fall into poverty with the increased fuel tax.

Source: http://web.worldbank.org/archive/website00519/WEB/OTHER/COUNT-14.HTM; see also OECD DAC (2003b).

PRSPs emphasized the agreement between a government and citizens, the accountability in delivery of services, and donor assistance based on an assessment of credibility of those commitments. Key monitoring indicators included the accountability to parliaments/legislatures on PRSP implementation and external accountability to donors, coherence across government departments, and reduced fragmentation of project-driven reporting and monitoring requirements. The coordination of reporting requirements—and their integration into the country's budget cycles—was seen as a key element of program implementation. However, concerns were raised about the extent to which reporting requirements were reduced as intended and about national capacity to produce the necessary data and analysis.

Similarly, evaluation of budget support—as the instrument behind sectoral or national development plans—required a complex mix of indicators (Lawson et al. 2003). These related to policy processes in-country and to the aid relationship, including, for example, the reduced time senior government officials needed to devote to a large number of individual project missions. Indicators needed to measure the predictability of aid flows, improvements in the overall direction and consistency of budget allocations, the effectiveness of the state and public administration and use of government systems, domestic accountability and transparency, and government capacity to reduce poverty.

Although these program approaches were intended to streamline aid processes, it became evident that the requirements for monitoring could be overly complex. The indicators were often hard to quantify, and the expanding lists of indicators stretched the capacity of monitoring systems.

Aid and Economic Growth

Starting in the 1960s, the number of studies on the impact of aid at the macrolevel and on economic growth has been growing. In 1987, Mosley (1987) found a "micro-macro paradox," which stated that aid was efficient at the project level but had no clear effect on the overall economy. This paradox greatly influenced subsequent work on aid effectiveness. In this section, I focus on the way this impact has been assessed and the debates that have arisen around the question (Arndt, Jones, and Tarp 2016; Mahembe and Odhiambo 2019b).

The key question in these analyses is about the correlation between amount of aid, and sometimes the way it is provided (for example, as project or as program aid), and economic growth or other economic indicators such as savings. Economists have been concerned about this correlation because it can help answer the question of whether aid has a positive impact. However, large-scale funding also can have negative impacts: it may lead to appreciation of the exchange rates and decreasing competitiveness of the economy (the Dutch disease), and it can have negative effects on government budgeting processes and rent seeking.

David Roodman's (2007) "guide for the perplexed" describes how the research on the effects of aid at the macrolevel has grown and quality data have become more widely available alongside improved computing, which makes it possible to test to establish links between different factors. Controversy already existed in the 1970s: some concluded aid did well, others said it did no harm, and yet others could not see any positive impact of aid. After Mosley produced his findings showing that there was no effect of projects at microlevel on macrolevel indicators, a paper from the London School of Economics showed there was no significant effect of aid on savings or growth, which in turn "launched a thousand regressions of growth" (Roodman 2007, 5).

A key contribution came from the World Bank with papers in 1997 and 2000 by Craig Burnside and David Dollar (the latter is also one of the main authors emphasizing how important economic growth is for poverty reduction). They argued that aid did work, but only in good policy environments with openness to trade, low inflation, and balanced government budgets. Subsequently, many analyses have added to this argument, each looking at slightly different conditions that make aid effective: stronger government institutions and economic policies, democracy, countries emerging from civil war, and so forth (Bräutigam and Knack 2004).

The apparently straightforward finding that aid works in the right environment has been criticized, but it remains influential. The independent evaluation of World Bank research referred to in Chapter 3 listed this contribution as an example of the unbalanced way in which the institution has used research results.[12] William Easterly, Ross Levine, and David Roodman (2003), using slightly different data that added countries and years of observation, came to a different conclusion: that there was no evidence that aid was effective, and that more research was needed. Others were particularly concerned with the question of causality, and it remains difficult to decide whether providing aid causes economic growth or whether economic growth leads to receiving more aid (Mahembe and Odhiambo 2019a).

Many variants of the argument exist. For example, the complexities have led to calls to focus on "reduced form estimates": Bourguignon and Sundberg (2007) showed that aid works via physical capital investments and health improvements. Others have looked at whether the volatility of aid matters for the impact of aid on growth (Liu and Li 2022). Some have shown that aid works in some countries and not others, some have focused on short- versus long-term aid and impacts, and other studies have focused on the impact of donors' strategic motives behind aid provision.[13] The statistical techniques continue to improve, but these usually lead to more questions being asked. The question of whether the aid industry contributes to economic growth will remain an important one, but perhaps the issues involved are too complex to be summarized in the simple indicators used in the regressions.

Conclusion

There are good reasons why it will remain very difficult to assess whether aid has worked or not. First, the objectives of aid vary, and it would be of limited value to assess all forms of aid or all aid providers using the same measures. Given the diversity of motivations and perspectives, and the diversity of agencies that all have their own reporting rules, accountability, stakeholders, and evaluation needs and uses, it should come as no surprise that measurement is and probably will remain imprecise.

Second, generalized conclusions about the impact of aid on global poverty would be extremely misleading. For example, would the knowledge that in the second half of the twentieth century more people were lifted out of poverty than before be a sign that the global aid architecture that developed during the same period was working? Or, conversely, is the failure to meet some of the 2000 Millennium Development Goals, or the failure to meet them in some regions, proof of the industry's failure? Put simply, the aid industry is different from other industries in that it does not have a simple bottom line of success and failure. One should not try to push this question too far, either, because a need to "show results" may drive agencies away from longer-term projects of capacity building into areas where results are more immediate and easier to achieve.

The question of whether aid "works," even asked in this simple fashion, is perhaps just too difficult to answer. The proposed outcomes of international development are manifold and oft-changing. What is being measured often is not clearly defined or agreed upon, or if there are agreements such as in the SDGs framework, there are simply too many goals. Even if the focus of evaluation is one of the variables—such as economic growth—the technical complexities for answering the question clearly remain.

However, there are instruments that allow insight into whether certain forms of support have worked and whether some have worked better than others. The important issue may not be finding the perfect science but improving the ways in which the industry can be held to account within the parameters of political and commercial motives. Much more may need to be done to strengthen accountability and develop instruments for making decisions on how to allocate aid, but progress is being made.

Notes

1. John Norris, "Opinion: USAID at 60," DevEx, November 3, 2021, https://www .devex.com/news/opinion-usaid-at-60-101934.

2. OECD (2021b); GIZ (2021); GEI (2022). Mitchell and McKee (2018) discussed the "Quality of Official Development Assistance" index.

3. "Evaluation of Development Programmes," OECD, https://www.oecd.org /dac/evaluation/; "GPEDC at a Glance," Global Partnership for Effective Development Co-operation, September 21, 2020, https://www.effectivecooperation.org/content /gpedc-glance-0; Global Partnership for Effective Development Co-operation (2019).

4. The World Bank Independent Evaluation Group (2015) provided a good overview of its strategy and an interesting example of how it approaches learning.

5. Independent Commission for Aid Impact, https://icai.independent.gov.uk/. For example, it carried out a rapid review of the UK's aid response to the pandemic ("The UK Aid Response to COVID-19," Independent Commission for Aid Impact, https://icai.independent.gov.uk/review/the-uk-aid-response-to-covid-19).

6. Key resources are Dutta and Williamson (2019) and Mitchell (2020).

7. There is a related but different strand of literature that looks at why aid may flow to richer parts of countries (Briggs 2021).

8. Rawlings, Sherburne-Benz, and Van Domelen (2004). This World Bank evaluation compared social funds in different countries using a variety of methods to assess success in reaching the poor, impact on living standards, quality of the infrastructure created in the context of social funds, and the costs of social funds as compared to institutions undertaking similar investment.

9. Chen, Mu, and Ravallion (2008); the evaluation also showed that the impacts were different on income than on consumption poverty because people saved additional income.

10. A volume by Bush and Duggan (2015) provides important examples of research in fragile contexts.

11. The assertion by Abhijit Banerjee (2007, 7, 16) that aid institutions are lazy and resist knowledge, because they do not use randomized trials enough, neglects the diverse nature of the aid industry.

12. "Bank reports prepared for Monterrey did not present a balanced picture of the research, with appropriate reservations and skepticism, but used it [World Bank research on aid effectiveness] selectively to support an advocacy position" (Banerjee et al. 2006, 56).

13. Bearce and Tirone (2010) showed that such motivations do not deter effectiveness as long as the share of these strategic benefits is small.

9

Ongoing Challenges

IN THIS BOOK, I HAVE DESCRIBED HOW DEVELOPMENT AID WORKS. To put it simply, what happens with the $150 billion or so official aid disbursed annually? I have discussed the numerous institutions involved, their histories, politics, and incentives; the often rapidly changing trends in international development; and the instruments that are available to the aid industry.

It has not been my intention to decide whether aid "works," "really works," or "fails." In fact, as I described in the last chapter, there are good grounds to conclude that it is almost impossible to come to an agreed-on assessment of whether aid works. There are many instruments and measurements with which assessments can be made, each with its merits; indeed, the assessment of aid has become a cottage industry of its own. There is no one standard way of measuring success and failure. Many perhaps unresolvable technical questions remain, and an overall assessment of such a complex venture may be too difficult. There may even be negative side effects of focusing on results, particularly if results need to be shown quickly. In particular, the political nature of the aid industry and development and the always-present diplomatic and commercial motives alongside charitable ones make assessments of success very difficult indeed.

By now, I hope you understand the challenges that exist and have an insight into the variety of aid agencies and approaches. In this final chapter, I describe major challenges for the aid industry over the coming years.

Has Aid Become Irrelevant?

As discussed in the introductory chapter, many have questioned the relevance of aid. In the context of globalization and increases in international trade and migration, does aid still provide value? Also, whereas the global economic context and political context have changed enormously, the foundations of the aid industry are still largely those created in the mid-twentieth century. The short answer regarding the relevance of aid, which I hope has been justified by the text in this book, is: seen in its proper context, with both its political and humanitarian motives, the aid industry is still relevant.

The 2020 pandemic highlighted the critical importance of global cooperation. The spread of infectious diseases in an interconnected world has shown the need for global cooperation in health, the critical role of the World Health Organization (WHO), Centers for Disease Control and Prevention (CDC), vaccine initiatives, and so forth. This situation has renewed calls for transfers of technology to lower-income countries so they can produce vaccines and medical equipment. Further, the growing climate crisis is reinforcing the need for global cooperation, funding, and technical assistance and transfers to help mitigate the severe impacts of climate change in low-income countries and to transition to lower-carbon economies. During the pandemic, these challenges were reinforced by growing public debt, which renewed the role of the International Monetary Fund (IMF), even though a large part of countries' debt is owed to private creditors. Although on all these fronts the aid industry can do better than it currently does, its objectives remain as important as before.

Over the last thirty years, many countries in the Global South have made significant economic progress, but the growth of emerging economies has not made the aid industry less important. China is an example. It has progressed with relatively little aid and donors gradually phased out aid programs there. As China grew, it integrated into the global economy, and the role of organizations such as the World Trade Organization (WTO), International Labour Organization (ILO), and WHO has remained as relevant as before. Emerging countries are slowly but clearly expanding their presence in these global institutions, and with that, calls for reform of these institutions have increased. Emerging economies have started their own aid programs, reinforcing the need for coordination and affecting the way the earlier donors operate—but not making the latter less important.

The private sector and finance industry have become increasingly important in growing economies and in the programming by aid agencies. New ways of working have emerged that mobilize private sector actors, including through blended finance. These have expanded the types of modalities in the aid industry and created new partnerships. However, these new ways of working do not imply a decreased significance of aid because in major areas of development private sector investment remains limited and mobilization of private sector investment requires public agencies' input, finance, and regulation.

The aid industry continues to go through episodes of aid fatigue, either times of disinterest or strong political opposition, as under President Trump in the United States. Equally, there continue to be forces that maintain the functions of the aid industry, continuously reinventing it, as they have done through periods of the Cold War and the "end of history" in an increasingly multipolar global system. Ever more national-oriented political interests see the role of aid. The security agenda after 9/11 reoriented but did not diminish the importance of aid, and emerging economies are incorporating forms of aid into their growing international connections. Civil society in many countries and global cooperation relationships—increasingly focused on the impacts of climate change—continue to push for maintaining or increasing the levels of aid provided.

There is thus little evidence that the aid industry is becoming redundant. The total amount of money involved, the number of players—including those who graduate from recipient to donor—the public interest, and the numbers of students of international development have continued to grow. National politics are becoming increasingly interdependent at a global scale and in the process ascribing a larger role to the aid industry, alongside other forms of cooperation.

Is Aid About Poverty Reduction or Development?

In the 1990s, the aid industry focused on poverty reduction, whereas earlier this focus tended to be implicit in broader development objectives. With the agreements on the Millennium Development Goals (MDGs) and Sustainable Development Goals (SDGs) and pressures to show aid is or can be effective, the aid industry started to be measured against trends in well-being. As the impacts of climate change continue to grow, affecting many lower-income economies and poorer groups severely and disproportionally, the demand for poverty-oriented investments continues to increase.

Although this poverty focus may seem self-evident, it also creates challenges. A focus on reaching the poorest may skew aid support toward projects with directly identifiable outcomes and *targeted* poverty interventions in projects, as described in Chapter 5, rather than to countries' broader institutions that are required for development. The roles donors have played in the social sector of recipient countries may limit those countries' ability to develop their own approaches to and institutions for social policies. The focus on primary education based on research that showed primary education had high rates of return and benefited the poor has tended to ignore higher education, which is a central element for countries' development.

A narrow focus can limit a development agenda at the cost of less support for broader and inclusive institutions and services for entire populations. Most aid agencies recognize the need to support the institutions and conditions that enable sustained poverty reduction; the discussion of reforms and governance shows the dilemmas the aid industry tries to deal with.

The growing importance of new donors such as China has rebalanced the poverty focus to some extent. Although China subscribes to the importance of the SDGs, it simultaneously highlights the need for economic growth and infrastructure, as well as mutual cooperation rather than aid. This has contributed to similar moves within the agencies of the traditional donors, too, which some regard as a loss of poverty focus, and it is reflected in institutional priority setting in low-income countries.

Numbers of Donors Continue to Increase

The industry has put much focus on the harmonization of and multilateral approaches to aid, expressed in the Paris Consensus, as described in Chapter 3. This makes the important argument that donors need to work together and back plans for development that are formulated by recipient countries, the government in consultation with the citizens. The aid industry is serious about its outcomes and is prepared to learn the lessons of its past and implement steps to change its way of operating.

Multiple forces have challenged these efforts. First, national interests of donor countries, including the need to show results, often reduce opportunities for collaboration. Second, the growing emphasis on aid agencies' collaboration with the private sector and mobilizing private finance have complicated harmonization. Third, the number of donors has been increasing, and so are total financial aid flows. Newcomers such as China and the Gates Foundation and other private foundations are contributing significant amounts. These newcomers do not immediately join the old clubs, and when they do, they may try to change the club rules. The approaches of the newer donors may be complementary to those of the older ones, but they may also seem to conflict. For example, China's focus on infrastructure was welcomed because that is an area that the old donors tended to neglect, but its insistence on noninterference was felt to be at odds with the old donors' emphasis on promoting good governance as a precondition for development.

These opposing movements or forces do not fundamentally challenge the aid industry; it has been subjected to opposition again and again and reinvented itself since its origins. The key question is how the industry will manage them. For example, insisting on donor coordination if only a portion of donors join the debate may hamper the process of redefining the club rules, such as regarding the ways in which aid is provided and maybe even the way the international community understands how development and poverty reduction happen. Although many recipient countries are committed to the processes of harmonization, its political nature and national and international changes continue to limit such efforts.

Need Versus Capacity

Even though most donor countries are not achieving the goal of providing 0.7 percent of their GNI, total amounts of aid are increasing. New donors are adding significantly to total amounts, while the numbers of recipients are declining, as major countries such as India and China are "graduating." A key question in the industry remains whether this additional aid can be spent in an accountable way.

As this book describes, much debate about whether aid works continues. Some economists' analyses of aid and economic growth show that aid works. Others argue that one cannot prove aid causes growth and that such macroanalyses cannot be relied on. Influential people such as Easterly have provided convincing critiques regarding how grand planning is misguided and have argued for smaller and experimental approaches—which often do not allow for large increases in amounts of aid. Experience with different aid modalities such as budget support confirms magic bullets do not exist. Advocates for aid increases stress how deeply underfunded public systems in health and education are—and reject arguments that increases in aid should be conditional on governance requirements.

With the growth of emerging economies, the Global South is increasingly diverse and needs for support are more varied—perhaps that diversity was always there and insufficiently recognized in the earlier aid industry. Some have argued that aid should focus on the "bottom billion." This would include a focus on countries where specific modalities of aid are crucial for people to get out of the poverty trap. But a large share of the world's poorest live in large countries that, on average, are not poor. Moreover, the aid industry limits itself in focusing aid flows to the poorest countries, partly because of donors' political motives and partly because of agencies' need to show results.

A key concept these debates raise is *absorptive capacity*: the technical and political preconditions for aid to be effective in reducing poverty. The main dilemma shown in the aid effectiveness research is that aid worked where good policies existed. Experience in conflict and postconflict settings shows the risks of overambitious goals. Newer initiatives to fight AIDS, tuberculosis, and malaria, such as the Global Fund and the Millennium Challenge Account, put significant money behind countries' good or improved conditions of governance. Though the aid industry now has a much better understanding of the importance of good policies and good governance for development and poverty reduction, it has—at the same time—learned that it is extremely difficult to change these areas. There have been cases where large amounts of funding were put into supporting governments, for example, those emerging from war, but there are not many such cases. The different modalities of new donors complicate this equation.

Aid Is and Always Has Been Political

The aid industry is not only about funding for development or poverty reduction but also plays a part in international politics between North and South and South–South. As described in this book, while part of the aid allocation follows humanitarian motives and ideas about where aid would be most effective—variously defined—part of it is politically determined. Some aid agencies have been very explicit about the need for aid departments to support foreign policy objectives and donor countries' commercial interests so as to maintain political support. Strong commitments to humanitarian motives also have a political base and can and do change. The industry will likely continue to follow the interests and beliefs of politicians.

What this implies is that assessing aid on its technical impact is important, particularly to increase its accountability, but provides insufficient insight into the way the aid industry will move because it has multiple objectives. It is important to see aid in that context. This makes an informed advocacy by external agencies ever more important to ensure that the aid industry—within its political margins—is steered in the direction of global justice and becomes a stronger part of an international framework for promoting this.

Compared to other forms of public policy, the aid industry has been relatively unaccountable. The average voter knows very little about what aid does and has little base to judge either claims made by official aid agencies or those who criticize it. Even students in international development, I found, know little about the political parties' policies and manifestos on aid. Moreover, the aid industry is unaccountable to its beneficiaries—unlike, say, a national ministry that provides health services. Informed public debate that leverages voices from the Global South is essential to keep pushing the aid industry and other policies that impact global development in the best possible direction.

Can the Industry Decolonize?

Given that official aid is a key instrument with which the North contributes to global solidarity and justice, it has a key role in decolonizing North–South relations. Alongside broader political debates, advocacy within aid agencies for decolonization has been growing. Increasing diversity within aid agencies, as in countries' public agencies more broadly, can lead to a different engagement with the Global South.

The growing role of former aid recipients in the industry is changing the industry's make-up. South–South cooperation provides alternatives to the North–South relations that dominated the industry in its first half century. Frameworks such as the SDGs have explicitly formulated development objectives as global, somewhat reducing the focus on the Global South. The growing role of the private sector also is leading to different forms of collaboration. Each of these trends has created a more dispersed field of aid relationships and more dispersed ideologies and has gradually changed the club of old donors.

However, there is limited evidence that these trends and changes are altering the central modalities of the aid industry. Many of the relationships—through bilateral agencies, NGOs, and the new private philanthropy—remain on a charitable basis. In the debate of decolonization, it is important once again to highlight how aid is embedded in both national institutions and a global political economy, and that decolonization is likely to be slow and can be interrupted.

List of Acronyms

AERC	African Economic Research Consortium
AfDB	African Development Bank
AIIB	Asian Infrastructure Investment Bank
AsDB	Asian Development Bank
BRI	Belt and Road Initiative
BRICS	Brazil, Russia, India, China, South Africa
CCRT	Catastrophe Containment and Relief Trust
CDC	Centers for Disease Control and Prevention
CDD	community-driven development
CDF	Comprehensive Development Framework
CEDAW	Convention on the Elimination of All Forms of Discrimination Against Women
CEPI	Coalition for Epidemic Preparedness Innovations
CERF	Central Emergency Response Fund
CGD	Center for Global Development
CGI	Clinton Global Initiative
CGIAR	Consultative Group on International Agricultural Research
CIDA	Canadian International Development Agency (now GAC)
CIDCA	China International Development Cooperation Agency
CRC	Convention on the Rights of the Child
DAC	Development Assistance Committee
DFATD	Department of Foreign Affairs, Trade and Development
DFID	Department for International Development (now FCDO)

EITI	Extractive Industries Transparency Initiative
ESAF	Enhanced Structural Adjustment Facility
ESF	Emergency Social Fund (Bolivia)
EU	European Union
Eurodad	European Network on Debt and Development
FAO	Food and Agriculture Organization
FCDO	Foreign, Commonwealth and Development Office
FIAP	Feminist International Assistance Policy
GAC	Global Affairs Canada
GAD	Gender and Development
GATT	General Agreement on Tariffs and Trade
GBA+	Gender-based Analysis Plus
GCF	Green Climate Fund
GDP	gross domestic product
GDI	Gender Development Index
GEM	Gender Empowerment Measure
GIZ	Gesellschaft für Internationale Zusammenarbeit
GNI	gross national income
GPE	Global Partnership for Education .
GPEDC	Global Partnership for Effective Development Co-operation
GSDRC	Governance and Social Development Resource Centre
GTZ	Gesellschaft für Technische Zusammenarbeit
HDI	Human Development Index
HDR	Human Development Report
HIPC	heavily indebted poor countries
IADB	Inter-American Development Bank
IBRD	International Bank for Reconstruction and Development
ICAI	Independent Commission for Aid Impact
IDA	International Development Association
IDRC	International Development Research Centre
IDS	Institute for Development Studies
IFAD	International Fund for Agricultural Development
IFC	International Finance Corporation
IFI	International Financial Institutions
IFPRI	International Food Policy Research Institute
IILS	International Institute for Labour Studies
ILO	International Labour Organization
IMF	International Monetary Fund
IMFC	International Monetary and Finance Committee
IPA	Innovations for Poverty Action

IPCC	Intergovernmental Panel on Climate Change
IPEC	International Programme on the Elimination of Child Labour
IRD	Integrated Rural Development
IsDB	Islamic Development Bank
JASPA	Jobs and Skills Program for Africa
JICA	Japan International Cooperation Agency
LDCs	least developed countries
MCA	Millennium Challenge Account
MCC	Millennium Challenge Corporation
MDGs	Millennium Development Goals
MIGA	Multilateral Investment Guarantee Agency
MOFCOM	Ministry of Foreign Trade and Economic Cooperation
NDC	Nationally Determined Contribution
NIEO	New International Economic Order
NGO	nongovernmental organization
ODA	official development assistance
ODI	Overseas Development Institute
OECD	Organisation for Economic Co-operation and Development
PEAP	Poverty Eradication Action Plan (Uganda)
PEPFAR	President's Emergency Plan for AIDS Relief
PPA	participatory poverty analysis
PPP	purchasing power parity
PRA	participatory rural appraisal
PRCDP	Poor Rural Communities Development Project
PREALC	Programa Regional del Empleo para América Latina y el Caribe (Regional Employment Program for Latin America and the Caribbean)
PRGT	Poverty Reduction and Growth Trust
PRSP	Poverty Reduction Strategy Paper
PSIA	Poverty and Social Impact Analysis
RBM	results-based management
RCTs	randomized control trials
RST	Resilience and Sustainability Trust
SAP	structural adjustment program
SARS	severe acute respiratory syndrome
SDGs	Sustainable Development Goals
SEWA	Self-Employed Women's Association
Sida	Swedish International Development Cooperation Agency
SWAP	sector-wide approach
TA	technical assistance

TC	technical cooperation
UK	United Kingdom
UN	United Nations
UNCTAD	United Nations Conference on Trade and Development
UNDAF	United Nations Development Assistance Framework
UNDP	United Nations Development Programme
UNEP	United Nations Environment Programme
UNFCCC	United Nations Framework Convention on Climate Change
UNHCR	United Nations High Commissioner for Refugees
UNICEF	United Nations Children's Fund
UNRISD	United Nations Research Institute for Social Development
USAID	United States Agency for International Development
WEF	World Economic Forum
WEP	World Employment Programme
WFP	World Food Programme
WHO	World Health Organization
WID	Women in Development
WIDER	World Institute for Development Economics Research
WTO	World Trade Organization

References

Abi-Habib, Maria. 2021. "Why Haiti Still Despairs After $13 Billion in Foreign Aid." *New York Times,* August 16, 2021.

Ackva, Johannes, Luisa Sandkühler, and Violet Buxton-Walsh. 2021. *A Guide to the Changing Landscape of High-impact Climate Philanthropy.* London: Founders Pledge.

Adelman, Irma. 2000. "The Role of Government in Economic Development." In Tarp, *Foreign Aid and Development,* 48–79.

Ahmed, Sarah Jana, Alicia Bárcena, and Daniel Titelman. 2021. "The IMF's Misstep on Climate Finance." Project Syndicate, December 13, 2021. https://www.project-syndicate.org/commentary/imf-must-adjust-funding-criteria-in-response-to-climate-vulnerability-by-sara-jane-ahmed-et-al-2021-12?barrier=accesspaylog.

AidData. 2021. "Listening to Leaders." https://www.aiddata.org/ltl.

Alesina, Alberto, and David Dollar. 2000. "Who Gives Foreign Aid to Whom and Why?" *Journal of Economic Growth* 5, no. 1: 33–63.

Al-Iryani, Lamis, Alain De Janvry, and Elisabeth Sadoulet. 2013. *Delivering Good Aid in Hard Places: The Yemen Social Fund for Development Approach.* WIDER Working Paper no. 2013/080. Helsinki: UNU-WIDER.

Alston, Philip, and Mary Robinson, eds. 2005. *Human Rights and Development: Towards Mutual Reinforcement.* Oxford: Oxford University Press.

Amarante, Verónica, Ronelle Burger, Grieve Chelwa, John Cockburn, Ana Kassouf, Andrew McKay, and Julieta Zurbrigg. 2021. "Underrepresentation of Developing Country Researchers in Development Research." *Applied Economics Letters.* https://doi.org/10.1080/13504851.2021.1965528.

Amsden, Alice H. 2007. "Escape from Empire." In *The Developing World's Journey Through Heaven and Hell.* Cambridge, MA: MIT Press.

Anderson, Mary B. 1999. *Do No Harm: How Aid Can Support Peace—or War.* Boulder: Lynne Rienner Publishers.

Ang, Y. Y. 2016. *How China Escaped the Poverty Trap.* Ithaca, NY: Cornell University Press.

Antunes, Marta, and Jorge O. Romano. 2005. "Combating Infant Malnutrition—An Experience of Networking in the Social Struggle for the Human Right to Food and Sustainable Nutrition." In Gready and Ensor, *Reinventing Development?* 131–143.

Archibong, Belinda, Brahima Coulibaly, and Ngozi Okonjo-Iweala. 2021. "Washington Consensus Reforms and Lessons for Economic Performance in Sub-Saharan Africa." *Journal of Economic Perspectives* 35, no. 3: 133–156.

Arndt, Channing. 2000. "Technical Co-operation." In Tarp, *Foreign Aid and Development,* 154–177.

Arndt, Channing, Sam Jones, and Finn Tarp. 2016. "What Is the Aggregate Economic Rate of Return to Foreign Aid?" *World Bank Economic Review* 30, no. 3: 446–474.

Asian Development Bank, Operations Evaluation Department. 2007. *Effect of Microfinance Operations on Poor Rural Households and the Status of Women.* Manila: Asian Development Bank, Special Evaluation Study. https://www.adb.org/documents/effect-microfinance-poor-rural-households-and-status-women.

Asiimwe, Allen, Christian Eldon, David Greene, Karen Kenny, and Stella Mukasa. 2004. "Justice, Law and Order Strategic Investment Plan. Mid-term Evaluation 2001/2–2005/6." International Human Rights Network. https://www.ihrnetwork.org/files/Uganda_JLOS_MTE_Vol_One.pdf.

Aslam, Abid. 2008. "Watchdog Faults IMF Loan Conditionalities." Pambazuka News, January 11, 2008. https://www.pambazuka.org/global-south/global-watchdog-faults-imf-loan-conditions.

Autesserre, Séverine. 2014. *Peaceland: Conflict Resolution and Everyday Politics of International Intervention.* Cambridge: Cambridge University Press.

———. 2021. *The Frontlines of Peace: An Insider's Guide to Changing the World.* Oxford: Oxford University Press.

Ayers, Jessica, Saleemul Huq, Helena Wright, Arif M. Faisal, and Syed Tanveer Hussain. 2014. "Mainstreaming Climate Change Adaptation into Development in Bangladesh." *Climate and Development* 6, no. 4: 293–305.

Babb, S., and A. Kentikelenis. 2021. "Markets Everywhere: The Washington Consensus and the Sociology of Global Institutional Change." *Annual Review of Sociology* 47, no. 1: 521–541.

Baker, Andy. 2015. "Race, Paternalism, and Foreign Aid: Evidence from U.S. Public Opinion." *American Political Science Review* 109, no. 1: 93–109.

Baker, Judy L. 2000. *Evaluating the Impact of Development Projects on Poverty: A Handbook for Practitioners.* Directions in Development. Washington, DC: World Bank.

Banerjee, Abhijit Vinayak. 2007. *Making Aid Work.* Cambridge, MA: MIT Press.

Banerjee, Abhijit, Angus Deaton, Nora Lustig, Ken Rogoff, and Edward Hsu. 2006. "An Evaluation of World Bank Research, 1998–2005." *SSRN Electronic Journal,* January 2006. https://doi.org/10.2139/ssrn.2950327.

Banks, Nicola. 2021. "The Role and Contributions of Development NGOs to Development Cooperation: What Do We Know?" In Chaturvedi et al., *Palgrave Handbook of Development Cooperation,* 671–688.

Baranyi, Stephen, and Themrise Khan. 2016. "Canada and Development in Other Fragile States: Moving Beyond the 'Afghanistan Model.'" In Brown, den Heyer, and Black, *Rethinking Canadian Aid,* 237–254.

Bass, Stephen, Hannah Reid, David Satterthwaite, and Paul Steele, eds. 2005. *Reducing Poverty and Sustaining the Environment: The Politics of Local Engagement.* London: Earthscan.

Batliwala, Srilatha, and David Brown. 2006. *Transnational Civil Society: An Introduction*. Bloomfield, CT: Kumarian Press.

Bearce, David H., and Brandy J. Jolliff Scott. 2019. "Popular Non-support for International Organizations: How Extensive and What Does This Represent?" *Review of International Organizations* 14, no. 2: 187–216.

Bearce, David H., and Daniel C. Tirone. 2010. "Foreign Aid Effectiveness and the Strategic Goals of Donor Governments." *Journal of Politics* 72, no. 3: 837–851.

Bebbington, Anthony J., Michael Woolcock, Scott Guggenheim, and Elizabeth A. Olson. 2006. *The Search for Empowerment: Social Capital as Idea and Practice at the World Bank*. Bloomfield, CT: Kumarian Press.

Benner, C. 2020. "Competitive Cooperation: How to Think About Strengthing Multilateralism." Global Public Policy Institute, October 28, 2020. https://www.gppi.net/2020/10/28/competitive-cooperation-how-to-think-about-strengthening-multilateralism.

Berkman, Steve. 2008. *The World Bank and the Gods of Lending*. Sterling, VA: Kumarian Press.

Bermeo, Sarah Blodgett. 2017. "Aid Allocation and Targeted Development in an Increasingly Connected World." *International Organization* 71, no. 4: 735–766.

Biermann, Frank. 2022. "The End of Sustainability Summitry—Reflections on 'Stockholm+50.'" Planet Politics Institute, June 8, 2022. https://www.planetpolitics.org/ppi-blog/the-end-of-sustainability-summitry-.

Binnendijk, Annette. 2001. "Results-Based Management in Donor Agencies." Draft report presented at DAC Working Party on Aid Evaluation meeting, February 2000. https://www.oecd.org/development/evaluation/dcdndep/31950852.pdf.

Black, David R. 2016. "Humane Internationalism and the Malaise of Canadian Aid Policy." In Brown, den Heyer, and Black, *Rethinking Canadian Aid*, 17–36.

Blackburn, James, Robert Chambers, and John Gaventa. 2000. *Mainstreaming Participation in Development*. OED Working Paper Series no. 10. Washington, DC: World Bank, Operations Evaluation Department.

Blair, Robert A., and Matthew S. Winters. 2020. "Foreign Aid and State–Society Relations: Theory, Evidence, and New Directions for Research." *Studies in Comparative International Development* 55:123–142.

Bolton, Giles. 2007. *Poor Story: An Insider Uncovers How Globalisation and Good Intentions Have Failed the World's Poor*. London: Ebury Press.

Booth, David, A. Grigsby, and C. Toranzo. 2006. *Politics and Poverty Reduction Strategies: Lessons from Latin American HIPCs*. ODI Working Paper 262. London: Overseas Development Institute.

Booth, David, and Sue Unsworth. 2014. *Politically Smart, Locally Led Development*. Overseas Development Institute discussion paper. London: Overseas Development Institute.

Bos, Julie, and Joe Thwaites. 2021. "A Breakdown of Developed Countries' Climate Finance Contributions Towards the $100 Billion Goal." World Resources Institute, October 5, 2021. https://doi.org/10.46830/writn.20.00145.

Bourguignon, François, and Mark Sundberg. 2007. "Aid Effectiveness—Opening the Black Box." *American Economic Review* 97, no. 2: 316–321.

Bracho, Gerardo, Richard Carey, William Hynes, Stephan Klingebiel, and Alexandra Trzeciak-Duval, eds. 2021. *Origins, Evolution and Future of Global Development Cooperation: The Role of the Development Assistance Committee (DAC)*. Studies 104. Bonn: German Development Institute.

Brainard, Lael. 2007a. "Organizing US Foreign Assistance to Meet Twenty-First Century Challenges." In Brainard, *Security by Other Means*, 33–66.

————, ed. 2007b. *Security by Other Means: Foreign Assistance, Global Poverty, and American Leadership.* Washington, DC: Center for Strategic and International Studies, Brookings Institution Press.

Brandt, Willy. 1980. *North–South: A Programme for Survival.* London: Pan Books.

Brass, Jennifer N., Wesley Longhofer, Rachel S. Robinson, and Allison Schnable. 2018. "NGOs and International Development: A Review of Thirty-Five Years of Scholarship." *World Development* 112:136–149.

Bräutigam, Deborah. 2011. *The Dragon's Gift: The Real Story of China in Africa.* Oxford: Oxford University Press.

Bräutigam, Deborah, and Stephen Knack. 2004. "Foreign Aid, Institutions, and Governance in Sub-Saharan Africa." *Economic Development and Cultural Change* 52, no. 2: 255–285.

Briggs, Ryan C. 2021. "Why Does Aid Not Target the Poorest?" *International Studies Quarterly* 65, no. 3: 739–752.

Broberg, Morten, and Hans-Otto Sano. 2018. "Strengths and Weaknesses in a Human Rights-Based Approach to International Development—An Analysis of a Rights-Based Approach to Development Assistance Based on Practical Experiences." *International Journal of Human Rights* 22, no. 5: 664–680.

Brown, Adrienne, Mick Foster, Andy Norton, and Felix Naschold. 2001. *The Status of Sector Wide Approaches.* ODI Working Paper 142. London: Overseas Development Institute.

Brown, Mark Malloch. 2007. "Holmes Lecture: Can the UN Be Reformed?" Presentation at the Annual Meeting of Academic Council on the UN System (ACUNS).

Brown, Stephen. 2020. "The Rise and Fall of the Aid Effectiveness Norm." *European Journal of Development Research* 32:1230–1248.

Brown, Stephen, Molly den Heyer, and David R. Black, eds. 2016. *Rethinking Canadian Aid.* 2nd ed. Ottawa: University of Ottawa Press.

Browne, Stephen. 2007. *Aid to Fragile States: Do Donors Help or Hinder?* UNU-WIDER Discussion Paper no. 2007/01. Helsinki: UNU-WIDER.

Budlender, D. 2000. "The Political Economy of Women's Budgets in the South." *World Development* 28, no. 7: 1365–1378.

————. 2003. "Gender Budgets and Beyond: Feminist Fiscal Policy in the Context of Globalisation." *Gender and Development* 11, no. 1: 15–24.

Burnside, Craig, and David Dollar. 2000. "Aid, Policies and Growth." *American Economic Review* 90, no. 4: 847–868.

Bush, Kenneth, and Colleen Duggan, eds. 2015. *Evaluation in the Extreme: Research, Impact, and Politics in Violently Divided Societies.* New Delhi: Sage Publications India, and Ottawa: IDRC.

Buvinić, Mayra, and Jacqueline Mazza. 2008. "Addressing Exclusion: Social Policy Perspectives from Latin America and the Caribbean." In Dani and de Haan, *Inclusive States: Social Policy and Structural Inequalities*, 123–144.

Caballero, Paula, with Patti Londoño. 2022. *Redefining Development: The Extraordinary Genesis of the Sustainable Development Goals.* Boulder: Lynne Rienner Publishers.

CAFOD, Trócaire, and Christian Aid. 2006. *Monitoring Government Policies: A Toolkit for Civil Society Organisations in Africa.* https://gsdrc.org/document-library/monitoring-govenrment-policies-a-toolkit-for-civil-society-organisations-in-africa/.

Calleja, Mikaela, and Rachael Gavas. 2021. "The UK's Foreign, Commonwealth and Development Office One Year In." Center for Global Development, September 1,

2021. https://www.cgdev.org/blog/uks-foreign-commonwealth-and-development -office-one-year.

Carment, David, and Yiagadeesen Samy. 2016. "Canada's Fragile States Policy: What Have We Accomplished and Where Do We Go from Here?" In Brown, den Heyer, and Black, *Rethinking Canadian Aid*, 221–236.

Carter, Paddy. 2021. *Are Development Finance Institutions Good Value for Money?* CGD Policy Paper 235. Washington, DC: Center for Global Development.

Casey, Katherine, Rachel Glennerster, Edward Miguel, and Maarten J. Voors. 2021. *Long Run Effects of Aid: Forecasts and Evidence from Sierra Leone.* NBER Working Paper 29079. Cambridge, MA: National Bureau of Economic Research.

Cedergren, Jan. 2007. "We're Working on It: Development Partners' Efforts for Effective Aid." *Poverty in Focus*, October 2007, 26–27.

Chambers, Robert. 2005. *Ideas for Development.* London: Earthscan.

Chambers, Robert, and Gordon Conway. 1992. *Sustainable Rural Livelihoods: Practical Concepts for the 21st Century.* IDS Discussion Paper 296. Brighton, UK: Institute for Development Studies.

Chandy, Laurence. 2011. *Ten Years of Fragile States: What Have We Learned?* Policy Paper 2011–22. Washington, DC: Brookings Institution.

Chang, Ha-Joon. 2007. *Bad Samaritans: Rich Nations, Poor Policies and the Threat to the Developing World.* London: Random House.

Chang, Ha-Joon, and Antonio Andreoni. 2020. "Industrial Policy in the 21st Century." *Development and Change* 51:324–351.

Chaturvedi, S., H. Janus, S. Klingebiel, X. Li, A. D. Mello e Souza, E. Sidiropoulos, and D. Wehrmann, eds. 2020. *The Palgrave Handbook of Development Cooperation for Achieving the 2030 Agenda: Contested Collaboration.* London: Springer Nature.

Chatzky, A., and J. McBride. 2020. "China's Massive Belt and Road Initiative." Council on Foreign Relations, January 28, 2020. https://www.cfr.org/backgrounder /chinas-massive-belt-and-road-initiative.

Chen, Martha, Renana Jhabvala, Ravi Kanbur, and Carol Richards. 2007. *Membership-Based Organizations of the Poor.* London: Routledge.

Chen, Shaohua, Ren Mu, and Martin Ravallion. 2008. *Are There Lasting Impacts of Aid to Poor Areas? Evidence from Rural China.* Working Paper Series 4084. Washington, DC: World Bank.

Cheru, F. 2006. "Building and Supporting PRSPs in Africa: What Has Worked Well So Far? What Needs Changing?" *Third World Quarterly* 27, no. 2: 355–376.

Chu, Patti, and Olivia Yutong Wang. 2018. *Philanthropy in China.* New York: Rockefeller Foundation. https://www.rockefellerfoundation.org/wp-content /uploads/Philanthropy-in-China-Web-Version-April-5-2019-FINAL.pdf.

Chwieroth, Jeffrey M. 2013. "'The Silent Revolution': How the Staff Exercise Informal Governance over IMF Lending." *Review of International Organizations* 8, no. 2: 265–290.

Cichocka, Beata, Ian Mitchell, and Euan Ritchie. 2021. "Three Key Shifts on Development Cooperation in China's 2021 White Paper." Center for Global Development, February 9, 2021. https://www.cgdev.org/blog/three-key-shifts-development -cooperation-chinas-2021-white-paper.

Clemens, Michael, and Mariapia Mendola. 2020. *Migration from Developing Countries: Selection, Income Elasticity, and Simpson's Paradox.* CGD Working Paper no. 539. Washington, DC: Center for Global Development.

Clemens, Michael A., and Todd J. Moss. 2005. *Ghost of 0.7%: Origin and Relevance of the International Aid Target.* CGD Working Paper no. 68. Washington, DC: Center for Global Development.

Clements, Mary Ann, and Caroline Sweetman. 2020. "Introduction: Reimagining International Development." *Gender & Development* 28, no. 1: 1–9.

Clifton, Judith, Daniel Díaz Fuentes, and David Howarth, eds. 2021. *Regional Development Banks in the World Economy.* Online edition. Oxford Academic.

Collier, Paul. 2007. *The Bottom Billion: Why the Poorest Countries Are Failing and What Can Be Done About It.* Oxford: Oxford University Press.

———. 2008. *Wars, Guns and Votes: Democracy in Dangerous Places.* New York: Vintage Books.

Collier, Paul, and David Dollar. 1999. *Aid Allocation and Poverty Reduction.* World Bank Policy Research Working Paper no. 2041.Washington, DC: World Bank.

Collier, Paul, V. L. Elliott, Håvard Hegre, Anke Hoeffler, Marta Reynal-Querol, and Nicholas Sambanis. 2003. *Breaking the Conflict Trap: Civil War and Development Policy.* World Bank Policy Research Report. Washington, DC: World Bank.

Collier, P., and N. Okonjo-Iweala. 2002. *World Bank Group Work in Low-Income Countries Under Stress: A Task Force Report.* Washington, DC: World Bank.

Commission for Africa. 2005. *Our Common Interest: Report of the Commission for Africa.* London: Penguin Books.

Commonwealth Secretariat. 1999. *Gender Budget Initiative.* London: Commonwealth Secretariat.

Convergence. 2021. *The State of Blended Finance 2021: Time to Scale.* Toronto: Convergence.

Cook, Bill, and Uma Kothari. 2001. *Participation: The New Tyranny.* London: Zed Books.

Cordella, Tito, and Giovanni Dell'Ariccia. 2003. *Budget Support Versus Project Aid.* IMF Working Paper no. 03/88. Washington, DC: International Monetary Fund.

Cornia, Giovanni Andrea. 1999. *Social Funds in Stabilization and Adjustment Programmes.* Helsinki: UNU/WIDER, Research for Action 48.

Cornia, Giovanni Andrea, Richard Jolly, and Frances Stewart. 1987. *Adjustment with a Human Face.* Oxford: Clarendon Press.

Cornwall, Andrea. 2007. "Buzzwords and Fuzzwords: Deconstructing Development Discourse." *Development in Practice* 17, nos. 4–5: 471–484.

Cummings, Sarah, and Paul Hoebink. 2017. "Representation of Academics from Developing Countries as Authors and Editorial Board Members in Scientific Journals: Does This Matter to the Field of Development Studies?" *The European Journal of Development Research* 29, no. 2: 369–383.

Custer et al. 2021. *Tracking Chinese Development Finance: An Application of AidData's TUFF 2.0 Methodology.* Williamsburg, VA: AidData at William & Mary.

Dani, Anis A., and A. de Haan. 2008. *Inclusive States: Social Policy and Structural Inequalities.* Washington, DC: World Bank.

Das, Vidya. 2003. "Kashipur: The Politics of Underdevelopment." *Economic and Political Weekly,* January 4, 2003.

Davies, Thomas. 2014. *NGOs: A New History of Transnational Civil Society.* Oxford: Oxford University Press.

Davis, Gloria. 2004. *A History of the Social Development Network in the World Bank.* Social Development Paper no. 56. Washington, DC: World Bank.

Dawson, Andrew, and Liam Swiss. 2020. "Foreign Aid and the Rule of Law: Institutional Diffusion Versus Legal Reach." *British Journal of Sociology* 71, no. 4: 761–784.

Degnbol-Martinusse, John, and Poul Engberg-Pedersen. 2005. *Aid: Understanding International Development Cooperation*. London: Zed Books.

De Haan, Arjan. 2007. *Reclaiming Social Policy: Globalization, Social Exclusion and New Poverty Reduction Strategies*. London: Palgrave Macmillan.

———. 2008. "Disparities Within India's Poorest Region: Why Do the Same Institutions Work Differently in Different Places?" In *Institutional Pathways to Equity: Addressing Inequality Traps*. Edited by Anthony Bebbington, Anis Dani, Arjan de Haan, and Michael Walton. Washington, DC: World Bank.

De Haan, Arjan, and Max Everest-Phillips. 2006. "Can New Aid Modalities Handle Politics?" Paper presented at the World Institute for Development Economics Research Annual Conference, Helsinki.

Delgado, Christopher L. 1997. *Africa's Changing Agricultural Development Strategies*. IFPRI 2020 Brief 42. Washington, DC: International Food Policy Research Institute.

Demeter, Marton. 2021. "Development Studies in the World System of Global Knowledge Production: A Critical Empirical Analysis." *Progress in Development Studies* 22, no. 3. https://doi.org/10.1177/14649934211060155.

Dercon, Stefan. 2022. *Gambling on Development: Why Some Countries Win and Others Lose*. London: Hurst Publishers.

Desai, Vandana. 2002. "Role of Non-Governmental Organizations." In Desai and Potter, *Companion to Development Studies*, 495–499.

Desai, Vandana, and Robert B. Potter. 2002. *The Companion to Development Studies*. London: Hodder Arnold.

De Silva, S., and J.-W. Sum. 2008. *Social Funds as an Instrument of Social Protection: An Analysis of Lending Trends. FY 2000–2007*. Social Protection Discussion Paper. Washington, DC: World Bank.

De Soto, Hernando. 1986. *El Otro Sendero: La Revolución Informal*. Lima: Instituto Libertad y Democracia.

DFID (Department for International Development). 1997. *Eliminating World Poverty: A Challenge for the 21st Century*. London: Stationary Office.

———. 2000a. *Eliminating World Poverty: Making Globalisation Work for the Poor*. London: Stationary Office.

———. 2000b. *Realising Human Rights for Poor People: Strategies for Achieving the International Development Targets*. London: DFID.

———. 2006. *Eliminating World Poverty: Making Governance Work for the Poor*. London: Stationary Office.

———. 2015. *UK Aid: Tackling Global Challenges in the National Interest*. London: Stationary Office.

———. 2016. *Bilateral Development Review. Technical Note*. London: DFID.

———. n.d. *Annual Report* (various years). London: Stationary Office.

Dijkstra, Geske. 2005. "The PRSP Approach and the Illusion of Improved Aid Effectiveness: Lessons from Bolivia, Honduras and Nicaragua." *Development Policy Review* 23, no. 4: 443–464.

Dodd, A., D. Knox, and D. Breed. 2021. *Aid Data 2019–2020: Analysis of Trends Before and During Covid*. Bristol, UK: Development Initiatives. https://devinit.org/documents/905/Aid_data_2019-2020_Analysis_of_trends_before_and_during_Covid.pdf.

Dollar, David, Tatjana Kleineberg, and Aart Kraay. 2013. *Growth Still Is Good for the Poor*. Policy Research Working Paper 6568. Washington, DC: World Bank.

Dollar, David, and Aart Kraay. 2002. "Growth *Is* Good for the Poor." *Journal of Economic Growth* 7, no. 3: 195–225.

Donaghy, G., and D. Webster. 2019. *A Samaritan State Revisited: Historical Perspectives on Canadian Foreign Aid*. Calgary: University of Calgary Press.

Dreher, Alex, Sarah Langlotz, and Silvia Marchesi. 2016. "Budget Versus Project Aid: A Tradeoff Between Control and Efficiency." Vox EU, December 2, 2016. https://voxeu.org/article/donors-don-t-budget-aid-they-should.

Drèze, Jean. 2022. "On the Perils of Embedded Experiments." Ideas for India, March 10, 2022. https://www.ideasforindia.in/topics/miscellany/on-the-perils-of -embedded-experiments.html.

Driscoll, R., with Alison Evans. 2005. "Second-Generation Poverty Reduction Strategies: New Opportunities and Emerging Issues." *Development Policy Review* 23, no. 1: 5–25.

Duffield, M. R. 2007. *Development, Security and Unending War: Governing the World of Peoples*. Cambridge, UK: Polity.

Dutta, Nabamita, and Claudia R. Williamson, eds. 2019. *Lessons on Foreign Aid and Economic Development: Micro and Macro Perspectives*. London: Palgrave Macmillan.

Easterly, William. 2006. *The White Man's Burden: Why the West's Efforts to Aid the Rest Have Done So Much Ill and So Little Good*. New York: Penguin.

———. 2014. *The Tyranny of Experts: Economists, Dictators, and the Forgotten Rights of the Poor*. New York: Basic Books.

Easterly, William, Ross Levine, and David Roodman. 2003. "New Data. New Doubts: A Comment on Burnside and Dollar's 'Aid, Policies, and Growth.'" National Bureau of Economic Growth, July 2003. https://www.nber.org /papers/w9846.

Economic Research Forum and Finance for Development Lab. 2022. *Embarking on a Path of Renewal. MENA Commission on Stabilization and Growth*. Cairo: Economic Research Forum, and Paris: Finance for Development Lab.

Edwards, Michael. 2020. *Civil Society*. 4th ed. Cambridge: Polity.

Edwards, Sophie. 2019. "As Jim Kim Steps Down, a Tumultuous World Bank Presidency Comes to an End." DevEx, February 4, 2019. https://www.devex.com /news/as-jim-kim-steps-down-a-tumultuous-world-bank-presidency-comes-to -an-end-94247.

Eurodad. 2008. *Turning the Tables: Aid and Accountability Under the Paris Framework. A Civil Society Report*. Brussels: European Network on Debt and Development.

Eyben, Rosalind. 2008. *Power, Mutual Accountability, and Responsibility in the Practice of International Aid: A Relational Approach*. IDS Working Paper 305. Brighton: Institute for Development Studies.

Eyoh, Dickson, and Richard Sandbrook. 2003. "Pragmatic Neo-liberalism and Just Development in Africa." In *States, Markets, and Just Growth: Development in the Twenty-first Century*. Edited by A. Kohli, C. Moon, and G. Sörensen, 227–257. Tokyo: United Nations University Press.

FAO (Food and Agriculture Organization). 2019. FAOLEX Database. Kenya National Agriculture Investment Plan 2019–2024. https://www.fao.org/faolex /results/details/en/c/LEX-FAOC189052/.

Fasulo, Linda. 2004. *An Insider's Guide to the UN*. New Haven, CT: Yale University Press.

Filmer, Deon, and Norbert Schady. 2006. *Getting Girls into School: Evidence from a Scholarship Program in Cambodia*. Policy Research Working Paper 3910. Washington, DC: World Bank.

Findlay, June. 2020. "Yes #WeHaveAProblem—and Not Just Because of Trudeau." *Fashion*, July 21, 2012. https://fashionmagazine.com/.

Flickner, Charles. 2007. "Removing Impediments to an Effective Partnership with Congress." In Brainard, *Security by Other Means,* 225–253.

Focus 2030. 2021. "Generation Equality Forum: Overview of the Commitments." Focus 2030, August 3, 2021. https://focus2030.org/Generation-Equality-Forum -overview-of-the-commitments.

Foster, Mike. 2000. *New Approaches to Development Co-operation: What Can We Learn from Experiences with Implementing Sector Wide Approaches.* Working Paper 140. London: Overseas Development Institute.

Foster, Mike, and Jennifer Leavy. 2001. *The Choice of Financial Aid Instruments.* Working Paper 158. London: Overseas Development Institute.

Fritz, Verena, and Alina Rocha Menocal. 2007. "Development States in the New Millennium: Concepts and Challenges for a New Aid Agenda." *Development Policy Review* 25, no. 5: 531–552.

Gabor, Daniela. 2020. "The Wall Street Consensus." July 2, 2020. https://osf.io /preprints/socarxiv/wab8m/.

Gaspart, Frédéric, and Jean-Philippe Platteau. 2006. "The Perverse Effect of Cheap Aid Money." Paper presented at WIDER Conference, Helsinki, June 2006.

GEI (Global Evaluation Initiative). 2022. "Who We Are." https://www.global evaluationinitiative.org/who-we-are.

Gender and Development Network. 2021. "Decolonising Aid." https://gadnetwork .org/gadn-resources/decolonising-aid.

Ghani, Ashraf, and Clare Lockhart. 2008. *Fixing Failed States: A Framework for Rebuilding a Fractured World.* Oxford: Oxford University Press.

Gill, Indermit A., Ana Revenga, and Christian Zeballos. 2016. *Grow, Invest, Insure: A Game Plan to End Extreme Poverty by 2030.* Policy Research Working Paper 7892. Washington, DC: World Bank Group. https://documents1.worldbank.org/curated /en/924111479240600559/pdf/WPS7892.pdf.

GIZ. 2021. *Indicators Matter to LNOB.* Bonn: GIZ.

Glassman, Amanda, and Suddhansho Handa. 2021. "Retooling UNICEF: New Leadership Needs to Couple Humanitarian Initiatives with Systems Reform." CGD blog, August 16, 2021. https://www.cgdev.org/blog/retooling-unicef-new -leadership-needs-couple-humanitarian-imperatives-systems-reform.

Glassman, Amanda, and Miriam Temin. 2016. *Millions Saved: New Cases of Proven Success in Global Health.* Washington, DC: Brookings Institution Press and Center for Global Development.

Glennie, Jonathan. 2020. *The Future of Aid: Global Public Investment.* Milton Park, UK: Routledge.

Global Partnership for Effective Development Co-operation (GPEDC). 2019. *Kampala Principles on Effective Private Sector Engagement in Development Co-operation.* https://www.effectivecooperation.org/system/files/2019-07/KampalaPrinciples –final.pdf.

Global Witness. 2007. *Cambodia's Family Trees. Illegal Logging and the Stripping of Public Assets by Cambodia's Elite.* Washington, DC: Global Witness Publishing.

Gore, Al. 2006. *An Inconvenient Truth.* Documentary. Directed by Davis Guggenheim.

Goris, Yannicke, and Kiza Magendane. 2021. "Taking a Historical Perspective on the Decolonization of Aid." The Broker, May 26, 2021. https://www.thebrokeronline .eu/taking-a-historical-perspective-on-the-decolonization-of-aid/.

Government of Canada. 2008. *Independent Panel on Canada's Future Role in Afghanistan.* Ottawa: Government of Canada.

———. 2019. "Feminist Approach—Innovation and Effectiveness Guidance Note." https://www.international.gc.ca/world-monde/issues_development-enjeux _developpement/priorities-priorites/fiap_ie-paif_ie.aspx?lang=eng.

———. 2021. "Canada's Feminist Approach to Addressing Unpaid and Paid Care Work Through International Assistance." https://www.international.gc.ca/world-monde/issues_development-enjeux_developpement/priorities-priorites/fiap_care_work-paif_prestation_soins.aspx?lang=eng.

GPE (Global Partnership for Education). 2021. "Results Report 2021." https://www.globalpartnership.org/content/results-report-2021.

Gready, Paul, and Jonathan Ensor. 2005. *Reinventing Development? Translating Rights-Based Approaches from Theory into Practice.* London: Zed Books.

Grillo, Ralph. 2002. "Anthropologists and Development." In Desai and Potter, *Companion to Development Studies,* 54–60.

Grindle, Merilee. 2002. *Good Enough Governance: Poverty Reduction and Reform in Developing Countries.* Cambridge, MA: Kennedy School of Government, Harvard University.

———. 2007. "Good Enough Governance Revisited." *Development Policy Review* 25, no. 5: 533–574.

Grove, Natalie J., and Anthony B. Zwi. 2008. "Beyond the Log Frame: A New Tool for Examining Health and Peacebuilding Initiatives." *Development in Practice* 18, no. 1: 66–81.

Gulrajani, Nilima. 2011. "Transcending the Great Foreign Aid Debate: Managerialism, Radicalism and the Search for Aid Effectiveness." *Third World Quarterly* 32, no. 2: 199–216.

Gulrajani, Nilima, and E. Silcock. 2020. *Principled Aid in Divided Times.* Working Paper 596. London: Overseas Development Institute.

Habraken, Rik, Lau Schulpen, and Paul Hoebink. 2017. "Putting Promises into Practice: The New Aid Architecture in Uganda." *Development Policy Reviews* 35, no. 6: 779–795.

Hallaert, Jean-Jacques. 2020. "The Tragedy of International Organizations in a World Order in Turmoil." European Centre for International Political Economy, July 2020. https://ecipe.org/publications/tragedy-of-international-organizations/.

Hancock, Graham. 1989. *Lords of Poverty.* London: Macmillan.

Hanlon, J., D. Hulme, and A. Barrientos. 2010. *Just Give Money to the Poor: The Development Revolution from the Global South.* Boulder, CO: Kumarian Press.

Harriss, John. 2002. *De-politicizing Development: The World Bank and Social Capital.* London: Anthem Press.

Hart, Jason, Jo-Anna Russon, and Jessica Sklair. 2021. "The Private Sector in the Development Landscape: Partnerships, Power, and Questionable Possibilities." *Development in Practice* 31, no. 7: 857–871.

Hart, Keith. 1973. "Informal Income Opportunities and Urban Employment in Ghana." *Journal of Modern African Studies* 11, no. 1: 61–89.

Haslam, Paul A., Jessica Schafer, and Pierre Beaudet, eds. 2012. *Introduction to International Development: Approaches, Actors and Issues.* Don Mills, ON: Oxford University Press.

Hatton, Michael J., and Kent Schroeder. 2007. "Results-Based Management: Friend or Foe?" *Development in Practice* 17, no. 3: 426–432.

Hedger, Edward, and Zainab Kizilbash Agha. 2007. *Reforming Public Financial Management When the Politics Aren't Right: A Proposal.* Opinion no. 89. London: Overseas Development Institute.

Heinrich, Tobias, Yoshiharu Kobayashi, and Edward Lawson. 2021. "Populism and Foreign Aid." *European Journal of International Relations* 27, no. 4: 1042–1066.

Heinzel, Mirko, and Andrea Liese. 2021. "Managing Performance and Winning Trust: How World Bank Staff Shapes Recipient Performance." *Review of International Organizations* 16:625–653.

Hettne, Bjorn. 2010. "Development and Security: Origins and Future." *Security Dialogue* 41, no. 1: 31–52.

Hill, Jonathan. 2005. "Beyond the Other? A Postcolonial Critique of the Failed State Thesis." *African Identities* 3, no. 2: 139–154.

Hjertholm, Peter, and Howard White. 2000. "Foreign Aid in Historical Perspective." In Tarp, *Foreign Aid and Development*, 80–102.

Hoebink, Paul, and Olav Stokke, eds. 2005. *Perspectives on European Development Co-operation: Policy and Performance of Individual Donor Countries and the EU*. New York: Routledge.

Hossain, N. 2017. *The Aid Lab: Understanding Bangladesh's Unexpected Success*. Oxford: Oxford University Press.

Hulme, David. 2016. *Should Rich Nations Help the Poor?* New York: Wiley.

Iancu, Alina, Seunghwan Kim, and Alexei Miksjuk. 2021. "Global Financial Safety Net—A Lifeline for an Uncertain World." IMF blog, September 30, 3033. https://blogs.imf.org/2021/11/30/global-financial-safety-net-a-lifeline-for-an-uncertain-world/.

ICAI (Independent Commission for Aid Impact). 2013. "DFID's Livelihoods Work in Western Odisha." https://icai.independent.gov.uk/review/dfids-livelihoods-work-western-odisha/review/.

———. 2021. "The UK Aid Response to COVID19." https://icai.independent.gov.uk/review/the-uk-aid-response-to-covid-19/.

IFAD (International Fund for Agricultural Development). 1999. "India: Completion Evaluation of Orissa Development Project: Seven Lessons Learned." https://www.ifad.org/en/web/ioe/-/india-completion-evaluation-of-orissa-development-project-seven-lessons-learned.

ILO (International Labour Organization). 1972. *Employment, Income and Equality: A Strategy for Increasing Productive Employment in Kenya*. Geneva: International Labour Office.

———. 2002. "Definition of Gender Mainstreaming." http://www.ilo.org/public/english/bureau/gender/newsite2002/about/defin.htm.

———. 2013. *Labour Rights: Preventing Trafficking for Labour Exploitation in China (CP-TING Phase 2)—Final Evaluation*. Project Code CPR/09/01/CAN. https://www.ilo.org/global/docs/WCMS_432833/lang—en/index.htm.

IMF (International Monetary Fund). 2021. "Fund Concessional Financial Support for Low-Income Countries—Responding to the Pandemic." https://www.imf.org/en/Publications/Policy-Papers/Issues/2021/07/22/Fund-Concessional-Financial-Support-For-Low-Income-Countries-Responding-To-The-Pandemic-462520.

IMF Independent Evaluation Office. 2007. *An IEO Evaluation of Structural Conditionality in IMF-Supported Programs*. Washington, DC: IMF.

IMF and World Bank. 2005. *PRS Review: Balancing Accountabilities and Scaling Up Results*. Washington, DC: World Bank.

Institute for Health Sector Development. 2003a. *Mapping of Sector Wide Approaches in Health*. Report for the Swedish International Development Cooperation Agency (Sida). London: IHSD.

———. 2003b. *Sector-Wide Approaches in Education*. Background paper for a UNICEF workshop. Institute for Health Sector Development, London.

International Development Committee. 2022. *Racism in the Aid Sector*. UK Parliament. https://publications.parliament.

Isbister, John. 2003. *Promises Not Kept: Poverty and the Betrayal of Third World Development*. 5th ed. Bloomfield, CT: Kumarian Press.

Janus, Heiner, and Lixia Tang. 2020. "Conceptualising Ideational Convergence of China and OECD Donors: Coalition Magnets in Development Cooperation."

In Chaturvedi et al., *Palgrave Handbook of Development Cooperation*, 217–243.

Jerve, Alf Morten, and Machiko Nissanke. 2008. *Aid Effectiveness to Infrastructure: A Comparative Study of East Asia and Sub-Saharan Africa*. Research Paper 36-4. Tokyo: Japan Bank for International Cooperation.

Johnsson, Urban. 2005. "A Human Rights–Based Approach to Programming." In Gready and Ensor, *Reinventing Development?* 47–62.

Jones, Andrew. 2005. "The Case of CARE International in Rwanda." In Gready and Ensor, *Reinventing Development?* 79–98.

Judd, K., ed. 2002. *Gender Budget Initiatives*. New York: UNIFEM.

Kabeer, Naila. 2003. *Gender Mainstreaming in Poverty Eradication and the MDGs: A Handbook for Policy-Makers and Other Stakeholders*. London: Commonwealth Secretariat/IDRC/CIDA.

Kanbur, Ravi. 2001. "Economic Policy, Distribution and Poverty: The Nature of Disagreements." *World Development* 29, no. 6: 1083–1094.

———, ed. 2005. *Q-Squared: Qualitative and Quantitative Methods of Poverty Appraisal*. Delhi: Permanent Black.

Kaufman, Daniel, Aart Kraay, and Pablo Zoida-Lobaton. 1999. *Governance Matters*. World Bank Policy Research Working Paper 2196. Washington, DC: World Bank.

Keller, Janeen Madan, Rachel Silverman, Julia Kaufman, and Amanda Glassman. 2021. "Moving Toward Smarter Health Spending: The Role of the Global Financing Facility." Center for Global Development, December 17, 2021. https://www.cgdev.org/blog/moving-toward-smarter-health-spending-role-global-financing-facility-world-bank#.YeL91s9dPQE.twitter.

Kenny, Charles. 2020. *Official Development Assistance, Global Public Goods, and Implications for Climate Finance*. Policy Paper no. 188. Washington, DC: Center for Global Development.

———. 2022. "When You Say Foreign Assistance Is Corrupt, Where Are You Pointing the Finger?" Center for Global Development blog, June 28, 2022. https://www.cgdev.org/blog/when-you-say-us-foreign-assistance-corrupt-where-are-you-pointing-finger.

Kentikelenis, Alexander, and Paul Stubbs. 2021. "Austerity Redux: The Postpandemic Wave of Budget Cuts and the Future of Global Public Health." *Global Policy* 13, no. 1: 5–17.

Kessler, Timothy. 2005. "Social Policy Dimensions of Water and Energy Utilities: Knowledge Gaps and Research Opportunities." Paper presented at World Bank Arusha Conference, "New Frontiers of Social Policy."

Khan, Themrise, Seye Abimbola, Catherine Kyobutungi, and Madhukar Pai. 2022. "How We Classify Countries and People—and Why It Matters." *BMJ Global Health* 7:e009704.

Kharas, Homi, John W. McArthur, and Dennis Snower. 2022. "From Vertical Funds to Purpose-Driven Funds: A New Approach to Multilateralism." In *Essays on a 21st-Century Multilateralism that Works for All*. Edited by Brahima S. Coulibaly and Kemal Dervis, chap. 5. Washington, DC: Brookings Institution.

Killick, Tony. 1999. *Making Adjustment Work for the Poor*. ODI Poverty Briefing 5. London: Overseas Development Institute.

———. 2002. "Aid Conditionality." In Desai and Potter, *Companion to Development Studies*, 480–484.

———. 2005. "Don't Throw Money at Africa." *IDS Bulletin* 36, no. 3: 14–19.

Kindornay, S., and F. Reilly-King. 2013. *Investing in the Business of Development: Bilateral Donor Approaches to Engaging with the Private Sector.* Ottawa: North-South Institute.

Korten, David C. 1980. "Community Organization and Rural Development: A Learning Process Approach." *Public Administration Review* 40, no. 5: 480–511.

Kothari, Uma. 2006. "From Colonialism to Development: Continuities and Divergences." *Journal of Commonwealth and Comparative Politics* 44, no. 1: 118–136.

Kothari, Uma, and Martin Minogue, eds. 2002. *Development Theory and Practice: Critical Perspectives.* Basingstoke, UK: Palgrave.

Krawczyk, Kelly Ann. 2019. "International NGOs, Transnational Civil Society, and Global Public Policy: Opportunities and Obstacles in the Twenty-First Century." In *The Oxford Handbook of Global Policy and Transnational Administration.* Edited by Diane Stone and Kim Moloney, chap. 9. Oxford: Oxford University Press.

Lammers, Ellen. 2008. "Aiming Global. Swedish Debates on International Development." The Broker, July 28, 2008. https://www.thebrokeronline.eu/aiming-global -d26/.

Lancaster, Carol. 2007. *Foreign Aid. Diplomacy, Development, Domestic Politics.* Chicago: University of Chicago Press.

———. 2008. *George Bush's Foreign Aid: Transformation or Chaos?* Washington, DC: Center for Global Development.

Land, T., and V. Hauck. 2003. *Building Coherence Between Sector Reforms and Decentralization: Do SWAPs Provide the Missing Link?* ECDPM Discussion Paper no. 49. Maastricht: European Centre for Development Policy Management.

Lang, Valentin. 2021. "The Economics of the Democratic Deficit: The Effect of IMF Programs on Inequality." *Review of International Organizations* 16:599–623.

Lauridsen, L. S. 2018. "New Economic Globalization, New Industrial Policy and Late Development in the 21st Century: A Critical Analytical Review." *Development Policy Review* 36, no. 3: 329–346.

Lavergne, Réal, and Anneli Alba. 2003. *CIDA Primer on Program-Based Approaches.* Gatineau, Quebec: CIDA Policy Branch.

Laws, Edward. 2016. "Branding and Communication of Development Assistance." Helpdesk Report K4D. http://gsdrc.org/wp-content/uploads/2017/10/011-Branding -and-communication-of-development-assistance.pdf.

Lawson, A., David Booth, A. Harding, and F. Naschold. 2003. *General Budget Support Evaluability Study Phase 1: Synthesis Report.* Evaluation Report EV643. East Kilbride, Scotland: Department for International Development.

Levy, Hernan. 2004. *Rural Roads and Poverty Alleviation in Morocco.* Washington, DC: International Bank for Reconstruction and Development/World Bank. http://web.worldbank.org/archive/website00819C/WEB/PDF/MOROCCO_.PDF.

Lewis, David, and David Mosse, eds. 2006. *Development Brokers and Translators: The Ethnography of Aid and Agencies.* Bloomfield, CT: Kumarian.

Lewis, Stephen. 2005. *Race Against Time.* Toronto: House of Anansi Press.

Lewis, W. Arthur. 1954. "Economic Development with Unlimited Supplies of Labour." *Manchester School* 22, no. 2: 139–191.

Lin, Justin Yifu. 2007. "Development and Transition: Idea, Strategy and Viability." Cambridge University Marshall Lectures, October 31–November 1, 2007.

Lipton, Michael. 1977. *Why Poor People Stay Poor: Urban Bias in World Development.* London: Temple Smith.

Liu, Qiaoqiao, and Zenggang Li. 2022. "Aid Instability, Aid Effectiveness and Economic Growth." *Development Policy Review* 40, no. 1.

Lucas, Brian. 2013. *Effectiveness of Sector-wide Approaches in Fragile Contexts.* GSDRC Helpdesk Research Report no. 1031. Birmingham, UK: GSDRC, University of Birmingham. http://gsdrc.org/docs/open/hdq1031.pdf.

Lundberg, Matthias, and Lynn Squire. 1999. "The Simultaneous Evolution of Growth and Inequality." Mimeograph. Washington, DC: World Bank.

Lynch, Leah, Sharon Andersen, and Tianyu Zhu. 2020. *China's Foreign Aid: A Primer for Recipient Countries, Donors, and Aid Providers.* CGD Notes. Washington, DC: Center for Global Development.

Machen, Ronald C., Matthew T. Jones, George P. Varghese, and Emily L. Stark. 2021. *Investigation of Data Irregularities in* Doing Business 2018 *and* Doing Business 2020: *Investigation Findings and Report to the Board of Executive Directors.* Washington, DC: WilmerHale. https://thedocs.worldbank.org/en/doc/84a922cc9273b7b120d49ad3b9e9d3f9-0090012021/original/DB-Investigation-Findings-and-Report-to-the-Board-of-Executive-Directors-September-15-2021.pdf.

Mahembe, Edmore, and Nicholas M. Odhiambo. 2019a. "Foreign Aid, Poverty and Economic Growth in Developing Countries: A Dynamic Panel Data Causality Analysis." *Cogent Economics & Finance* 7, no. 1. https://doi.org/10.1080/23322039.2019.1626321.

———. 2019b. "Foreign Aid and Poverty Reduction: A Review of International Literature." *Cogent Social Sciences* 5, no. 1. https://doi.org/10.1080/23311886.2019.1625741.

Malik, Rabia, and Raqndall W. Stone. 2018. "Corporate Influence in World Bank Lending." *Journal of Politics* 80, no. 1: 103–118.

Mallaby, Sebastian. 2005. *The World's Banker: A Story of Failed States, Financial Crises, and the Wealth and Poverty of Nations.* New Haven, CT: Yale University Press.

Maluccio, John, and Rafael Flores. 2004. *Impact Evaluation of a Conditional Cash Transfer Program: The Nicaraguan Red de Proteccion Social.* Discussion Paper 184. Washington, DC: International Food Policy Research Institute.

Manji, Firoze. 2003. "The Missionary Position: NGOs and Development in Africa." Paper presented at Futures for Southern Africa conference, Namibia. *International Affairs* 78, no. 3: 567–583.

Manor, James. 2005. Introduction. *IDS Bulletin* 36, no. 3: 1–7.

———, ed. 2007. *Aid That Works: Successful Development in Fragile States.* Washington, DC: World Bank.

Mansuri, Ghazala, and Vijayendra Rao. 2004. "Community-Based and -Driven Development: A Critical Review." *World Bank Research Observer* 19, no. 1: 1–39.

———. 2013. *Localizing Development: Does Participation Work?* Policy Research Report. Washington, DC: World Bank.

Martin, Courtney. 2016. "The Reductive Seduction of Other People's Problems." BRIGHT Magazine. https://brightthemag.com/the-reductive-seduction-of-other-people-s-problems-3c07b307732d.

Masaki, T., Bradley C. Parks, Jörg Faust, Stefan Leiderer, and Matthew D. DiLorenzo. 2021. "Aid Management, Trust, and Development Policy Influence: New Evidence from a Survey of Public Sector Officials in Low-Income and Middle-Income Countries." *Studies in Comparative International Development* 56:364–383.

Masters, Jonathan, Andrew Chatzky, and Anshu Siripurapu. 2021. "The IMF: The World's Controversial Financial Firefighter." Council on Foreign Relations, September 8, 2021. https://www.cfr.org/backgrounder/imf-worlds-controversial-financial-firefighter?cid=ppc-Google-Backgrounder-IMF-contect_ad.

Mawdsley, Emma. 2018. "'From Billions to Trillions': Financing the SDGs in a World 'Beyond Aid.'" *Dialogues in Human Geography* 8, no. 2: 191–195.

Mawdsley, Emma, Warwick E. Murray, John Overton, Regina Scheyvens, and Glenn Banks. 2018. "Exporting Stimulus and 'Shared Prosperity': Reinventing Foreign Aid for a Retroliberal Era." *Development Policy Review* 36, no. S1: O25–O43.

Maxwell, Simon. 2006. *What's Next in International Development? Perspectives from the 20% Club and the 0.2% Club*. Working Paper 270. London: Overseas Development Institute.

McGann, James. 2021. "2020 Global Go To Think Tank Index Report." University of Pennsylvania Library, January 28, 2021. https://repository.upenn.edu/think_tanks/18/.

McVeigh, Karen. 2021. "How Covid Could Be the 'Long Overdue' Shake Up Needed by the Aid Sector." *The Guardian*, February 5, 2021.

Miller, Mark, Lionel Roger, Annalisa Prizzon, and Tom Hart. 2021. *Multilateral Finance in the Face of Global Crisis*. London: Overseas Development Institute.

Ministry of Foreign Affairs, the Netherlands. 2018. *Investing in Global Prospects: For the World, for the Netherlands*. The Hague: Government of the Netherlands.

Mitchell, Ian. 2020. "Measuring Development Cooperation and the Quality of Aid." In Chaturvedi et al., *Palgrave Handbook of Development Cooperation*, 247–270.

Mitchell, Ian, and Caitlin McKee. 2018. "How Do You Measure Aid Quality and Who Ranks Highest?" Center for Global Development blog, November 15, 2018. https://www.cgdev.org/blog/how-do-you-measure-aid-quality-and-who-ranks-highest.

Mkandawire, Thandika, and Charles C. Soludo, eds. 2002. *African Voices on Structural Adjustment: A Companion to "Our Continent, Our Future."* Dakar, Senegal: Copublished by the Council for the Development of Social Science Research in Africa and the Africa World Press.

Moncrieffe, Joy. 2004. "Uganda's Political Economy: A Synthesis of Major Thought." London: Overseas Development Institute. http://www.gsdrc.org/docs/open/doc44.pdf.

Monga, Célestin. 2020. "Discrimination and Prejudice in Development." Brookings Institution, July 15, 2020. https://www.brookings.edu/blog/future-development/2020/07/15/discrimination-and-prejudice-in-development/.

Morrison, D. R. 1998. *Aid and Ebb Tide: A History of CIDA and Canadian Development Assistance*. Waterloo, ON: Wilfrid Laurier University Press.

Moser, Caroline. 2020. "From Gender Planning to Gender Transformation: Positionality, Theory and Practice in Cities of the Global South." *International Development Planning Review* 43, no. 2: 205–229.

Mosley, Paul. 1987. *Overseas Aid: Its Defence and Reform*. Brighton, UK: Wheatsheaf Books.

Mosley, Paul, and Marion J. Eeckhout. 2000. "From Project Aid to Programme Assistance." In Tarp, *Foreign Aid and Development*, 131–153.

Mosse, David. 2005. "Global Governance and the Ethnography of International Aid." In Mosse and Lewis, *The Aid Effect*, 1–36.

———. 2013. "The Anthropology of International Development." *Annual Review of Anthropology* 42, no. 1: 227–246.

Mosse, David, and David Lewis, eds. 2005. *The Aid Effect: Giving and Governing in International Development*. London: Pluto Press.

———. 2006. "Theoretical Approaches to Brokerage and Translation in Development." In Lewis and Mosse, *Development Brokers and Translators*, 1–26.

Moyo, Dambisa. 2009. *Dead Aid: Why Aid Is Not Working and How There Is a Better Way for Africa.* Vancouver: Douglas & McIntyre.

Mross, Karina. 2021. "Disaggregating Democracy Aid to Explain Peaceful Democratisation After Civil Wars." *European Journal of International Security* 7, no. 2: 1–25.

Muller, Sean Mfundza, Grieve Chelwa, and Nimi Hoffman. 2019. "How Randomised Trials Became Big in Development Economics." The Conversation, December 9, 2019. https://theconversation.com/how-randomised-trials-became-big-in-development-economics-128398.

Munk, Nina. 2013. *The Idealist: Jeffrey Sachs and the Quest to End Poverty.* Toronto: McLelland & Stewart.

Nadelman, Rachel. 2021. *How Do World Bank Staff Perceive the Institutional Environment for Building Citizen Engagement into Projects.* Accountability Working Paper no. 9. Washington, DC: Accountability Research Center. https://accountabilityresearch.org/publication/how-do-world-bank-staff-perceive-the-institutional-environment-for-building-citizen-engagement-into-projects/.

Nankani, Gobind, John Page, and Lindsay Judge. 2005. "Human Rights and Poverty Reduction Strategies: Moving Towards Convergence?" In Alson and Robinson, *Human Rights and Development: Towards Mutual Reinforcement,* 475–497.

Narayan, Deepa. 1997. *Voices of the Poor: Poverty and Social Capital in Tanzania.* ESSD Studies and Monographs Series no. 20. Washington, DC: World Bank.

Nastase, A., A. Rajan, B. French, and D. Bhattacharya. 2021. "Technical Assistance: A Practical Account of the Challenges in Design and Implementation." *Gates Open Research* 4:177.

Natsios, Andrew S. 2006. "Five Debates on International Development: The US Perspective." *Development Policy Review* 24, no. 2: 131–139.

New York Times. 2021. "Foreign Aid Is Having a Reckoning" (Editorial). *New York Times,* February 13, 2021.

Nicola, Fernanda G. 2021. "Scandal Involving World Bank's 'Doing Business' Index Exposes Problems in Using Sportslike Rankings to Guide Development Goals." The Conversation, October 15, 2021. https://theconversation.com/scandal-involving-world-banks-doing-business-index-exposes-problems-in-using-sportslike-rankings-to-guide-development-goals-169691.

Norris, John. 2021. "Opinion: USAID at 60." DevEx, November 3, 2021. https://www.devex.com/news/opinion-usaid-at-60-101934.

OECD (Organisation for Economic Co-operation and Development). 2007. *Aid Effectiveness: 2006 Survey on Monitoring the Paris Declaration. Overview of the Results.* Paris: OECD.

———. 2013. *Perspectives on Global Development 2013: Industrial Policies in a Changing World.* Paris: OECD.

———. 2016. "Taking Stock of Aid to Least Developed Countries (LDCs)." https://www.oecd.org/dac/financing-sustainable-development/Taking-stock-of-aid-to-least-developed-countries.pdf.

———. 2017. "10 Learning Areas for SDG Communications." OECD Development Communication Network. https://www.oecd.org/dev/pgd/DevCom_10_Learning_Areas_SDG_Communications.pdf.

———. 2018. *Climate-Resilient Infrastructure.* OECD Environment Policy Paper no. 14. Paris: OECD.

———. 2019. *Perspectives on Global Development 2019.* Paris: OECD.

———. 2021a. *Achieving SDG Results in Development Co-operation.* Paris: OECD.

———. 2021b. *Integrating Environmental and Climate Action into Development Co-operation.* Paris: OECD.

———. 2022. "Methodological Notes on the Development Co-operation Profiles 2022." In *Development Co-operation Profiles.* Paris: OECD. https://doi.org/10 .1787/5d646dd8-en.

OECD DAC (Development Assistance Committee). 1996. *Shaping the 21st Century: The Contribution of Development Co-operation.* Paris: OECD.

———. 2002. *Gender Equality in Sector Wide Approaches: A Reference Guide.* Paris: OECD.

———. 2003a. *Harmonising Donor Practices for Effective Aid Delivery: Good Practice Papers.* Paris: OECD..

———. 2003b. *Promoting Pro-Poor Growth: Practical Guide to Ex Ante Poverty Impact Assessment.* DAC Guidelines and Reference Series. Paris: OECD.

———. 2006. *2006 Survey on Monitoring the Paris Declaration.* Paris: OECD.

———. 2007a. *Development Cooperation Report 2007.* Paris: OECD.

———. 2007b. *2006 Development Co-operation Report.* Paris: OECD.

———. 2009. *Managing Aid: Practices of DAC Member Countries.* Paris: OECD.

———. 2016. "History of the 0.7% ODA Target." https://www.oecd.org/dac/financing -sustainable-development/development-finance-standards/ODA-history-of-the -0-7-target.pdf.

———. 2018a. *Cooperation Peer Reviews: Canada 2018.* Paris: OECD.

———. 2018b. "OECD Statistics on Private Philanthropy for Development." https://www.oecd.org/dac/Private-Philanthropy-for-Development-Flyer-2018 -19.pdf.

———. 2021. "COVID-19 Spending Helped to Lift Foreign Aid to an All-Time High in 2020." https://www.oecd.org/dac/financing-sustainable-development /development-finance-data/ODA-2020-detailed-summary.pdf.

———. n.d. "Official Development Assistance—Definition and Coverage." https:// www.oecd.org/dac/financing-sustainable-development/development-finance -standards/officialdevelopmentassistancedefinitionandcoverage.htm.

OECD DAC, Network on Development Evaluation. 2006. "Evaluation of General Budget Support." In *A Joint Evaluation of General Budget Support 1994–2004.* Paris: OECD.

OECD DAC, Network on Governance. 2006. *The Challenge of Capacity Development: Working Towards Good Practice.* Paris: OECD.

Oshima, Kaori. 2013. *What Have Been the Impacts of World Bank CDD Programs? Operational and Research Implications.* Social Development Notes no. 136. Washington, DC: World Bank.

Osterfeld, David. 1990. "The Failures and Fallacies of Foreign Aid." Foundation for Economic Education, February 1, 1990. https://fee.org/articles/the-failures-and -fallacies-of-foreign-aid/.

Ottenhof, Jenny. 2011. *Regional Development Banks.* CGD Brief. Washington, DC: Center for Global Development.

Owusu, Francis. 2003. "Pragmatism and the Gradual Shift from Dependency to Neoliberalism: The World Bank, African Leaders and Development Policy in Africa." *World Development* 31, no. 10: 1655–1672.

Oxfam. 2020a. "Climate Finance Shadow Report 2020." https://policy-practice.oxfam .org/?tab=all&s=Climate+Finance+Shadow+Report+2020.

———. 2020b. "The EU Trust Fund for Africa: Trapped Between Aid Policy and Migration Politics." https://policy-practice.oxfam.org/resources/the-eu-trust -fund-for-africa-trapped-between-aid-policy-and-migration-politics-620936/.

———. 2021. "Adding Fuel to Fire. How IMF Demands for Austerity Will Drive Up Inequality Worldwide." https://policy-practice.oxfam.org/resources/adding-fuel-to-fire-how-imf-demands-for-austerity-will-drive-up-inequality-worl-621210/.

Paris, Roland. 2010. "Saving Liberal Peacebuilding." *Review of International Studies* 36, no. 2: 337–365.

Park, Katrin. 2019. "The Great American Food Aid Boondoggle." *Foreign Policy*, December 10, 2019.

Parks, Bradley. 2019. "Where Has the Millennium Challenge Corporation Succeeded and Failed to Incentivize Reform—and Why?" Brookings Institution, April 1, 2019. https://www.brookings.edu/blog/future-development/2019/04/01/where-has-the-millennium-challenge-corporation-succeeded-and-failed-to-incentivize-reform-and-why/.

Parks, Bradley C., Takaaki Masaki, Jörg Faust, and Stefan Leiderer. 2016. *Aid Management, Trust, and Development Policy Influence: New Evidence from a Survey of Public Sector Officials in Low-Income and Middle-Income Countries.* Aid Data Working Paper no. 30. Williamsburg, VA: College of William & Mary.

Parry, Martin. 2009. "Climate Change Is a Development Issue, and Only Sustainable Development Can Confront the Challenge." *Climate and Development* 1, no. 1: 5–9.

Patel, Smruti. 2021. "Localisation, Racism, and Decolonisation: Hollow Talk or Real Look in the Mirror?" Humanitarian Practice Network, September 29, 2021. https://odihpn.org/publication/localisation-racism-and-decolonisation-hollow-talk-or-real-look-in-the-mirror/.

Peace Direct. 2021. *Time to Decolonise Aid.* Peace Direct, Adeso, the Alliance for Peacebuilding, and Women of Color Advancing Peace and Security. https://www.peacedirect.org/wp-content/uploads/2021/05/PD-Decolonising-Aid-Report.pdf.

Pearson, Lester. 1969. *Partners in Development: Report of the Commission on International Development.* New York: Praeger Publishers.

Pennarz, Johanna, Song Haokun, Deng Weijie, and Jianping Wang. 2011. *Wagging the Dragon's Tail.* Participatory Learning and Action no. 62. London: International Institute for Environment and Development.

Petrikova, Ivica, and Melita Lazell. 2022. "'Securitized' UK Aid Projects in Africa: Evidence from Kenya, Nigeria and South Sudan." *Development Policy Review* 40, no. 1: e12551.

Piattifuenfkirchen, Moritz Otto Maria Alfons, Ali Hashim, Sarah Alkenbrack, and Sriniva Gurazada. 2021. *Following the Government Playbook Channeling Development Assistance for Health Through Country Systems.* Washington, DC: World Bank.

Poku, Nana K., and Alan Whiteside. 2002. "Global Health and the Politics of Governance: An Introduction." *Third World Quarterly* 23, no. 2: 191–195.

Power, Samantha. 2021. "USAID Administrator Samantha Power on a New Vision for Global Development." YouTube video, 1:35:10. https://www.usaid.gov/news-information/speeches/nov-4-2021-administrator-samantha-power-new-vision-global-development.

Pralahad, C. K. 2004. *The Fortune at the Bottom of the Pyramid: Eradicating Poverty Through Profits.* Upper Saddle River, NJ: FT Press.

Prinsen, Gerard, and Saskia Nijhof. 2015. "Between Logframes and Theory of Change: Reviewing Debates and a Practical Experience." *Development in Practice* 25, no. 2: 234–246.

Radelet, Steven. 2007. "Strengthening U.S. Development Assistance." In Brainard, *Security by Other Means,* 93–119.

Rappeport, Alan. 2021. "Out of Trump's Shadow: World Bank President Embraces Climate Fight." *New York Times,* April 9, 2021. https://www.nytimes.com/2021 /04/09/us/politics/david-malpass-world-bank-climate.html.

Rawlings, L. B., L. Sherburne-Benz, and J. Van Domelen. 2004. *Evaluating Social Funds: A Cross-Country Analysis of Community Investments.* Regional and Sectoral Studies. Washington, DC: World Bank.

Reeves, Hazel, and Sally Baden. 2002. *Gender and Development: Concepts and Definitions.* Bridge Report no. 55. Brighton, UK: Institute for Development Studies.

Reinsberg, Bernard, Alexander E. Kentikelenis, Thomas H. Stubbs, and Lawrence P. King. 2019. "The World System and the Hollowing Out of State Capacity: How Structural Adjustment Programs Affect Bureaucratic Quality in Developing Countries." *American Journal of Sociology* 124, no. 4: 1222–1257.

Rice, Condoleezza. 2008. "Rethinking the National Interest: American Realism for a New World." *Foreign Affairs,* July/August 2008, 2–26.

Riddell, Abby. 2002. "Synthesis Report on Development Agency Policies and Perspectives on Programme-based Approaches." Paper prepared for the Forum on Accountability and Risk Management Under Program-Based Approaches, organized by the Learning Network on Program-Based Approaches, Ottawa.

———. 2008. "Issues and Challenges Raised by Development Agencies in Implementing the New Modalities of Aid to Education." *Prospects* 38:363–376.

Riddell, Roger C. 2007. *Does Foreign Aid Really Work?* Oxford: Oxford University Press.

Ritchie, Euan, Ina Mitchell, and Sam Hughes. 2021. "Assessing the UK's ODA Focus on Poverty and Africa." Center for Global Development, December 2, 2021. https://www.cgdev.org/publication/assessing-uks-oda-focus-poverty-and-africa.

Rogerson, Andrew, with Adrian Hewitt and David Waldenberg. 2004. *The International Aid System 2005–2010. Forces For and Against Change.* ODI Working Paper 235. London: Overseas Development Institute.

Rogerson, Andrew, and Euan Ritchie. 2020. *ODA in Turmoil: Why Aid Definition and Targets Will Come Under Pressure in the Pandemic Age, and What Might Be Done About It.* Policy Paper 198. Washington, DC: Center for Global Development.

Rogoff, Kenneth. 2002. "An Open Letter to Joseph Stiglitz, by Kenneth Rogoff, Economic Counsellor and Director of the Research Department, IMF." International Monetary Fund, July 2, 2002. https://www.imf.org/external/np/vc/2002/070202 .HTM?source=content_type:react|first_level_url:article|section:main_content |button:body_link.

———. 2022. "Why Is the IMF Trying to Be an Aid Agency?" Monitor, January 4, 2022. https://www.monitor.co.ug/uganda/special-reports/why-is-the-imf-trying -to-be-an-aid-agency-3672240.

Roodman, David. 2007. *Macro Aid Effectiveness Research: A Guide for the Perplexed.* Working Paper 135. Washington, DC: Center for Global Development.

Rostow, Walt Whitman. 1960. *The Stages of Economic Growth: A Non-communist Manifesto.* Cambridge: Cambridge University Press.

Roth, Silke. 2015. *The Paradoxes of Aid Work: Passionate Professionals.* Milton Park, UK: Routledge.

Ruger, J. P. 2005. "The Changing Role of the World Bank in Global Health." *American Journal of Public Health* 95, no. 1: 60–70.

Runde, Daniel F. 2020. *Defending the 'Global Spoils System' of Leadership Jobs in Multilaterals Is in the U.S. Interest.* CSIS Briefs. Washington, DC: Center for Strategic and International Studies.

Sachs, Jeffrey. 2005. *The End of Poverty: Economic Possibilities for Our Times.* New York: Penguin Press.

Sage, Caroline, and Michael Woolcock. 2007. *Breaking Legal Inequality Traps: New Approaches to Building Justice Systems for the Poor in Developing Countries.* BWPI Working Paper 17. Manchester: Manchester University.

Salemink, Oscar. 2006. "Translating, Interpreting, and Practicing Civil Society in Vietnam: A Tale of Calculated Misunderstandings." In Lewis and Mosse, *Development Brokers and Translators,* 101–126.

Sandefur, Justin, and Dev Patel. 2016. "World Bank Presidents, Ranked: From McNamara to Kim." Center for Global Development blog, September 9, 2016. https://www.cgdev.org/blog/world-bank-presidents-ranked-mcnamara-kim.

Sayeh, Antoinette M. 2021. "A New Agenda for Macro Stability." International Monetary Fund, September 21, 2021. https://www.imf.org/en/News/Articles/2021/09/21/sp092121-a-new-agenda-for-macro-stability-dmd-sayeh.

Schulpen, Lau. 2005. "All in the Name of Quality: Dutch Development Co-operation in the 1990s." In Hoebink and Stokke, *Perspectives on European Development Co-operation,* 406–447.

Scoones, Ian. 1998. *Sustainable Rural Livelihoods: A Framework for Analysis.* IDS Working Paper 72. Brighton, UK: Institute for Development Studies.

SD21 (Sustainable Development in the 21st Century). 2012. *Review of Implementation of Agenda 21 and the Rio Principles.* https://sustainabledevelopment.un.org/content/documents/641Synthesis_report_Web.pdf.

Seers, Dudley. 1967. *The Meaning of Development.* IDS Communication 44. Sussex, UK: Institute for Development Studies.

Seguino, Stephanie. 2007. "Plus Ça Change? Evidence on Global Trends in Gender Norms and Stereotypes." *Feminist Economics* 13, no. 2: 1–28.

Sen, Amartya. 1981. *Poverty and Famines: An Essay on Entitlement and Deprivation.* Oxford: Oxford University Press.

———. 1999. *Development as Freedom.* New York: Alfred A. Knopf.

Shaffer, Paul. 2013. *Q-Squared: Combining Qualitative and Quantitative Approaches in Poverty Analysis.* Oxford: Oxford University Press.

Shah, Mohammad Qadam. 2021. "What Did Billions in Aid to Afghanistan Accomplish? 5 Questions Answered." *The Conversation,* October 26, 2021. https://theconversation.com/what-did-billions-in-aid-to-afghanistan-accomplish-5-questions-answered-166804.

Shanks, Edwin, and Carrie Turk. 2003. *Refining Policy with the Poor: Local Consultations on the Draft Poverty Reduction and Growth Strategy in Vietnam.* Policy Research Working Paper 2968. Washington, DC: World Bank.

SIDA (Swedish International Development Agency). 2003. *Country Strategy Development: Guide for Country Analysis from a Democratic Governance and Human Rights Perspective.* Stockholm: SIDA.

———. 2006. *Power Analysis—Experience. Concept Note.* Stockholm: SIDA.

Simon, David. 2002. "Neo-liberalism, Structural Adjustment and Poverty Reduction Strategies." In Desai and Potter, *Companion to Development Studies,* 86–92.

———, ed. 2019. *Key Thinkers on Development.* London: Routledge.

Singer, Peter. 2009. *The Life You Can Save: Acting Now to End World Poverty.* New York: Random House.

Smets, L., and S. Knack. 2018. "World Bank Policy Lending and the Quality of Public-Sector Governance." *Economic Development and Cultural Change* 67, no. 1: 29–54.

Smyth, Ines. 2007. "Talking of Gender: Words and Meanings in Development Organisations." *Development in Practice* 17, no. 4-5: 582–588.

Sobocinska, A. M. 2017. "How to Win Friends and Influence Nations: The International History of Development Volunteering." *Journal of Global History* 12, no. 1: 49–73.

Sommerer, Thomas, Theresa Squatrito, Jonas Tallberg, and Magnus Lundgren. 2022. "Decision-Making in International Organizations: Institutional Design and Performance." *Review of International Organization* 17: 815–845. https://doi.org/10.1007/s11558-021-09445-x.

Sou, Gemma. 2021. "Aid Micropolitics: Everyday Southern Resistance to Racialized and Geographic Assumptions of Expertise." *Environment and Planning C: Politics and Space* 40, no. 4: 876–894.

Sriskandarajah, Danny. 2020. "NGOs Must Decolonise Aid Relief, Says Oxfam UK CEO." Open Democracy, December 8, 2020. https://www.opendemocracy.net /en/ngos-must-decolonise-aid-relief-says-oxfam-uk-ceo/.

Sserumaga, S. 2002. "Sector-Wide Approaches in the Administration of Justice and Promoting the Rule of Law: The Ugandan Experience." Seminar on the Rule of Law, European Initiative for Democracy and Human Rights, July 3–4, 2002, Brussels.

Steinmetz, Katy. 2020. "She Coined the Term 'Intersectionality' Over 30 Years Ago. Here's What It Means to Her Today." *Time*, February 20, 2020.

Stern, Nick. 2002. "Dynamic Development: Innovation and Inclusion." Munich Lectures in Economics, Munich, November 19, 2002.

———. 2006. *The Economics of Climate Change: The Stern Review*. London: HM Treasury.

Stevens, M., and S. Teggeman. 2004. "Comparative Experience with Public Service Reform in Ghana, Tanzania and Zambia." In *Building State Capacity in Africa: New Approaches, Emerging Lessons*. Edited by B. Levy and S. Kpundeh. https://gsdrc.org/document-library/comparative-experience-with-public-service -reform-in-ghana-tanzania-and-zambia/.

Stewart, Frances, and Michael Wang. 2003. *Do PRSPs Empower Poor Countries and Disempower the World Bank, or Is It the Other Way Around?* Queen Elizabeth House Working Papers Series. Oxford: University of Oxford.

Stiglitz, Joseph. 2002. *Globalization and Its Discontents*. New York: W. W. Norton.

Subramanian, Arvind. 2007. "A Farewell to Arms." *Wall Street Journal*, August 22, 2007.

Subramanian, Arvind, and Rajan, Raghuram G. 2005. *What Undermines Aid's Impact on Growth?* IMF Working Paper WP/05/126. Washington, DC: International Monetary Fund.

Swedlund, Heley J., and Malte Lierl. 2020. "The Rise and Fall of Budget Support: Ownership, Bargaining and Donor Commitment Problems in Foreign Aid." *Development Policy Review* 38, no. S1: O50–O69.

Tarp, Finn, ed. 2000. *Foreign Aid and Development*. London: Routledge.

Taylor, John. 2005. "Environment–Poverty Linkages: Managing Natural Resources in China." In Bass et al., *Reducing Poverty and Sustaining the Environment*, 73–99.

Tendler, Judith. 1975. *Inside Foreign Aid*. Baltimore: Johns Hopkins University Press.

———. 2000. "Why Are Social Funds so Popular?" In *Local Dynamics in an Era of Globalization: 21st Century Catalysts for Development*. Edited by Simon J. Evenett, Weiping Wu, and Shahid Yusuf. New York: Oxford University Press, World Bank.

Thanh, Hoangh Xuan. 2005. *Participatory Poverty Research and Policy Influencing in PRSP Processes: The Vietnam Case*. Participatory Learning and Action 51. London: International Institute for Environment and Development.

Theis, Joachim, and Claire O'Kane. 2005. "Children's Participation, Civil Rights and Power." In Gready and Ensor, *Reinventing Development?* 156–170.

Thérien, Jean-Philippe. 2002. "Debating Foreign Aid: Right Versus Left." *Third World Quarterly* 23, no. 3: 449–466.

Thobani, M. 1983. *Charging User Fees for Social Services: The Case of Education in Malawi*. World Bank Staff Working Paper 572. Washington, DC: World Bank.

Thompson, Lyric, Spogmay Ahmed, and Tanya Khokhar. 2021. *Defining Feminist Foreign Policy: A 2021 Update*. Washington, DC: International Center for Research on Women. https://www.icrw.org/wp-content/uploads/2021/09/Defining-Feminist-Foreign-Policy-2021-Update.pdf.

Thorbecke, Erik. 2000. "The Evolution of the Development Doctrine and the Role of Foreign Aid." In Tarp, *Foreign Aid and Development*, 17–47.

Tiessen, Rebecca, Katelyn Cassin, and Benjamin J. Lough. 2021. "International Development Volunteering as a Catalyst for Long-Term Prosocial Behaviours of Returned Canadian Volunteers." *Citizenship Teaching and Learning* 16, no. 1: 95–114.

Timperley, Jocelyn. 2021. "The Broken $100-billion Promise of Climate Finance—and How to Fix It." *Nature,* October 20, 2021.

UN (United Nations). 2002. *Report of the International Conference on Financing for Development Monterrey*. New York: UN. http://archive.ipu.org/splz-e/ffd08/monterrey.pdf.

———. 2004. *A More Secure World: Our Shared Responsibility, Report of the Secretary-General's High-Level Panel on Threats, Challenges and Change*. New York: UN.

———. 2008. *Doha Declaration on Financing for Development: Outcome Document of the Follow-up International Conference on Financing for Development to Review the Implementation of the Monterrey Consensus*. New York: UN.

———. 2009. *Framework Convention on Climate Change*. New York: UN.

———. 2015. *Addis Ababa Action Agenda of the Third International Conference on Financing for Development*. New York: UN.

———. 2021. *Inter-agency Taskforce on Financing for Development: Financing for Sustainable Development Report 2021*. New York: UN.

UN Commission on the Legal Empowerment of the Poor. 2008. *Making the Law Work for Everyone*. New York: Commission on Legal Empowerment of the Poor and UNDP.

UNCTAD (United Nations Conference on Trade and Development). 2021. *Digital Economy Report 2021: Cross-Border Data Flows and Development. For Whom the Data Flow*. New York: UN.

UNDESA (United Nations Department of Economic and Social Affairs). 2021. *Effective Blended Finance in the Era of COVID-19 Recovery*. UNDESA Policy Brief no. 100. New York: UN.

UNDP (United Nations Development Programme). 2003. *Poverty Reduction and Human Rights: A Practice Note*. New York: UNDP.

———. 2004. *Sources for Democratic Governance Indicators*. Oslo: UNDP.

————. 2005. *Human Development Report 2005: International Cooperation at a Crossroads: Aid, Trade and Security in an Unequal World*. New York: UNDP.

————. 2021. "The 2021 Global Multidimensional Poverty Index (MPI)." http://hdr.undp.org/en/2021-MPI.

————. n.d. *Human Development Report* (various years). New York: Oxford University Press.

UNICEF (United Nations Children's Fund). 2021. *Investing in Justice, Law and Order*. Budget Brief 2021/2. https://www.unicef.org/uganda/media/9891/file/Investing%20in%20JLOS.pdf.

UN Millennium Project. 2005. *Investing in Development: A Practical Plan to Achieving the Millennium Development Goals*. London: Earthscan.

UN Uganda. 2005. *United Nations Development Assistance Framework of Uganda, 2006–2010*. Kampala: United Nations System.

Uvin, Peter. 2004. *Human Rights and Development*. Bloomfield, CT: Kumarian Press.

————. 2007. "From the Right to Development to the Rights-Based Approach: How Human Rights Entered Development." *Development in Practice* 17, no. 4: 597–606.

Veltmeyer, Henry. 2012. "Civil Society and Development." In Haslam et al., *Introduction to International Development*, 217–234.

Vorisek, Dana, and Shu Yu. 2020. *Understanding the Cost of Achieving the Sustainable Development Goals*. Policy Research Working Paper no. 9164. Washington, DC: World Bank.

Wahlberg, Katarina. 2008. "Food Aid for the Hungry?" *Global Policy Forum*, January 2008. www.globalpolicy.org.

Walford, Veronica. 2003. *Defining and Evaluating SWAps: A Paper for the Inter-Agency Group on SWAps and Development Cooperation*. London: Institute for Health Sector Development.

WEF (World Economic Forum). 2021. *Global Gender Gap Report*. Geneva: WEF.

Wei, Qian, and Liam Swiss. 2022. "Filling Empty Promises? Foreign Aid and Human Rights Decoupling, 1981–2011." *Sociological Quarterly* 63, no. 1: 134–153.

Wenham, Clare. 2017. "What We Have Learnt About the World Health Organization from the Ebola Outbreak." *Philosophical Transactions of the Royal Society of London. Series B, Biological Sciences* 372:20160307. https://doi.org/10.1098/rstb.2016.0307.

White, Howard. 2005. "The Case for Doubling Aid." *IDS Bulletin* 36, no. 2: 8–13.

Williams, Martin. 2017. "The Political Economy of Unfinished Development Projects: Corruption, Clientelism, or Collective Choice?" *American Political Science Review* 111, no. 4: 705–723.

Wolf, Martin. 2019. "The IMF Today and Tomorrow." International Monetary Fund, June 2019. https://www.imf.org/external/pubs/ft/fandd/2019/06/the-future-of-the-imf-wolf.htm.

Wolfensohn, James, and Stanley Fischer. 2000. "The Comprehensive Development Framework (CDF) and Poverty Reduction Strategy Papers." http://www.imf.org/external/np/prsp/pdf/cdfprsp.pdf.

Woodward, Susan L. 2017. *The Ideology of Failed States: Why Intervention Fails*. Cambridge: Cambridge University Press.

Woolcock, Michael. 2007. "Higher Education, Policy Schools, and Development Studies: What Should Master Degree Students Be Taught?" *Journal of International Development* 19, no. 1: 55–73.

World Bank. 1989. *Sub-Saharan Africa: From Crisis to Sustainable Growth.* Washington, DC: World Bank.

———. 1994. *Governance: The World Bank's Experience.* Washington, DC: World Bank.

———. 1998. *Assessing Aid: What Works, What Doesn't, and Why.* Oxford: Oxford University Press.

———. 2002. *A Sourcebook for Poverty Reduction Strategies.* Washington, DC: World Bank.

———. 2004a. *Reducing Poverty, Sustaining Growth: Scaling Up Poverty Reduction. A Global Learning Process and Conference in Shanghai.* Washington, DC: World Bank.

———. 2004b. *Integrated Safeguards Data Sheet (Updated).* Report no. AC 1074. Washington, DC: World Bank.

———. 2007. *China and the World Bank: A Partnership for Innovation.* Washington, DC: World Bank.

———. 2015. *Gender Strategy: 2016–2023.* Washington, DC: World Bank.

———. 2018. *The State of Social Safety Nets 2018.* Washington, DC: World Bank.

———. n.d. *World Development Report* (various years). New York: Oxford University Press.

World Bank Development Finance. 2021. *A Changing Landscape: Trends in Official Financial Flow and the Aid Architecture.* Washington, DC: World Bank.

World Bank Independent Evaluation Group (IEG). 2015. *Learning and Results in World Bank Operations: Toward a New Learning Strategy.* Washington, DC: World Bank.

———. 2021. *Morocco—Community-Based Rural Roads Maintenance.* Washington, DC: World Bank.

———. 2022. *The Development Effectiveness of the Use of Doing Business Indicators, Fiscal Years 2010–20. An Independent Evaluation.* Washington, DC: World Bank.

World Bank Operations Evaluation Department. 2003. *Toward Country-Led Development: A Multi-partner Evaluation of the Comprehensive Development Framework.* Washington, DC: World Bank.

World Bank Social Development Department. 2003. *Social Analysis Sourcebook: Incorporating Social Dimensions into Bank-Supported Projects.* Washington, DC: World Bank.

World Neighbors. 1995. *The Quiet Revolution: Bangladesh: Microcredit.* Documentary. World Neighbors, CASID.

Yamey, Gavin, Diana Gonzalez-Garcia Pharos, Ipchita Bharali, Kelly Flanagan, and Robert Hecht. 2018. *Transitioning from Foreign Aid: Is the Next Cohort of Graduating Countries Ready?* Working Paper. Durham, NC: Center for Policy Impact in Global Health.

Zehra, Maheen. 2005. "Creating Space for Civil Society in an Impoverished Environment in Pakistan." In Bass et al., *Reducing Poverty and Sustaining the Environment,* 20–43.

Zhou, Pingjian. 2022. "China's Africa Debt Deals Guided by Transparency." *Business Daily,* July 1, 2022. https://www.businessdailyafrica.com/bd.

Zhou, Xizhou. 2019. "China Is Committed to Multilateralism." *Project Syndicate,* September 4, 2019.

Zimmerman, Robert A. 2007. "The Determinant of Foreign Aid: An Inquiry into the Consequences of Welfare Institutions and Public Opinion." University of Amsterdam, August 2007. https://www.oecd.org/dev/40699467.pdf.

Index

About the Book

INTERNATIONAL DEVELOPMENT ASSISTANCE—WHAT ARJAN DE HAAN calls the aid industry—continues to be critical for overcoming the world's development challenges, perhaps more so than ever given the global realities of climate change and the Covid-19 pandemic. But how does this industry actually work? What practices does it follow, and to what effect? De Haan addresses these questions, providing a concise introduction to the business of development.

This new edition reflects fifteen years of increasing complexity in the aid industry: heightened polarized debates about appropriate approaches; the involvement of new donors, such as China; adoption of the Sustainable Development Goals; the blending of public- and private-sector investment; tensions among charitable, political, and commercial considerations. The list goes on. De Haan incorporates these factors in a succinct overview that is an ideal introduction for students encountering the subject of development for the first time, as well as a handy overview for development practitioners.

Arjan de Haan is a senior program specialist at the International Development Research Centre (IDRC).